MAGOMERO

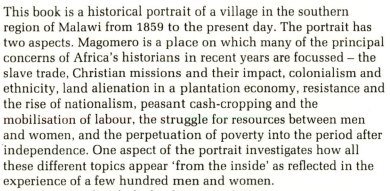

This book is a historical portrait of a village in the southern region of Malawi from 1859 to the present day. The portrait has two aspects. Magomero is a place on which many of the principal concerns of Africa's historians in recent years are focussed – the slave trade, Christian missions and their impact, colonialism and ethnicity, land alienation in a plantation economy, resistance and the rise of nationalism, peasant cash-cropping and the mobilisation of labour, the struggle for resources between men and women, and the perpetuation of poverty into the period after independence. One aspect of the portrait investigates how all these different topics appear 'from the inside' as reflected in the experience of a few hundred men and women.

On the other hand, the book's overriding concern is to capture something of the tone and tenor of village life since 1859. It records the changes that have taken place in the economy, in custom, in relationships both personal and political, and in the village's changing relationship with the broader Malawian and southern African context. Above all, it explores the different perceptions of the world that have animated village life over a century and a quarter.

The village story intertwines with two others. David Livingstone is viewed from a fresh angle as his doctrine of Christianity and Commerce came to be applied by his son-in-law and grandson using Magomero as their testing ground. Fresh light is thrown, too, on John Chilembwe and the Nyasaland rising of 1915, which drew most of its support from villages in the Magomero area.

But the book's real heroes are ordinary men and women, powerless in their poverty, whose names and voices and contribution to history are resurrected in this portrait of a village community.

MAGOMERO

Portrait of an
African village

LANDEG WHITE

Centre for Southern African Studies
University of York

CAMBRIDGE
UNIVERSITY PRESS

Published by the Press Syndicate of the University of Cambridge
The Pitt Building, Trumpington Street, Cambridge CB2 1RP
40 West 20th Street, New York, NY 10011–4211, USA
10 Stamford Road, Oakleigh, Melbourne 3166, Australia

First published 1987
First paperback edition 1989
Reprinted 1990, 1993, 1996

British Library cataloguing in publication data

White, Landeg
Magomero: portrait of an African village.
1. Magomero (Malawi) – social life and customs
I. Title
968.97   DT865.M3

Library of Congress cataloguing in publication data

White, Landeg
Magomero: portrait of an African village.
Includes index.
1. Magomero (Malawi) – History.   I. Title.
DT865.M35W44   1987   968.97   86-24427

ISBN 0 521 32182 4 hard covers
ISBN 0 521 38909 7 paperback

Transferred to digital printing 2000

CE

For Martin and John

Contents

Figures

(*Where no source is cited the photographs are the author's.*)

Maps

Preface

This book is a historical portrait of a village in the southern region of Malawi between 1859 and the present day.

More precisely, it is a portrait in two parts of two village communities, one of which succeeded the other on the same site. Neither was actually called Magomero. The first, which was destroyed in warfare in 1863, was called Chigunda's. It was a Mang'anja village of twelve huts occupying a peninsula formed by a loop in the Namadzi river. This peninsula was called Magomero. Chigunda was the chief of a dozen tiny settlements straddling the Namadzi river over an area of eight square kilometres and by kinship and politics his story involves theirs. In c.1901, this same stretch of the Namadzi river was cleared of bush and settled by Lomwe-speaking immigrants from Mozambique. Eight villages, once again linked by kinship and politics, were built under two chiefs on the east and west banks of the river, one of them occupying the same peninsula as Chigunda's. The immigrants settled as labour tenants on an estate which had been given the name Magomero. It is the name Magomero and all it came to signify which makes this a single story.

Twice Magomero has briefly become known to the outside world. The first occasion was in 1861, when it was chosen by David Livingstone as the site of the ill-fated Universities' Mission to Central Africa under Bishop Mackenzie. The mission found itself stranded in the middle of wars generated by the Indian Ocean slave trade and was forced to withdraw after becoming involved in fighting and after the deaths of several of its members, including the Bishop himself. The episode provoked controversy in Britain. The second occasion was in 1915 after the area had become part of the large estate owned by Livingstone's grandson Alexander Livingstone Bruce. Magomero was the centre of the rising led by John Chilembwe, when the estate manager, W. J. Livingstone, and two of his colleagues were killed. Chilembwe was a proto-nationalist and the circumstances of the rising were again widely publicised.

Otherwise, over the past century and a quarter, Magomero has been a place of the utmost unimportance. Situated in a poor region of one of the world's poorest countries, it is off the main road, far from the line of rail, and has no mineral or natural resources beyond moderately fertile soil and a perennial stream. Yet this is the point of the book. The majority of people in Malawi, as indeed in much of Africa, continue to live in such villages or to maintain strong rural ties. What I have tried to recover, working so far as I could from the inside, is the experience of living in such a place since the mid-nineteenth century. The record of these villagers, shut out of history or locked into their alternative history, is without charity or patronage fascinating in its own terms.

Writing this book was made possible by a generous grant from the Leverhulme Trust, which provided a salary over two years and the costs of two visits to Malawi, for six months in 1982 and a further three weeks in 1985. I must also thank Dzimani Kadzamira, Louis Msukwa, Steve Mwiyeriwa and Kings Phiri for constant advice and practical help in Malawi. Coretta M'meta, Doris Kadzamira and Irene Machowa conducted and translated my Lomwe interviews. The village headmen and the people of Bowadi, Komiha, Mpawa, Mpotola, Nasawa, Nazombe, Njenjema and Ntholowa tolerated my requests for information, interrupting their work and offering hospitality and entertainment long after my own entertainment value was exhausted. At different stages of the research, Anne Akeroyd, Jonathan Kydd and Robin Palmer commented in ways which made me acutely aware of my ignorance and of the need for drastic improvements.

Of my other innumerable debts, five are outstanding – to Jack Mapanje for generosity and biting satire, to Martin Chanock and Megan Vaughan for the fertility of their ideas, and to Leroy Vail for never wavering in his perception that the key to Malawi's history is poverty. As before, Alice White, whom I first met in Malawi, was with me throughout the work, guiding my interpretations when insight was needed. This book, though, is dedicated to Martin and to John, Chanock's and Mapanje's namesakes, in the hope that growing up in Thatcher's Britain they will not lose sight of the real world.

The Mang'anja village

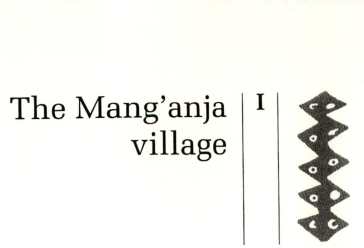

1859–1863

'One of the neatest we have ever seen'

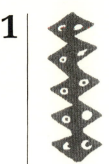

In the middle of the village between the road and the river is a bald hill, a dome of polished gneiss thirty-five metres high. Some of the villagers call it Magomero, but the older men know that this name, in the language of the people who lived here before them, is usually given to a dome twice as high 2 km to the north-west. Asked about their own hill they shrug their shoulders, until one of them dredges from his memory the word Nanyungwi. This first Sunday in September, as the cold season drags on, Nanyungwi has only the charred vestiges of vegetation. Fire swept over it in July, and the ash has been blown from the crevices or washed into them by the drizzle which comes up from Mozambique, leaving only the blackened roots of coarse grass and some burnt-off bushes on the lower slopes. The white-flecked rock is otherwise quite bare.

From the summit, the patterns of the landscape are clear. From a jumble of rounded hills to the west, a wide plain undulates east-wards, falling two hundred metres in the 50 km that are visible. Occasionally, stone hills push upwards – Bikuni, Machereni, Chanda and Chikomwe – but otherwise the land falls evenly, marked by the zigzag folds of stream courses. It looks an ancient landscape, de-forested, overcropped and heavily eroded.

The horizons are dramatic. To the south-east, at the farthest point of vision, there rises without preamble the massif of Mulanje moun-tain. From this angle it presents itself as a vast shining cliff 1,700 m. high and 25 km long, floating in the clouds and looking strangely insubstantial, a vision of ice and sunlight. On the northern horizon is Zomba plateau, a flatter version of Mulanje. Zomba is sombre-coloured, its slopes and summit planted with pine forests, and above it seems to hang a perpetual rain cloud. The space separating Zomba from Mulanje is filled in the distance by Lake Chilwa and the

3

Phalombe plain, though on the clearest days of all, in December after a storm, mountains in Mozambique can be seen like a breath on a pane of glass. These are the Namuli hills, where the Lomwe people who now possess the village once had their home and where a flat rock contains the footprints of their first ancestors.

To the south-west the horizon is much closer. Chiradzulu, a sleeping lion of a mountain, appears side-on as a broad pyramid rising 900 m from its base with a shorter pyramid to the left. It, and the town which bears its name, are 10 km distant. The village is in Zomba district but it is to Chiradzulu that its history connects it in suppression and in revolt.

Behind Chiradzulu are clustered other peaks of the Shire Highlands – Ndirande, Soche, Bangwe, Maravi and Mikolongwe. Between them and Mulanje, completing the southern circle and looking across the tea plantations of Thyolo district, is another flat horizon where the Highlands plunge to the valley of the Shire river. For this wide basin is itself a plateau a thousand metres above sea level. This fact, which to the British made it suitable for white settlement, together with one other, explains much of the region's history since the middle of last century. The other fact is the Shire river itself. Flowing from the southern tip of Lake Malawi through Lake Malombe, it follows the boundary curve of the highlands, round the back of Zomba mountain, behind the hills to the west, far behind Chiradzulu, Ndirande, Bangwe, Maravi and Mikolongwe, before flowing directly south into Mozambique and the vast delta of the Zambesi. It formed, according to David Livingstone, a route into the Highlands for Christianity and Commerce.

On Nanyungwi hill, as a marsh harrier circles overhead, we are at the centre of this wide curve and at the heart of the Shire Highlands.

The road to the village, a dirt road with gullies impassable during the rains, cuts south towards the river from the Young Pioneers' base at Nasawa. The base is 13 km off the main Blantyre–Zomba road and 2 km north of the village. Its buildings are hidden in a plantation of trees with only occasional flashes of corrugated iron, but the trees themselves indicate something imported and extraneous, since nowhere else in the neighbourhood is there such a dense clump of woodland. Leaving the base, the road crosses a patch of waste ground before passing through the village of Nasawa. From this point onwards, it is hard to distinguish where one village ends and the next begins. Every now and then, though, houses and trees are more heavily concentrated and Nasawa has given way to Njenjema, and

Njenjema to Ntholowa, and Ntholowa to Mpawa, and Mpawa to Nazombe, and Nazombe to Komiha 2 km to the south-east.

Sprouting like thick grey mushrooms the houses blend with the cold season yellows and browns. It is the trees that catch the eye. Most are mango trees, each one growing separately, its bottle-green silhouette rising sturdily from the dark pool of its shadow and washed with pink-tipped spiky blossoms. Clumps of bright bamboo look like green fountains spurting from leaks in the hard red earth, and along the roadside are yellow-leaved *malimo* trees and occasionally a sweet-smelling Pride of India or a jacaranda smouldering with blue fire. A strip of bright green to the north-east indicates the Congress Party's 'scheme' at Chimwalira, where dry-season maize can be grown on the *dambo* or marsh soil. Clumps of trees mark the separate village graveyards. In the homesteads themselves, the most popular trees are pawpaw and banana or plantain.

The village surrounding Nanyungwi hill is called Mpawa. Between the boundary of Ntholowa to the left and Nazombe to the right, there are eighty-one different mud buildings spread out along the road and these make up forty-seven homesteads.

Closest to the hill is one of the largest. The compound, fenced with grass, contains one rectangular house some 20 by 15m, its untrimmed thatch overhanging on all sides, and two more buildings half the size, one of them newly thatched with yellow grass, the other dilapidated and used as a hen house. Raised off the ground on stilts is a circular thatched *nkokwe* for storing grain. There is also a small thatched kitchen, a washroom covered with sacking and a latrine. Sheaves of thatching grass are piled in two stooks, for this is the season for house building and repairs. On the roof of the largest house is a splash of maroon and yellow, bright as a new cotton print, where bundles of millet have been spread out to dry. The compound where the hens scratch is beaten hard and swept clean with a broom of twigs. Against the grass fence is a single pawpaw tree.

Outside the compound, following the curve of the hill towards the stream, are the homestead's 'gardens', irregularly shaped plots divided by footpaths and fitting together like a jigsaw. One garden still contains the tall dry stalks of last year's millet and the turquoise-blue thistles that spring up everywhere when given the chance. Others have already been prepared for the new season, ridged along the lines of contour with a precision that is pleasing to look at.

A few houses, such as village headman Mpawa's, have rusty zinc roofs with stones on them to resist the wind, giving them a shanty-like appearance. Others have a doll's house neatness with razor-edged thatch and a red wooden door between two red-framed windows, all on a raised platform of polished earth. Many of the houses are built in line facing the road and some distance from their garden plots. There is a sharp contrast, in fact, between the 'built-up' area within 50 km of the road and the gardens beyond, where there are no houses but fields separated by footpaths or by rows of bananas or *malimo* trees. These plots, again, form a varied patchwork. Some are planted with dry-season cash crops – an acre of sunflowers, dazzlingly yellow as their faces begin to droop, or rows of cowpeas in lush turquoise lines against the red soil. Some food crops await harvesting. There are straggling clumps of *nandolo* or pigeon peas, one of the village staples, and of cassava whose spindly stems are intertwined with the green vines of sweet potatoes. Other fields are already ridged for the new season, and others still are half cultivated. The trash has been chopped down and laid in the gulleys between last year's ridges and the new ridges will be hoed over them, forming a compost which will have decomposed when the rains arrive in November.

Towards the river, the red soil darkens until the steep slopes of the far bank, which belongs to the opposite village of Bowadi, are black with rich cotton-based soil. The river is the Namadzi, which rises in the foothills of Zomba mountain to the north and flows in a wide semi-circle – south, east and north-east – to join the Phalombe river and flow into Lake Chilwa. It is a small river, at this season no more than a few centimetres deep, but it is perennial. From here come sounds of activity as men and women share the task of cultivating tomatoes, peppers and Chinese cabbage.

The day is Sunday, however, and not everyone is working. As well as the sound of women talking and goats bleating and children crying and rock doves croodling, all surprisingly audible on the hilltop, there are the lugubrious cadences of a hymn. It comes from by far the ugliest building in the village, the clay-brick *Chiyembekezo* (Adventist) church, and is recognisable as the Lomwe version of 'What a friend we have in Jesus'.

This is not the only church in Mpawa. Directly south of Nanyungwi hill, the Namadzi river rounds on itself to form a peninsula 270m long and 135m wide, an invaluable addition to the village's land. It is here, where the curve of the river forms several large pools, that women do their washing and that the best dry-season gardens are found. At the centre of the peninsula, among *nandolo* bushes and castor-oil plants,

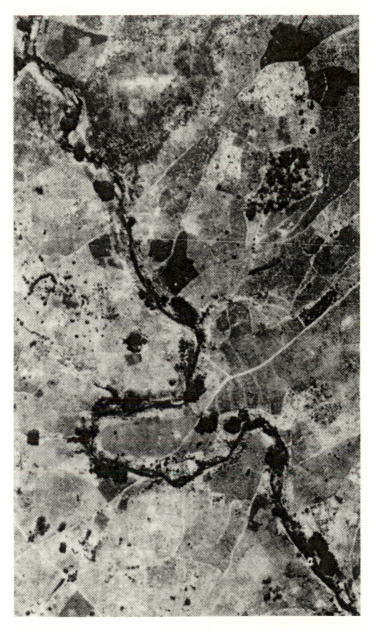

Fig. 1. The Magomero peninsula: Nanyungwi hill is the bare rock top right.
Scale 1:4500

on a beaten platform of earth between five tall blue gums, is a cross of white marble marking the grave of Henry de Wint Burrup, who died here in February 1862. Around the grave has been built of grass and poles a tiny Anglican church with a clay altar.

This is the site of the ill-fated Universities' Mission to Central Africa, guided to this spot and settled here by David Livingstone in the dry season of 1861.

Livingstone had been to the spot two years earlier. Accompanied by his brother Charles and the young John Kirk, he had spent the night of 2 September 1859 in a village of twelve huts on this horseshoe-shaped peninsula. His *Journal*, laconic in its shorthand, notes that the village was Chibaba's, that the people were Mang'anja, and that *Pambe* was the name of God. In quotation marks is the sentence 'Shire passes only: sometimes cuts its way through rocks, sometimes runs smooth, but there it passes and passes only.' – a disappointingly obscure reply to his persistent questioning about a huge lake to the north. Livingstone's other preoccupation emerges in the comment that 'Bajana' people from the east 'are buying hoes and slaves with salt' but that (heavily under-scored) 'all are ashamed of slave selling'. It was a sign that Chibaba had won Livingstone's approval. Later in print he described Chibaba as 'the most manly and generous Manganja Chief we had met'.

John Kirk was less complicated. He, too, kept a journal and his emphasis was different:

we turned aside to a large village, the chief named Tshibabe, a fat jolly fellow who took our present and returned it handsomely in food and drink.

He had never seen white men but had heard of our having passed not long ago, from Tshinsunze to Kankombe. He was very talkative and seemed to give an account of the neighbouring countries to the best of his knowledge. He informs us that the Bajawa are confined to the east of the Lake, while in the west are now the Mang'anja.

The beer which is very common at this season is made of any of the cereals such as *Penisetum* which communicates its bitter taste to it, or Indian corn which is reputed to give headaches. Most frequently, however, it is made of *Sorghum* or *Mabisa*. The grain is caused to sprout when it is dried, powdered in a wooden mortar into fine meal, boiled and allowed to ferment. At first it is sweet and very refreshing but after a few days becomes sour and at the same time intoxicating. When left for seven days it is valued highly, being then at its strongest.

The village of this man, Tshibabe, was one of the neatest we have ever seen. The huts as usual are made of a circular form with conical roof overhanging, thatched by long grass and the whole group of one man's huts surrounded by a fence similarly constructed.

Neatness, hospitality, good humour, from a fat jolly fellow, advice about beer making, and a warning against hangovers: it is a charming first picture. Could any first encounter between races have been less suspicious, more agreeable? Were these people in need of missionaries?

Kirk was a botanist, delighted with the Shire Highlands as a naturalist's paradise. Almost everyone, though, seeing Chibaba's village for the first time, found something about it to approve.

After the triumph and honours which followed his trans-African journey, Livingstone had returned to Africa in 1858 as leader of an expedition commissioned by the Foreign Office to explore the Zambesi valley. By the time he and his party entered the Shire river in January 1859 and first glimpsed the Shire Highlands, he was already enmeshed in a tangle of misunderstandings. The story is a complicated one to unravel, not least because much of the testimony is his own. It begins with a fatal miscalculation on Livingstone's earlier journey.

In May 1853, Livingstone for the fourth time crossed the eastern Kalahari desert and arrived at Linyanti, the territory of the Kololo people on the Chobe river in what is now the Caprivi Strip. The Kololo, under their chief Sebitoane, had established themselves at Linyanti after a series of migrations during the wars generated by the rise of the Zulu empire in the south-east. By the time they reached the Chobe river, the Kololo were cut off from their contacts in the south. They had ivory for sale, and they needed guns and powder, especially to protect themselves against Mzilikazi's Ndebele, their nearest and most recent enemy. But guns were obtainable only from the coast and the route lay through hostile territory. When Livingstone arrived at Linyanti with his talk of missionary settlement and trade, the idea appealed at many levels. The fact that Livingstone's wife, Mary, was the daughter of Robert Moffat, who was known to have great influence with Mzilikazi, was a bonus. But it was the prospect of trade with the coast, of access to firearms, that mattered. Thus Seleketu, Sebitoane's successor, became the sponsor of Livingstone's great journey, equipping him with food, trade goods and a team of carriers as he travelled first to the west coast to Luanda and then, following the Zambesi river, to the Indian Ocean at Quelimane. Without this sponsorship, the journeys would have been impossible, though the

9

Kololo never gained the benefits they anticipated, and following Seleketu's death in 1863 ceased to exist as a nation.

Meanwhile, Livingstone had travelled west to Luanda and then eastwards to Quelimane. His companions, who never deserted him and who at least once saved his life profoundly impressed him. The Kololo, though, had their own motives. On the one hand, they were fulfilling Seleketu's orders. On the other, their loyalty was negotiable. It was precisely because they were not originally of Kololo stock but were from peoples the Kololo had themselves subdued and absorbed during their migrations that they had been chosen to make the journey. If Livingstone had more to offer than Seleketu, there was no reason why the carriers should not attach themselves to him or use their association with him to seek out new opportunities for survival elsewhere. This was to happen, with consequences for Chibaba's people.

It is not surprising that Livingstone, dispirited with his years of unsuccessful preaching at Kolobeng, should have responded to the friendship of the Kololo with the feeling that his life's purpose was at hand. While still on his journey, he worked out his plan. It was to move the Kololo people across the Zambesi river from Linyanti to the Batoka plateau and to establish them at the heart of Africa under a Christian mission.

Then in February 1856 he made his miscalculation. Learning that the Zambesi river flowed in a wide arc and that he could save himself 80 km by taking the direct route, he missed seeing the cataracts at Cabora Bassa. 'I anticipate', he wrote from Tete to the astronomer Thomas Maclear, 'water carriage to within 2° of the Makololo by means of flat bottomed boats.'

Livingstone's reception on his return to Britain in December 1856 was ecstatic. His message that Africa was open, that at the heart of the continent there existed a people of loyalty and talent, eager for Commerce and Christianity, was flattering to the businessman and irresistible to the philanthropist. By May 1858 he was back on the Zambesi as the leader of a government sponsored expedition. By November he had seen the cataracts at Cabora Bassa and his plans were in ruins. There was no highway to Kololo territory.

Instead, Livingstone turned his attention to the Shire river, which joins the Zambesi below the town of Sena. Warily, since his previous despatch had lied about Cabora Bassa, Livingstone ordered John Kirk to write the report of their discovery of a territory 'capable of growing not only cereals but also cotton and sugar cane of excellent quality and in almost unlimited amount'. The arguments were as before: a navigable river, a peaceful agricultural people, an equitable climate and rich soil. By shifting them 1,200 km to the east, Livingstone was able to add another powerful inducement to British involvement in the possibility of striking a fresh blow against the Indian Ocean slave trade.

In 1842 the British government had established an anti-slaving naval patrol in the Mozambique Channel. This was in imitation of the patrol established in 1807 off the coast of West Africa to stop trading in slaves between British possessions, and was also partly its consequence. One of the effects of the West Africa patrol had been to drive the slave trade into the south Atlantic where, because of complications arising from the Napoleonic wars, Britain had found it expedient to recognise the trade in slaves between Portuguese possessions. The coast of Mozambique held special attractions for slave traders in that Portuguese possessions along the Zambesi river provided an established chain of suppliers along routes that extended deep into the interior and included a vast catchment area. By 1842, it is estimated that upwards of 300,000 men and boys had been drained from the Zambesi valley to markets in Brazil and Cuba, to the islands of the Indian Ocean and to the Persian Gulf.

In stemming this haemorrhage, the naval patrol had limited success. One frigate with four sloops and three or four brigs were hopelessly inadequate to patrol the Mozambique coastline. When the navy confined its attentions to Quelimane, the port serving the Zambesi valley, slavers shipped their cargoes from the mouths of the rivers of the Zambesi delta or from creeks along the coast to the north. Although the slave trade had been declared illegal by the Portuguese government in 1836, it remained entirely legal in Zanzibar to the north. Slaves were shipped in hundreds of dhows operating from the coastal inlets, or simply marched overland to territory north of the Rovuma river and hence beyond the reach of the naval patrol. Not surprisingly, the British and Foreign Anti-Slavery Society recommended that the patrol should be withdrawn.

This did not mean that the fight against slavery was being abandoned. Instead, adopting Thomas Buxton's curious formula that the causes of the slave trade were to be found in Africa rather than the New World, in the supply rather than in the demand, the abolitionists' aim became to provide African suppliers with an alternative source of revenue. The trade in slaves was to be replaced by 'legitimate commerce'. By shifting the location of his vision to an area

11

threatened by the Indian Ocean slave trade, Livingstone supplemented the appeal of his belief in the civilising effects of Christianity and Commerce with all the moral impetus of the fight against slavery.

With gratifying speed Livingstone's plan seemed to be fulfilled. In February 1861, just two years after his first voyage up the Shire river, there arrived at the mouth of the Zambesi two sloops bearing Charles Frederick Mackenzie, newly consecrated Bishop to the Tribes dwelling in the neighbourhood of Lake Nyasa and the River Shire, together with members of the Universities' Mission to Central Africa, including a gardener and a carpenter. Ladies were expected as soon as a settlement had been established.

This mission party was a large one, large enough to be an embarrassment. By the time it settled in Chibaba's village six months later it had swelled to 184 people. Its origins lay in Livingstone's triumphal tour of Britain in 1857 when, in lectures at Oxford and Cambridge, he had appealed to young men to devote themselves to a lifetime of service in Africa. Even before his first voyage up the Shire river, plans were being drawn up to create a central African mission backed by the universities of Oxford, Cambridge, Durham and Dublin. The leader was Charles Mackenzie, a man of high-church views whose reputation for muscular swashbuckling Christianity was at odds with his gentleness and a profound innocence. There had been argument about his consecration as the Church of England's first 'missionary Bishop'. Could there be a Bishop without a See? What was the relation between Church and State where there was no state? Yet no one who worked under him found him in the least controversial.

By contrast, the Bishop's deacon, Henry Rowley, was inclined to be needlessly combative. He was a little feared by the rest of the party for his intelligence and for a suspicion that of all the mission members he was the one to regard the adventure as an episode only in his life. All of them kept journals, but it was Rowley who worked hardest at preserving the history as it unfolded and who got his account into print.

Lovell Procter and Horace Waller were both twenty-seven years of age and both travelling outside England for the first time. Procter, who had served in parishes close to York, was the most colourless and parsonical of the missionaries. He had distinguished himself, however, by falling in love with a seventeen-year-old girl during the long voyage out to South Africa. By the time they reached the Cape he was engaged to be married. When Procter left for the Shire, his fiancée

Frances stayed behind in Natal. To the work of the mission Procter brought a dogged commitment that won his colleagues' respect, but all the romance of the enterprise remained with Frances. For Horace Waller, the romance of the mission lay in the cause itself. He was not ordained and was given the title lay superintendent. His enthusiasm never waned, nor his belief in Livingstone, whom he hero-worshipped, nor his devotion to the Africans who became the mission's charges. Yet typically he acted from high, passionate, philanthropic concern. It was the pale curate Procter who knew everybody's name.

The fifth university member of the party was the Rev. H. C. Scudamore. No one recounting the story of the mission found a role to assign to Scudamore. Neither his actions nor his words gave scope to anecdote and it was somehow typical that he alone of the main group left no journal. Yet it was Scudamore, especially as their disasters accumulated, on whose calmness of spirit everyone came to depend. Significantly, he was the most popular of all the party with their African dependents.

The party also included five black Christians. Four of these were recruited in Cape Town, where there existed a congregation of Africans who had been freed by the anti-slavery naval patrol. The leader was Charles Thomas, named after a retired merchant captain who had become his patron in Cape Town after his release. Thomas was originally from northern Mozambique and spoke fluent Makua. His English was excellent after almost twenty years residence in South Africa, but his Mang'anja was poor. William Ruby, his compatriot, spoke excellent Makua and Mang'anja, but little English. Henry Job, originally from Sena, and Apollos le Paul, originally from Tete, proved invaluable in various practical capacities. The fifth member of this group was Lorenzo Johnson, a Jamaican cook who had once been a slave in the United States. He too brought a practicality to the mission's arrangements which was badly needed.

By the time of Mackenzie's consecration in Cape Town the mission's destination had been fixed as the neighbourhood of Lake Nyasa and the Shire river. This was not where they had originally expected to go and when the party disembarked in the Zambesi delta in February 1861 their faith in Livingstone's judgement was further undermined. 'Nothing', noted Rowley in his diary, 'could look more impracticable for ordinary commercial purposes than the entrance to the Zambesi.' Even more disquieting was Livingstone's news. The Portuguese had built a fort and a customs' post in the mouth of the

13

Shire and were regulating access. Instead of transporting the missionaries up the Shire, he intended to explore another route to the Shire Highlands by the Rovuma river which flowed into the Indian Ocean far to the north.

It was not until 1 May, the Rovuma having proved navigable for only 30 km, that the missionaries again assembled at the mouth of the Zambesi to begin their voyage up the Shire river. They anticipated a journey of seventeen days. In the event it took them until 8 July to reach Chibisa's village below the first of the rapids, the river proving too shallow for a ship of the *Pioneer's* draught. It was Rowley who noted the mounting evidence. The Shire was not 'the splendid stream for navigation it was described to be'. The valley was beautiful but 'its fertility has been much overrated'. Its population was 'scant – that it could ever have been thickly peopled seems to be impossible'. As for cotton growing, it was a little surprising that the missionaries' own calico should have proved so much in demand, but perhaps that was a matter of 'fashion'. None of these criticisms were voiced to Livingstone, but the missionaries argued between themselves. Rowley was scornful; Procter was worried; Waller was passionately defensive.

When finally they disembarked and began to transport their baggage through morning mist up the steep escarpment to the Highlands, they were oppressed by a further difficulty. Livingstone had spoken of a peaceful, agricultural people awaiting the stimulus of trade. Among their goods was a second-hand cotton gin manufactured by Jameson of Ashton-under-Lyne and sold them by Livingstone himself. But every village they had visited coming up-river had been heavily fortified. Some had been surrounded by stockades of stakes or thorn trees, some hidden in the crevices of rocky outcrops, some concealed in clumps of woodland or in the papyrus of the marshes. The need for security was paramount and was reflected in other ways. No man left his village without carrying a bow and arrows. They became accustomed to lying and misdirection, and although they interpreted this as heathen behaviour awaiting correction it left a deposit in their minds that emerged in an anxious debate about guns. Should they carry firearms as they advanced into the Highlands? It was an aspect of the argument about Church and State. Assured by Livingstone that the mere show of force would be sufficient, Bishop Mackenzie entered his diocese carrying his shepherd's crook in one hand and a shotgun in the other.

On 16 July there occurred the event which determined all else that befell the mission. Their party had advanced in separate groups to

Fig. 2. The caravan of slaves at Mbame's: from the Livingstone memorial volume, 1874

Mbame's village where, Livingstone being too ill to continue, they halted for the day. There are numerous accounts of what followed – by Livingstone himself, by John Kirk, by the Bishop, by Rowley, by Procter and by Horace Waller. As the story was told and retold, it was polished into myth. Repeated in mission journals, in published memoirs and official accounts, and in propaganda literature with dramatic illustrations, it became part of the iconography of colonialism in central Africa. In fact, of the whole party only Livingstone, his brother, Kirk and Waller were actually present and of these only Waller's account has the authenticity of a writer addressing only himself. His breathless, unstudied, ungrammatical account is as follows:

A sudden whisper amongst our men who were seated round their fires told us something was going on of more than common interest. I soon learned that a large string of slaves was descending the slope into the village accompanied by the slave dealers who were returning with them from higher up the country. I went to the Dr who was lying down in his hut and found he had heard the report also. I could see he had a great mind to interfere although it would of course involve most serious interests. I had barely time to think much about it when the sound of horns and the tramp of feet ushered the long winding string of slaves into the village. The owners, or rather the drivers, were evidently uneasy at the sight of us, and pressed them on, intending to pass through without stopping. On they came, men, women and children, some with bark thongs from neck to neck, the men with their necks in heavy forked sticks fastened with an iron pin behind them, thus

I have a piece of one of them 6 feet long, as thick as a man's thigh above the knee and weighing about 30 lbs. A sickening sight it was!

Their masters came along jauntily enough, one of them especially, who had a scarlet Arab-looking cap. I was standing at the time among our black servants from Cape Town who, being themselves liberated slaves, never missed an opportunity for expressing their opinion on the subject. It did not require their taunts to make our position, as a looker-on, an irksome one, and right glad was I to see a sudden halt in their march and the blue jacket of the Doctor visibly an obstacle to further progress. He laid his hand on the shoulder of one of them who seemed to be the chief and recognised him, it appears, as the servant of a worthy at Tette. The men did not wait for a hint but snatched up their guns, the signal for a precipitate bolt on the part of those who had come with him. Bewildered and amazed the poor slaves were unable to comprehend what was the matter. They crouched down in a closely packed group and witnessed what was going on. One by one they seemed to get a glimpse of its import and then, slowly at first, but in its own unmistakable way, rose the measured sound of thankfulness. None who have not heard a multitude clapping the hands together in time hollowed in the palm to make a low deep sound – and at what is called slow time in marching – can understand the effect it produces. Slowly it rose, louder and louder till its solemn sound told gratitude was coming to hearts whose hope was well nigh dead in its long long sickness ...

At it we went, my poor old fishing knife well nigh getting his back broken cutting the thongs from the women and children, saws too came to use – their first use in this country – and many a hard five minutes was there as the poor patient captive held his head on one side to be eased of his burden which had galled him many a day. The only remaining captive had an opportunity given him also, not (I have omitted to say 84 were liberated) before he had been cross-examined, and he was not long in taking advantage of it. The fellows left 4 guns and a great quantity of things in the hands of the Senna men and the Makololo, hoes and beads especially. We were told by some of the liberated slaves that 3 of the drove had had their throats cut on the route, they being an encumbrance to the march from their weakness. One poor woman, unable to carry her child, had it taken away and its brains were dashed out on the spot. Two refractory ones were shot we were told also, this served as a warning to the rest. Can the crime of man much further go? Can anyone blame the excuse of that free will God has given to all? We served out 4 pieces of calico amongst the women and clad them in their own way with it ... To make the table turning a fait accompli we bade them gather their thongs and sticks together and we had the satisfaction of hearing the laugh so long unheard amongst them as they cooked their night's meal by the blazing piles.

It was a momentous intervention. Though by Portuguese law the slave trade was illegal, the ownership of slaves was not and there was nothing to forbid the movement of slaves overland. The humanity of the action seemed unquestionable, but the fact remained that Livingstone had challenged Portuguese jurisdiction on the mission's behalf. There were also eighty-four freed captives, mainly women and children, to be dealt with. To cast them adrift far from their homes would be irresponsible. More likely than not, most of them would be captured and sold again. Livingstone's solution was to offer them to Bishop Mackenzie as his first congregation. He accepted and the Africans acquiesced.

Next morning, leaving five of the released captives at Mbame's, the missionaries continued their journey. They were told of another slave gang and sent four of the Kololo in pursuit. Eight more women and boys were added to the party. That evening, it was decided there was no point in marching everyone round the countryside. The freed captives would remain with Procter and Scudamore at Soche's village while the others advanced into the Highlands to search for a mission site. Next day, Waller and Charles Livingstone went ahead, reaching the village of Mbona, south of Chiradzulu, late in the afternoon. Entering by a winding path, they found 300 men preparing for a dance. Despite such numbers, they still ransacked the village hunting for slaves. Six more were set free and the dealers captured (though they escaped during the night). Livingstone and the Bishop, joining them a little afterwards, wholeheartedly approved. The total under their protection was now ninety-eight.

The missionaries saw themselves as liberators. But they were advancing as an armed group into a region torn by warfare. Back at Soche's village Procter and Scudamore had an experience which threw some light on how their actions were perceived. On the night of 19 July, several of the women and children disappeared. Then Mbame paid them a visit, asking for gifts. The missionaries were puzzled, but Mbame got most of what he requested – cloth, beer, some goat meat, a ribbon for his hat – before setting off on the long walk back to his village. Next morning, the missing women were returned under escort by one of Mbame's sons. The implication was disturbing. Mbame, and probably the women too, believed the missionaries to be slavers.

Meanwhile, the advance party were continuing their search for a site for the mission. Following Livingstone's path of two years earlier, they passed east of Chiradzulu mountain and headed towards Zomba. The next village in line was Chibaba's, the village of neat huts on the horseshoe of land surrounded by the river. Waller's account is once again the unofficial one;

On our way to Chibaba's we passed a great many fugitives retreating southwards, driven out by the Achawas who are making sad havoc in front we are told. Nothing could exceed the woebegone appearance of these poor people. Mothers overladen with their poor children strapped to their backs and a heavy basket of corn on their head provision for the journey, the father walking before them perhaps leading the one poor goat they own on a leash or carrying another child unable to march for itself. It was a piteous sight and as we advanced it became more sorrowful still. We found Chibaba had died since the Dr's last visit to the place and Chigoonda, a civil inoffensive man, was chief in his stead.

Despite the warfare the village was still intact. Next morning, spontaneously, Chigunda pressed them to stay.

Chibaba, the fat jolly fellow who warned Kirk against hangovers, had died late in 1860. His grave was marked by a prayer hut at the western end of the peninsula.

Chigunda did not succeed him automatically. By Mang'anja custom, Chibaba's successor would have been chosen from any of the sons of his mother or eldest sister. In fact, Chigunda appears to have been Chibaba's brother. But there would have been much discussion between the women and the older men of the village before the choice fell on him. This goes some way towards explaining Chigunda's eagerness for the missionaries to stay in his village. For Chigunda had a nephew who, in the circumstances of the time, might have made a better chief.

This was Zachurakamo, a blacksmith and a flamboyant man, always at the centre of local dramas. The missionaries liked him. As Rowley put it, Zachurakamo 'had plenty of courage and energy and vivacity for twenty'. He was, though, a tragic figure. His wife had borne him eight children and all had died in infancy. This was not just a private grief. Zachurakamo was regarded in the village as a *mfiti*, a devil.

Chigunda had been a safer choice as chief. Describing him independently of each other the missionaries all used the same negatives. 'Civil and inoffensive' was Waller's impression. 'Of no very striking appearance or manner' was Procter's. 'Neither old, tall or stout', was Rowley's, 'a mild intelligent-looking man' with 'a very nerveless mouth'.

Chigunda was in his early thirties and had been chief for less than a year. He was not an important Mang'anja chief. He had twelve villages under him, strewn out along both sides of the river. But they were tiny villages, each consisting of about a dozen homesteads. Perhaps he governed four to five hundred men and women in all. Later on, the missionaries modified their initial judgement of him. When, as the weeks passed, Zachurakamo began to lead the opposition to the missionaries, Chigunda would himself come to seem a tragic figure. In those first days he appeared merely timid and harassed, overwhelmed with problems of a kind he was not equipped by experience or temperament to handle.

Chigunda's superior was Chisunzi, the principal chief of the Highland Mang'anja. Chisunzi lived 23 km north of Chigunda in a large village called Mitande, shaded by trees with yams festooning their branches. He was a very old man, old enough to command

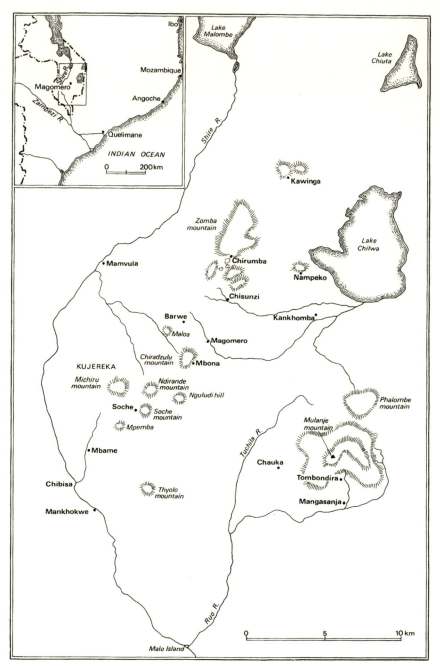

Map 1. The Shire Highlands 1861–3

respect for his age alone, and of a dried up appearence. His power was more than political. Close to Mitande, underneath Namilongo hill, was the most important of the rain shrines of the Highland Mang'anja, where Chisunzi annually would offer sacrifices of millet, ground-nuts, pigeon peas and beans to the spirit of his maternal ancestor, Nakoko. This ceremony, held before the rains in December, was attended by the whole district. Chisunzi, then, was a person to be reckoned with. Visiting him in April 1859 as the senior chief of the district, Livingstone and Kirk had found a group of Yao traders doing business in the village. By July 1861, the Yao had moved in in force, building a settlement of seventy huts in the next valley and raiding the vicinity for captives. Mitande was abandoned and Chisunzi had, in Chigunda's words, 'hid himself for fear'.

To Chigunda, living in the next village of any size in the line of attack, the arrival of men with guns apparently well-disposed towards the Mang'anja must have seemed like a gift from the ancestors. Repeatedly he pressed them to remain, promising, 'I will not run away if the English will stay with me.' For the mission-aries, too, the invitation seemed divinely purposed. It confirmed advice Livingstone had given them weeks before that Chibaba's would be a suitable site for the mission. Next day, a Sunday, the first sounds of prayer and praise' arose from their new mission settlement.

On the Monday morning, a large party led by Livingstone set off towards Zomba. Once again they passed streams of refugees on the path. Encountering a man they immediately took to be a slaver, they learned as he tried to exculpate himself of yet another caravan of slaves in Marongwe's village a mile or two further on. The Kololo, the Sena men and the Mang'anja rushed ahead, firing their guns and spreading panic. Forty-three more captives were added to the Bishop's responsibilities. Advancing further they came in sight of the Yao settlement. Livingstone tried to parley but the events he had precipitated were quickly out of control as a number of the huts were ransacked and burned. Most of the Yao men, however, were absent from the camp. As the remainder retreated they shouted 'how they would beat us if we would come again the next day'.

Back at Chigunda's, the missionaries did their arithmetic. They now had forty-four men and boys and thirty women and girls to add to the group of ninety-eight waiting with Procter and Scudamore at Soche's and the five left behind at Mbame's. The Bishop 'thought of Homeric battles and of David and Goliath'. Their estimates of the numbers they had killed fell with each review of the day's events until they believed it was only 'three, and three supposed'.

Chisunzi, whom they had yet to meet, was appalled. He sent men to request a visit, mentioning that he was too old and infirm to travel himself. Then, finding that his age and prestige made no impression on the white men, he walked the distance himself. His argument was straightforward. The attack had been made on the Mang'anja's behalf and had been inconclusive. The Yao would certainly respond by attacking him, the principal Mang'anja chief in the Highlands. The missionaries, therefore, should move to Mitande where he would offer them plenty of land for cultivation. Otherwise, he was 'already dead'. The white men would return to their own country leaving him to perish. Livingstone's response to this was cruelly inept. Confiscating Chisunzi's bow and arrows he joked that if the chief were dead he could have no further use for them.

For the first time they made a proper inspection of the site. The peninsula faced east, the river flowing on the north, west and south sides. Cutting diagonally across the top to the south-west ran a track leading through a ford to the opposite bank, and the twelve huts of Chigunda's village were grouped irregularly on either side of the track. The western end of the peninsula, beyond Chigunda's own hut and Chibaba's grave with its prayer hut, was covered with tobacco plants belonging to Zachurakamo. It was not an ideal site. After all they had experienced since reaching central Africa, the missionaries were keen to be protected. That afternoon Waller began cutting trees to build a stockade fence along the open side of the peninsula. Livingstone's argument was that the river would guard the other approaches. But the river was only knee-deep. Though the banks were high, suggesting a greater flow of water in the rainy season, a dam would be necessary to make the river an effective obstacle. The current, too, was sluggish and the Bishop had to abandon plans for a watermill.

There were two other objections to the site. It was in a hollow, approached downhill from all sides except the south. Chiradzulu mountain was just visible, but to see Zomba and Mulanje they would have to climb Nanyungwi hill a little way off. There was little wind on the peninsula and they all found it damp and dispiriting. It was also small. It was twice as large as Livingstone's estimate of 80 by 150 yards, but it was still a tiny patch of land on which to settle their current party of 184 people.

Not surprisingly, Chigunda began to have second thoughts. His first impulse when the white men turned up, to seize whatever protection was available, had been superseded by Chisunzi's request that the mission should settle at Mitande. Livingstone could afford to be cavalier in his treatment of the senior Mang'anja chief but Chigunda could not, and he can only have been acutely embarrassed that events had made him the agent of Chisunzi's humiliation. The return of the war party with their seventy-four new followers had given him an inkling of the numbers involved and he knew there were more to come from Soche's. Within the limits of his capacity for firmness he began to temporise. He refused to give up the whole peninsula, insisting to Bishop Mackenzie's displeasure on retaining three of the twelve huts. 'He says', noted the Bishop, 'they are the huts of his fathers: if he went away men would say he had been driven away.' The Bishop responded with his own rules. There would be no evening beer drinking within the stockade, which must be a 'a closed town at sundown'. The reception of Livingstone and John Kirk two years earlier was not to be repeated. Eventually, on the mission's second Sunday, the Bishop and Chigunda agreed to be 'co-proprietors of the soil'. In effect they were to become rival chiefs of different villages on the same plot of land. It was hardly a happy compromise.

Next morning, Livingstone returned to the *Pioneer*, his task of settling the missionaries on a suitable site accomplished. His advice on departure was that they should above all avoid getting involved in local conflicts.

Professionally, Livingstone was an explorer. Politically, he was an innocent. On his African journeys only sickness, bad weather or lack of essential supplies ever kept him in one place for more than a few days. He was a reliable and often acute observer of people, plants, animals and geographical features. But as an interpreter of local structures of power he was reliable only in the sense that he was usually wrong. He judged the chiefs he encountered by whether they welcomed him and whether they were responsive to his message about the slave trade and cotton growing. Invariably those who did so were vulnerable in some way and hoped for a profitable alliance. Those who didn't, who were strong enough to withhold judgement or even to oppose him, he wrote off as irrelevant. He never stayed long enough in any one place to need to learn more. After his action at Mbame's village and its sequels at Soche's, Mbona's and Morangwe's, after his humiliation of Chisunzi and his supervision of the building of fortifications in the village of one of Chisunzi's minor chiefs at the edge of a battlefield, only a politically innocent man could have departed advising non-involvement. The missionaries were out of their depth, but they were not fools.

Settling in, they discovered the peninsula was called Magomero, after the river which 'flows round it in the shape of a horseshoe'. This explanation meant nothing to them but the word 'magomero' means, idiomatically, 'journey's end', and it perhaps referred to the journey made by the river on its enormous loop before returning to its proper south-westerly course.

The missionaries had learned no Mang'anja. To communicate they had to depend on Charles, who spoke excellent English but poor Mang'anja, or on Thomas and William, who spoke Mang'anja fluently but whose English was haphazard. They planned to keep notebooks, making word lists as they went about their day's work and comparing notes each evening. Preaching though, or teaching the catechism were serious matters. These were Cambridge theologians trained in the classics. The Christian message they had come to impart was a gospel of scrupulously defined articles and precise paradoxes. They were much more afraid of planting false ideas than of failing to preach at all. On their first Sunday alone, the Bishop explained to everyone it was a day of rest but 'did not at present attempt to explain anything further'. The conversion of the Mang'anja was put off until they felt equipped for the task.

Civilising the Mang'anja was treated as a more straightforward affair. Whatever else Magomero might be it was plainly not 'civilised', and they threw themselves into improvements with a long-bottled-up energy. Waller, with Scudamore as woodcutter, completed the stockade in just four days. Procter, with some of the women and the boys, set about clearing scrub and weeds from the western end of the peninsula. It was rather symbolic labour – 'beginning to work on our new ground', Procter called it with deliberate metaphor – since without tools, which had yet to come up from the *Pioneer*, they could do no more than clear the surface, and with the rainy season not due for another four and a half months there was nothing they could plant. The futility of the work, in fact, provoked resistance from the women. If planting corn in the dry season was what the missionaries had come to teach them, they were not impressed. The workers did, however, make progress. They cleared Zachurakamo's tobacco plants which had just reached maturity, and they destroyed the prayer hut marking Chibaba's grave.

Of the nine houses given them by Chigunda, three were occupied by the missionaries. A few of the younger children were allowed to share this accommodation but the remaining mass of the people had to sleep where they could. On the Sunday they counted them: Waller made it 108, the Bishop and Procter 111 (61 men and boys, 44 women and 6 infants). Where the rest had gone they had no idea, though Scudamore had heard a rumour that some had run away because they 'believed their heads would be cut off and the brains turned into gunpowder', and the Bishop had the gravest doubts about the terms on which the women had found somewhere to sleep at nights. Housing was an immediate necessity and so the Bishop with Scudamore once more in attendance as woodcutter began building, getting in the corner posts and frames of two houses within the week.

Corner posts! It was as deliberate a metaphor as Procter's 'new ground'. All the huts presented by Chigunda were round, with conical thatched roofs supported on posts which provided each hut with a circular shaded veranda. As at the Cape, where straight lines of rectangular houses with neat gardens were the sign of Christian dwellings, so at Magomero 'civilisation' began by squaring the circle. As the house, and then the second larger one progressed, their people watched with astonishment, and villagers came from throughout the region to see the construction rise. While they had waited for the large house to be completed, they ate their meals in the open ...

to the infinite delight of the natives, who come round and look at us, apparently highly amused at our use of knives and forks. We had Chisunzi to dine with us today, and when we offered him one of these implements, he seemed utterly begone. After using his fingers, too, he asked for water to wash his fingers, and in consequence we offered him a towel to dry them with. At this, also, he seemed a good deal puzzled, and rubbed his fingers very awkwardly. He was rather an old man, certainly, to try our first lesson in civilisation upon ...

And they equipped themselves with personal servants. Though slavery was an abomination, the missionaries were firm believers in class. Thus, the Bishop selected a boy called Wakotane, Waller a young man called Chinsoro, and Procter fixed upon Combe from 'a certain Je ne sais quoi about him which pleased me'. All three were from the group freed at Mbame's village. They became personal attendants, odd-job boys and waiters.

Surprisingly quickly the days fell into a routine – a bathe in the river at six, prayers and breakfast at seven, followed by a roll call and work for the whole village from nine-thirty until five with a two-hour break for lunch. There was an evening meal at six, prayers at seven, and an hour or so language work in the Bishop's hut by the light of an oil lamp. This was not an African timetable and the women, who already objected to clearing land long before the rains, objected to starting so late and working so long into the afternoon. Waller had to summon Charles to 'get more work out of them'.

Routine did not resolve the security problem. There was plenty to keep them apprehensive. On the very day of Livingstone's departure Chigunda came flying into the half-built stockade with news that the Yao were close at hand burning villages. There was half an hour of general panic until the Bishop asserted his chieftaincy by climbing Nanyungwi hill with his field glasses and reporting they were merely hunting fires. A week later there was a further alarm at 10 o'clock at night. This time it was Zachurakamo who took the initiative, lighting a bundle of grass and searching the area for intruders while the white men assembled with their guns. Waller was amused to see the children imitating them:

The little fellows have made some most clever little toy guns out of bamboo. The great thing is to make a click for the lock and smoke. The first they do by inserting a splinter under the bark and the muzzle is filled with fine wood ashes: just like English boys.

Meanwhile, Chisunzi continued to visit them. His argument was as before, that the Yao were determined to punish the Mang'anja for 'bringing us against them'. It sounded plausible and made them uneasy. In any case, being members of an established church, they were more hierarchically minded than Livingstone and Chisunzi was the senior chief, the secular power of the region. Conversely, if they didn't recognise him as such, then who was the secular power? Was it themselves? Reluctantly, the Bishop agreed that the chiefs and the missionaries should confer.

The council or *mirandu* which took place behind the Bishop's hut impressed the missionaries profoundly. Chisunzi had brought with him his two most important sub-chiefs. These were Kankhomba who governed the area south and east of Lake Chilwa, and Barwe who came from a village fortified with thorn trees 20 km to their north-west. Kankhomba was about forty years old and struck them all as being vigorous and intelligent. Barwe had already on an earlier visit made the opposite impression. His pigtail and necklace and the profusion of brass rings on his ankles and wrists were hardly likely to appeal to Victorian clergymen. Behind Chisunzi, Kankhomba and Barwe were seated 150 other men, all minor chiefs and councillors, giving the assembly the status of the governing body of the Mang'anja of the Shire Highlands.

For Chisunzi and his followers the issues were simple. Their land had been invaded by the Yao and they wanted the help of English firepower in driving them out. This, at least, was their public stance. In private, warnings were already circulating among the Mang'anja about English ambitions. But the Yao were the immediate threat and the requirements of public diplomacy were straightforward. For the missionaries, what had to be said in public was more complicated. They had come to accept the logic of Chisunzi's argument that their previous attack, by being inconclusive, had only made matters worse. But they had no ambition to become the secular power in the land. What they longed for was a just and temporal state in which, like St Augustine, they would assume spiritual authority.

The missionaries gave their reply at a second council. Styling himself the chief of the English, the Bishop declared they would fight on four conditions. First was that all captives found with the Yao should be free to go where they pleased. This condition provoked much argument before Chigunda insisted that the Yao men should be killed but the women and children spared. It was a significant reply for, as the chiefs knew better than the missionaries, it would be cruel to turn the women and children loose once the men had been killed or driven off, and to take them into their own villages was not quite the same as enslaving them. Some doubt was left, too, whether this first condition had been agreed. Later, it was to cause trouble.

The second was that they should promise never to buy or sell men and women. This provoked laughter and Kankhomba, rubbing the cloth he had on replied, 'We do not sell our people for cloth; we make our own.' The whole neighbourhood had been treated to homilies about cotton growing, and plainly the Mang'anja found the English more than a little odd.

The third condition was that they should prevent the other chiefs from slave trading. 'If I know of anyone selling people,' Kankhomba declared, having clearly heard about Waller's behaviour, 'I will go against him and tie him up.' The fourth condition was that they should not receive slave traders into their villages. Once again there was a double edge of humorous complaint in Kankhomba's comment that the slave traders only dealt with the Yao.

By solemn covenant on the British side and by diplomacy edged with irony on the African, the agreement to fight was concluded. It was, however, above all Chigunda's day. His decision to settle the missionaries at Magomero had been vindicated and the effects showed in his energetic and animated appearance, his gleaming eyes and his great volubility.

Next morning Chigunda, dressed in the mantle of crimson velveteen the missionaries had given him for the nine huts, led out some fifty men armed with bows and arrows and spears while the Bishop, Waller, Rowley and Scudamore followed. After five miles he returned home, it 'not being the custom' for chiefs to go to war, and Zachurakamo took over the leadership of the Magomero men. Keyed up for battle the missionaries wrote him off as a coward, not appreciating that the Mang'anja, too, made a distinction between those who fought and those whose most important duties were religious. The relations of Church and State were indeed complex!

At Chisunzi's village one thousand men assembled, sitting in complete silence around their camp fires. Chisunzi was eager to surprise the Yao with a dawn attack but it was not until 4 o'clock in the morning that the missionaries set out. From the south, the last small hill before Zomba mountain is called Sazi hill and the Yao settlement of Chirumba was spread out between the foot of this hill and the slopes of Zomba itself. Approaching under cover of the hill, the Bishop destroyed all chance of surprise by insisting on a parley, and he went ahead to put the missionaries' terms – that the Yao must release all their captives, surrender their guns and leave the country. When these terms had been doubly translated – English to Mang'anja to Yao – they were instantly rejected on the grounds that the English 'were the enemies of the Yao', who were still looking for revenge for Livingstone's attack. While cries of 'shoot them' rang out from behind, the Bishop and his negotiators were forced to run back ignominiously towards their army.

The attack was made on two fronts, one downhill towards Chirumba, the other by a flanking movement to the right, in an attempt to cut off retreat, which met up with a Yao flanking column attempting to surround them. Both attacks were successful, the missionaries' Enfield rifles astonishing the Yao by their ability to kill at 600 yards. This part was exhilarating. The pursuit was a different matter. They were sickened by the results of what they had approved, by the burning huts and the looting and the panic-stricken people. The Bishop saw a woman killed as she tried to shield her three children. Unwilling to blame themselves after all the earnestness of their preparations, they could only blame the Mang'anja. 'I fear our friends', wrote Procter, 'are too generally but cowards, and cowards are often tyrants.' Gradually, and illogically, their sympathies began to shift towards the Yao.

That evening while the whole valley burned they returned one by one to Mitande. The Bishop led in some eighty women and children. He was carrying a boy he had found abandoned by the wayside. The boy was obviously dying and was baptised by the Bishop in the name of Charles Henry. Next morning he was given a Christian burial in Chisunzi's village.

They had released forty Mang'anja captives: they had separated forty Yao women and children from their families. The equation depressed them. So, too, did the subsequent wrangle over the fate of the people they had 'released'. The Mang'anja women, in Rowley's account, were restored to their friends and families; in Proctor's, they simply chose for themselves new protectors. The Yao women and children, having nowhere else to go, accompanied the missionaries to Magomero. But there were also children who were part Mang'anja and part Yao. There were other captives from a further group called Nguru, independent of both sides. It was not clear how these were covered by the terms the missionaries had agreed, and bitter arguments ensued with the chiefs and headmen over individual cases.

Back at Magomero, where the Bishop arrived carrying on his shoulders a little girl called Dauma, their mood settled into sober self-justification. They had struck 'a second blow' against the slave trade and had done so on terms which bound the Mang'anja chiefs to cooperate with them. They had united the Highlands Mang'anja and the population was flooding back into Chisunzi's capital at Mitande. Even the Yao women, separated from their homes, had been brought into a 'more perfect freedom' at Magomero. The Bishop gave them each a length of cloth to make them 'decent'.

Self-justification was not a problem for Chigunda. It was only a month since the white men had arrived and his decision to offer them land had been resoundingly vindicated. Almost daily, Chigunda played host to chiefs and headmen who came to offer tribute or to make further requests for help. His confidence showed. Procter noted he had lost 'the weak undecided manner he first had', showing 'especially in his public capacity much promptness and shrewdness and with a good deal of humour'.

He had other reasons to be satisfied. Though the missionaries had brought up considerable supplies of food, including huge quantities of Fortnum and Mason tinned meats, they expected eventually to live off the land. They were disappointed by the absence of game. They had assumed the Shire Highlands to be swarming with wild animals, mainly because Livingstone had never said explicitly they were not. But the region was much too heavily populated for game to survive and goat meat and chickens, with an occasional guinea fowl, were all they could obtain locally. It would be weeks before they could plant anything. Nor, frankly, were they quite sure that their wheat and barley, their coffee, parsnips and beetroot would actually grow in central Africa. Most important of all, they had expected to be feeding only themselves, not a whole congregation of some 200-odd dependents. For all these people, food had to be purchased with beads or with cotton or woollen cloth. During the second half of 1861, Magomero became the most important trading post in the Shire Highlands.

The economy of Chigunda's village was based on hoe agriculture. Finger-millet and sorghum were the most common crops and were used for making a porridge called *nsima* or, as Chibaba had advised John Kirk, for brewing the best varieties of beer. Maize was a relatively new crop, introduced from the east coast, and was beginning to be grown fairly widely. It had the advantage of giving higher yields and earlier harvests, but was less versatile in coping with variable rainfall. Rather than give over their main millet and sorghum gardens to maize, people were experimenting with growing it in marshy depressions or *dambos* during the dry season. There were several *dambos* along the river valley and Chigunda farmed one a kilometre east of the river.

Another crop on the increase was cassava. East of Lake Chilwa it was the staple food, and where pockets of Nguru people had settled in the Highlands moving west from Mozambique it was widely grown, the example spreading to the Mang'anja. One of Chigunda's villages, downstream towards Machereni, was known to the missionaries as 'the Anguru village' and it was surrounded by cassava gardens. The main root crops, however, were yams and sweet potatoes. Groundnuts were grown both for roasting as a breakfast relish and for manufacturing oil for cooking. Castor-oil was also manufactured but for cosmetic or medical purposes. There was a huge variety of peas and beans, and pumpkins were grown both for their leaves, used as a vegetable, and for their flesh which was an important food resource in the 'famine' months of December to February. Bananas were the only fruit available, but the missionaries were able to obtain a regular supply of tomatoes, grown in the *dambo* or in plots along the river bank.

In producing these crops the men and women worked together. Land was plentiful, though the red and yellow-red soils were not especially fertile, and so the quantities produced depended mainly on the labour available. The grass was burned off in late September and the ash hoed into the ground to await the first rains. By varying the crops and the periods of planting and harvesting, people produced and stored enough to last the year round. Chickens and goats added variety, and tobacco and hemp were grown for recreation. There was plenty of firewood available since, although the land was heavily cultivated, even on the slopes of the hills, the hills themselves were densely wooded.

Not everything could be produced within the household. Hoes, for instance, were bought from the blacksmith. But here, too, the Mang'anja were advantageously placed, for the Highlands were rich in iron ore and every village had its own smelting furnace and forge. Zachurakamo's were on the river bank half a kilometre upstream from the mission site. The smelting process took a couple of days' preparation. First, the furnace had to be rebuilt, with baked clay ventilation pipes laid like spikes forming a circle some two metres in diameter. Firewood was laid on top of them and then alternate layers of charcoal and of iron ore dug from the local mine. The outside of the furnace was sealed with clay, eventually forming a cone like an anthill two metres high. Into an opening at the base was inserted the bellows made from the skin of a goat turned inside out, with the clay nozzle fastened into the neck and bamboo splints each side of a narrow slit in the belly. When the furnace was lit, Zachurakamo or his assistant worked the bellows and his customers brought their own iron ore and fed it into the top of the furnace. The smelted iron collected in nuggets in the ashes at the bottom and was raked out.

The lumps of hot iron were beaten with a stone hammer to remove impurities and then taken to Zachurakamo's forge close by. There they were heated in a second fire and while the assistant pumped the bellows Zachurakamo worked the iron using a flat stone as his anvil and a variety of different stone hammers. Hoes manufactured in this manner were beaten into the shape of a half shield with a ridge up the middle ending in a sharp point which could be fitted into a wooden hoe-handle. These were the simplest items to make but were thoroughly efficient for their purpose. One might have expected blacksmiths to become relatively rich since their products were essential to survival. In practice, there were so many forges in the different villages offering such a variety of choice to the customers that none of the blacksmiths became wealthy. Zachurakamo would sell a hoe for a chicken or some millet beer. On the days when he was forging his smithy was a social centre where men gathered to share rumours about the missionaries.

Salt was another item normally purchased outside the household. It came from Lake Chilwa, a saline lake the shores of which were heavily impregnated with salt. Washing the soil and producing salt by evaporation was a semi-professional skill, but an inferior quality salt could also be manufactured from the mchudza reeds growing on the lake shore, which were burned and then the ash washed and evaporated. Dried fish was another important Lake Chilwa industry, and Mang'anja chiefs like Kankhomba and Nampeko exercised local monopolies. Traders who had obtained dried fish by purchase or by working for short periods would tour the Highlands on foot. It was an event when they arrived in a village and the missionaries who, despite their devotion to commerce found African traders 'most suspicious characters', were chagrined when they kept well clear of Magomero.

Hoes and salt were essentials. Fish were an occasional luxury. Goods such as charcoal for cooking, or earthenware pots, or the special waterproof baskets used for brewing, could all be made within the household, but were often purchased for the sake of convenience or quality. But the third essential item of purchase was clothing. Despite Livingstone's claims, very little cotton could be grown in the Highlands. The alternative was bark cloth, made from the inner bark of the njombo tree, which was soaked and beaten with a wooden hammer until it was stretched and soft enough for working. Bark cloth was made by professionals who travelled through the bush looking for suitable trees. It was warm but it was not decorative. Most of the men wore bark cloth but the women much preferred to wear cotton.

Cotton cloth could be obtained from the Shire valley where two varieties were grown, one a perennial bush and the other planted annually with seed originally imported. It was grown partly for the purpose of trade with the people of the Highlands, who supplied the valley Mang'anja with iron goods in return. But there was an alternative source, not only of cloth but also of salt, in trade with the Indian Ocean ports of Quelimane and Ibo. Communication with these ports was constant with traders passing through the Highlands selling beads or calico or salt made in the coastal salinas in exchange for tobacco, beeswax and wild rubber. These trade routes were long established. The new demand from the coast for slaves was not, as Livingstone thought, breaking an ancient isolation but rather corrupting a trade already in existence.

Into this economy the missionaries burst like a supermarket. With their knives, axes and mirrors, their brass wire and brass chains, their blue, red, pink and opaque white beads, and their rolls of drugget and baize and of white and coloured calicos, they set about purchasing sufficient food for 200 people for ten months. Their customers travelled over long distances. Initially the women were too nervous to go inside the stockade and sent their husbands instead. Each one was treated to a homily on the objects of the mission and Rowley made a particular point of paying for a goat or for ten fowls the two fathoms of calico which were the going price for a slave. Symbolism and their own dietary habits with meat three times a day made them extravagant. Procter was very soon worrying whether their cloth would last; Waller noted 'how fat the people have got since being with us ... really, some of the women are enough to smash the avoirdupois measure altogether'.

There is no evidence that Chigunda profited from his position by controlling this trade in any way. But the market on his doorstep was substantial, paying extravagant prices for the ordinary products of his village. Never before had he and his people been so conspicuously wealthy. As a consequence, they began themselves to acquire an interest in domestic slave holding.

In Mang'anja society, the custom was for a man to marry into his wife's home village. The land they cultivated was hers and the produce of their joint labour belonged nominally to her lineage, though it would normally be consumed within the household. In these circumstances, with land relatively plentiful, the main constraint on the production of food was labour. This raised two difficulties. The first was that the household was always vulnerable to the accidents of a low birth rate or of early death, and the practice had arisen by which children could be attached to the household as pawns, either by adoption or in settlement of disputes arbitrated by the chief. The second difficulty lay in the need for every household to acquire some goods, such as hoes, salt or clothing, by exchange. The larger the household, the more food could be produced and hence the more was available for trading. Supplementing the normal patterns of settlement and marriage it became the practice for men to acquire 'slave' wives who would do work in return for protection.

This practice seems to have been established before the coming of the slave trade. There were always some women left destitute by the turn of events, and there were advantages for men in becoming their owners. Apart from the sexual benefits and the extra labour they provided, the children of 'slave' marriages were under the direct control of their fathers and not of the male relatives of the mothers. With the coming of the slave trade, the numbers of women requiring such protection increased enormously. Mang'anja customs by 1861 were, in fact, breaking down, being rapidly superseded by a society in which, as Procter noted, 'a husband or a protector are considered essential'.

The missionaries had never asked themselves why it was that so many of the captives they had released were women. It was not women who were being traded from Quelimane to Brazil or Cuba or the United States. Some of them had probably been destined to travel up the Zambesi to Zumbo, where they would have been exchanged for ivory with traders from Mzilikazi's Ndebele kingdom where women were in short supply. But the majority were women who, by capture or through destitution, were already being forced into the kind of society which came to dominate the region for the next forty years – a society in which the men fought and raided and the women produced the bulk of the food crops. Once the women and children had been brought by the missionaries to Magomero, Chigunda's own people began to look at them covetously. The men had their eyes on the women and the women were interested in the children. Bishop Mackenzie was startled to discover that Chigunda already had a number of 'slave' wives and that Chigunda's principal wife had already appropriated one of their boys. The missionaries were horrified at how easily women entered into such relationships. A woman who sought a man's protection had only to put herself in his power by stealing something from him. But, while they noted their disquiet, they continued to buy up all the food available, and the benefits of 'slave' labour became every day more obvious to the Mang'anja.

In any case, it was hard for Chigunda's people not to conclude that the missionaries were in the same business. They had built a stockaded village. They had acquired by force a number of men, women and children whom they employed under pressure in cultivating the land. The rumour that they were slavers continued to circulate, and Waller found that women 'would resort to any subterfuge to avoid falling into our hands'. Another story was that they were cannibals, fattening their protégés before eating them. On the night of

31 August, seventeen of the women from Chirumba ran away. Letters had gone off to the *Pioneer* the previous day and they had caused panic. The rumour – marvellously suggestive in its imagery as African rumours usually are – was that below deck on the *Pioneer* were housed a group of cannibals perpetually engaged in making cloth. Four days later, a number of the women were brought back by Sachima, one of Chigunda's headmen. He anticipated a reward, and when the Bishop told him the women were perfectly free to come and go as they pleased, Sachima 'seemed staggered and smiled incredulously'.

The missionaries declared they had come to teach the people agriculture. But they had cleared land in the middle of the dry season. They told everyone to grow cotton, but cotton was a valley crop, unproductive in the Highlands. They lectured against slavery, yet had assembled the largest group of refugees in the whole region.

Why?

Inadvertently, the missionaries solved the problem and put paid to the rumours. While they were building their square houses accommodation remained a problem, with some people being crowded twenty to a hut. Though men and women were supposed to be separated, they, as Procter put it, 'mutually appeared to mistake the locality . . . almost every night'. The Bishop therefore decreed an absolute segregation of the sexes, with a dividing line down the middle of the peninsula. This 'astonished them not a little and they asked if it was the English custom for the women to live away from the men'. The Bishop explained the rules of Christian marriage. That evening, one of the young men presented himself at the Bishop's hut during their evening meal:

He sat at the door of the hut, and to our enquiry, said he came to talk; but he did not talk, we could not get him to talk, it was the last thing he seemed able to do, and at last we got out of him that he wished to have a certain woman for his wife. Upon our asking him if she wished to have him for a husband, he held down his head, and softly said: 'she says so'. And there was no doubt about it, for when he fetched her, she did say so.

Encouraged by this experiment, two other couples came forward. The Bishop declared them man and wife, and pointed out a plot of land outside the stockade where he intended the married people to live.

Marriage and land! At last, as the cultivation season approached, the rules were clarified. Five more couples came forward and within a few days 'all the men were provided for'.

The missionaries were charmed by this turn of events. For the first time they saw their charges as people rather than as anonymous unfortunates. One of the first to be married was Procter's servant Combe. Procter paid them 'a bridal visit' in their hut where he was welcomed 'with a grace and courtesy which, if not finished, reminded me singularly of many a similar visit I have made to newly married couples in England', and he rather envied Combe for his choice 'in the quiet demure little Winape'.

Another of the bridegrooms was Ndoka, a young man who had been among those released at Mbame's. His wife, Gwasala, a widow considerably older than him, was one of the eight released at Soche's. In being sold to the slavers she had been separated from her two-year-old child and was still grieving over her loss. Ndoka was a Nguru from beyond Lake Chilwa. He had been working in the gardens of his future mother-in-law, performing his bride labour, when she and her own brother sold him to the slavers for two yards of cloth and a brass bracelet. He had spent six weeks in the slave forks before the 'English came and said, you are free'.

Chasika's story was somewhat similar. He, too, had been sold while completing his bride labour. Later, though, his intended wife had been captured in a raid and they both found themselves together in the caravan released at Mbame's. At Magomero, they finally married. It was just the sort of coincidence to warm the missionaries' hearts.

All of them, however, felt sorry for Songanaga. She and her strikingly pretty daughter Malotta had been released at Mbame's after being sold by her husband and her sister's husband, who shared the proceeds. Later, this brother-in-law had come to Magomero selling food and wearing the actual fathom of cloth he had received for Songanaga. There had been a riot led by her and the missionaries had to intervene to prevent him being beaten to death. At Magomero, Songanaga had become attached to Demanje, another of the young men from Mbame's, and when the weddings began she expected to be his wife. Demanje instead married Dendijiwarero, a woman comically larger than himself, and was given his plot of land. When he built his hut and moved there with Dendijiwarero, Songanaga 'rushed about like a mad woman', and had to be forcibly restrained from attacking her rival. Later, when Ntula wished to marry her, he had to withdraw for fear of Demanje and shortly afterwards Songanaga left Magomero to become the 'slave' wife of a man from Soche's.

Preoccupied with this discovery that their people were individuals with feelings and personal histories, the missionaries missed the broader significance of what they had done. The Bishop's agreement with Chigunda was that they should be 'co-proprietors of the soil'. Now, without reference to Chigunda, he was allocating land to his own people. The land was outside the stockade, across the river to the north, and was not covered by the agreement. Nor was this all. Contrary to Mang'anja custom, the Bishop was allocating land to men on their marriage. In Chigunda's villages, it was the custom for land to be distributed to married women. Despite all the Bishop's homilies about equality and fidelity in marriage, what he had done in the eyes of the Mang'anja was to lend support to the pattern already evolving by which the most important rights and powers were vested in men, to whom the women became subordinate. As Songanaga's predicament illustrated, even as the missionaries attacked the system of 'slave' wives, their own actions upheld a new division of the sexes.

For the people of Magomero, both inside and outside the stockade, the issues were suddenly clear. The missionaries were not, after all, slave traders. They had come to take over the country. Immediately, there were consequences. Some of the women stole several baskets of peas from gardens belonging to Chigunda's people. Bishop Mackenzie treated it as a case of theft. Chigunda, to whom he referred the matter and who must have been puzzled why it was all right to take his land but not his peas, preferred to let the matter drop. A few days later, two of the new bridegrooms were accused of robbing a man of his amulet and some articles. It emerged that they had been extorting food and valuables from Chigunda's people on the grounds that they were 'the boys of the English' and entitled to gifts. Another contrivance was to waylay people bringing food for sale on Sundays and to declare the food forfeit on grounds of breaking the sabbath. These cases were not referred to Chigunda. Confirming the widespread assumption that he was now chief of the area, the Bishop had the culprits flogged.

The chiefs and headmen who visited the missionaries invariably brought presents of goats or chickens. At first, the missionaries had responded with gifts of calico. Then, just two days after the first weddings, they decided to accept the offerings without making any return. The presents became tribute, an acknowledgement of authority not just in Magomero but throughout the Highlands. Stories such as Waller's description of the headman who fell on his knees as he approached or Rowley's experience of having people prostrate themselves, calling him master, confirmed their new overlordship. Faced with these effects Chigunda was helpless. When trouble erupted it was with Zachurakamo and his family.

Fig. 3 Dr Meller's sketch of Magomero: October 1861

The day of the first marriages a little girl returned to Magomero saying she had been abducted three days earlier by a woman from a village across the river. Treating it as a case of slaving, the Bishop, with Chigunda and William, demanded to be taken to the spot a kilometre downstream. They found a woman called Akaswiri, who admitted to being 'the friend' of the woman responsible. Chigunda delivered a stern lecture and the party came home, debating appropriate punishments and full of praise for Chigunda.

Next day, they discovered Akaswiri to be Chigunda's sister-in-law and the woman who had taken the child to be her daughter, Zachurakamo's wife. With William as spokesman, the missionaries shouted at her, demanding how she would like to lose her own daughter. It was the wrong thing to say to a woman who had watched eight children die. She answered 'with affrontery and impertinence' and only when intimidated by the threat of being sold herself was she silenced. She took her revenge on her husband. He had lit his forge to repair the missionaries' hoes. His wife hid the hoes and, unable to leave his fire, Zachurakamo spent some time shouting across the village for the hoes, which 'after a considerable expenditure of breath on his part the wife was at last prevailed upon to produce'.

There was no punishment and, for the missionaries at least, the affair had ended in comedy. Ten days later, two of the Kololo men from the *Pioneer*, Mobita and Sesaho, who were on a visit, went out hunting. They stopped at Akaswiri's village to buy a chicken and Sesaho leant his shotgun against a tree. Some children playing nearby knocked it down and it went off, wounding one in the abdomen. By the time Procter arrived on the scene, the child was dying. The child was Akaswiri's grandchild, and Zachurakamo was its uncle. The Bishop sent a fathom of cloth for the burial, and William explained to Akaswiri that 'God had perhaps sent this as a punishment for stealing the child'.

Until the missionaries arrived it had been Zachurakamo who was *mfiti*. Now, as they were appropriating land and undermining custom there was added a new explanation of misfortune. Chigunda's villagers were divided and Zachurakamo's wife and mother were angry and resentful. Only the continued threat from the Yao and their dependence on the missionaries' firepower kept this resentment subdued.

The boldness of their followers infected the missionaries. In a mood of happy confidence they planned the station. The village they had inherited was felt to be 'irregular and inconvenient', the huts being scattered on both sides of a footpath which itself cut diagonally across the top end of the peninsula. There was a distressing absence of symmetry and straight lines. The Bishop decided that their own sleeping huts should extend in a row from the left of the stockade entrance with his own new 'palace', a hut measuring 40 by 15 feet where they took their meals, to the right. Behind the sleeping huts, work began on a large dormitory, capable of sleeping forty boys in separate cubicles with raised beds and bamboo partitions. Behind the palace there was to be a hut for the Bishop's sister, who was to join the settlement when it was established, and another for her Scottish maid.

The huts of their dependents would occupy the centre of the promontory, extending in parallel lines to Chigunda's three huts at the very edge of the new clearing. These huts, of which eventually they built thirty, were for the unmarried women, the married couples having been allocated land across the river to the north. The women were given gardens on the south side of the promontory. The framework of the new huts was constructed by the young men working under the Bishop's supervision, and the women, supervised by Charles, clayed the walls.

Waller took over the task of tending the sick. He had no medical training or experience, but no doctor had accompanied the mission and there were people needing attention. Most of his time was spent bathing and bandaging ulcers of the legs and feet. He had picked up a book at the Cape, Milligan on *Medicines and their Administration*, and found it 'the most valuable I could have hit on'. Later, his enthusiasm shifted to Martin's work on *Tropical Climates* and he experimented dangerously with recipes for diarrhoea. Fortunately, a visit from Dr Mellor who had joined Livingstone's expedition was in time to diagnose an outbreak of smallpox in September. The cases were successfully isolated in a hut 2 km away.

Rowley continued purchasing and distributing food. Maize continued to be very cheap but their cloth was running out alarmingly fast. One evening, the Bishop discovered with the excitement of an amateur how to grind pods in their maize mill, and from then on they bought no flour. Every evening, Rowley distributed food to their dependents, flour on weekdays and a goat or chickens for Sunday. The children's meals were cooked by Jessiwiranga, an 'excellent and motherly' woman who had been among those released at Mbame's.

This left Procter and Scudamore to supervise the education of the boys. There were three classes, each of twelve boys. The youngest were nominally Rowley's charge, but since he was fully occupied with bartering, the Bishop took responsibility, sitting every day under a tree trying to 'make them understand the difference in form and sound between A and B'. Rowley gave all three classes singing lessons, and Scudamore began each morning's schooling with drill. The boys were marched in line to the river and on Scudamore's order 'Off clouts!' were required to jump in.

Education involved reducing Mang'anja to writing and they worked a standard alphabet of twenty-four letters. Q and X were rejected, as better represented by Kw and Ks. The dental fricative ŵ eluded them. For the adult men, who were working through the day, it was planned to begin evening classes later. No one suggested educating the girls, though there was a prospect of sewing classes when Miss Mackenzie arrived.

On 1 October, the anniversary of the mission's inauguration in Canterbury Cathedral, they marked out the ground at the west end of the promontory for their church. Scudamore trimmed a tree trunk and the Bishop formally erected it as the corner post of the Church of St Paul. A bottle commemorating their action was buried next to the post. The surrounding land, which already contained Chibaba's grave was declared consecrated ground.

The church and graveyard, the boys' residential school, the singing lessons, the drill, the charitable health work, the refectory, even (in the 'admirable Jessiriwanga') an embryo Mothers' Union – these were signs of their confidence, not simply in their ability to bring Christianity and Civilisation to central Africa but in the particular accents of Anglicanism. In no way was their vision adapted to circumstances.

They all longed to begin preaching. Waller, surveying the village and dealing as always in generalities, wished 'to open all my brotherhood to them'. Procter, again typically, regretted the way his conversations with Combe or Jessiriwanga were cut short by his poor Mang'anja and their self-imposed embargo on religious teaching. Rowley's high-church vision was of 'the hills echoing to the voice of prayer and thanksgiving from numerous Christian communities'. Meanwhile, they concentrated their efforts on the men they had brought from the Cape. The attempt revealed something of the self-distrust already taught to these men from central Africa by their contact with Christianity:

In reading Genesis IV Charles asked me what was the nature of the mark set upon Cain. I said I believed it to be some visible token of his guilt impressed by God on his face or features, by which after generations should recognise and avoid the murderer. He had a strong impression that this mark was a change in the colour of the skin, Cain thus becoming the first black man, and so strong was it that it was some time before I could induce him to adopt my view, which I cannot help thinking a better one, and taken from a more literal interpretation than his.

William observed that he had often heard the following facts asserted with regard to this history. Cain, from being a tiller of the ground, and consequently exposed to sun and air, became dark in colour, which peculiarity was handed down to his posterity, and in this way he was made father of the black and coloured races. Seth, on the other hand, from being occupied, as it was asserted, in works connected with books and writing, which belonged to a more confined mode of life, never lost the lightness of his complexion, and so became the father of the whites. He quite saw, however, that the history of the deluge upset this theory!

Procter was not warned by this response. He felt there was a need to collect such traditions.

Livingstone's original proposal had been that the mission should be established among Seleketu's Kololo on the Batoka plateau. Now several of the Kololo porters came to Magomero. They wanted to settle with the missionaries. Mobita, acting as spokesman, told the Bishop those parts of his story which were likely to appeal to a man of his sensibility. Mobita was not a Kololo but a captive. Though Seleketu had been generous to him with cattle, land and wives, he had no wish to return. He and the others wished to marry Magomero women and to join the settlement. This request was repeated over the following weeks, each time more urgently, and each time the Bishop promised to discuss the matter with Livingstone. In effect, this was a refusal. One of Livingstone's most stubborn intentions, arising from comment in England about his having left his loyal companions at Tete on his departure for England, was to return them to Seleketu. Thirty of them had already been led there rather against their will in 1860. His intentions for those still employed by the expedition were obscure, but so long as Seleketu was alive an obligation had to be assumed, whatever the Kololo themselves wanted. In fact, by the time the expedition was recalled in 1864 the Kololo state no longer existed and the remainder were left in the Shire valley to fend for themselves.

Meanwhile, the Bishop was caught up in a second miscalculation. The diplomatic seige of the settlement continued. Barwe called the day after their return from Chirumba. It was a bad moment to choose. They were still trying to justify to each other the battle they had just fought, and the wrangle with Chisunzi over the captives soured the atmosphere. He was also an unsatisfactory petitioner. With his brass rings and necklaces and his elaborately greased hair, he raised all their Victorian hackles. When he introduced 'the old story of the Ajawa', they were disgusted. It was, though, a worrying story. His village was a morning's walk distant and much nearer than Zomba. Scudamore, with Charles and the Kololo, were sent to investigate. Creeping forward at dusk through the long grass they came close enough to hear conversations as the Yao sat round their fires. There was no doubt that Barwe's Yao existed, and that their numbers had increased following the burning of Chirumba.

Then Nampeko arrived with a similar petition. Nampeko Mpoto was from the west side of Lake Chilwa, where he exercised control over fishing and the manufacture of salt, a monopoly which made him as important economically as Chisunzi was in ritual terms. The Yao raiding his territory were based in the Chikala hills to the north. They were burning his villages and taking food and slaves. The Bishop decided to make another tour of inspection. First, he visited Barwe's village and confirmed that 'the people were afraid and with reason'. Next, the Bishop dropped in on Chisunzi at Mitande, confirming that the village had been resettled and that the first battle had achieved its objectives. Finally, he made the long hot trek across the Chilwa floodplain to Nampeko's village at the foot of Mpyupyu hill. A short distance to the north he saw burning villages and the familiar columns of pathetic refugees. The Yao, he determined, were 40 km inside Mang'anja territory and should be driven out.

Back at Magomero, the Bishop made a sharp distinction. The Yao village he had seen beyond Barwe's was very large but essentially peaceful. The people had been there for three years and were cultivating the land. At Nampeko's the opposite was the case. The Yao based at Chikala were invaders who lived by raiding and enslaving Nampeko's people. Reinforcing this moral distinction was a tactical consideration. The Chikala hills were the northern gateway to the Highlands. If the Yao could be driven off and the border of Mang'anja territory secured, the whole area would be pacified. Thus, the Bishop's plan was this: to capture the Chikala hills and establish a second mission station at Nampeko's.

It was a bold plan and the climax of the missionaries' month of confidence. Then Nampeko returned with news that his village had been destroyed. Another council of chiefs was summoned. It was a very different affair from the earlier councils. There were no formalities, and the Bishop was clearly in charge. Briefly, he laid down their conditions. No slave traders were to be welcomed in their villages. No people were to be sold. Chiefs were to punish people involved in slave trading. The third condition caused laughter, which was quickly suppressed with a stern lecture from Chigunda. The agreement to fight was concluded.

Then came disaster. The Bishop asked where they should all assemble.

'Where Nampeko now lives.'

'In the bush?'

'No, at his village, where you slept before.'

'Is it not burned then?'

'No.'

The Bishop shook his fist in Nampeko's face. 'If a dog could do as you have done I should kick it. The tongue of the liar should be pulled out!' He stormed from the meeting, sending William back to break off negotiations. 'What, not go to war?' said Nampeko in utter astonishment.

The missionaries returned to their routine of building, bartering, doctoring and teaching. They had few interruptions. A little girl who had fallen in the fire was baptised on her deathbed by the Bishop and given the first Christian burial at Magomero. People began burning the long grass to prepare their gardens. Chimula, one of Chigunda's men, was caught 'misbehaving' with Katichona, one of their women. The Bishop consecrated their new church. Then, a fortnight after the disastrous conference, Chisunzi and Nampeko returned.

They were kept waiting. It was 3 o'clock on the following day before the Bishop received them. Nampeko abased himself and was pardoned. There was no question now of Church dealing with State. The missionaries were the real power in the land. Yet now the Bishop temporised. He despatched Scudamore to Nampeko's for a further assessment. Three days later, Scudamore's letter arrived. It was the same story. Six villages had been burned, the 'ruins were still smoking and the gardens ravaged'. The Bishop decided to fight. He took with him Adams and Gamble, and Mellor, the doctor from the *Pioneer*. Procter, Rowley and Waller remained behind.

It was a dispiriting action. At Nampeko's, they found a force of two thousand Mang'anja drawn there by Scudamore's presence. The Bishop loaded thirty of their guns and they advanced. Nampeko remained behind. Complaining bitterly about cowardice and falsehood, the Bishop repeated over and over again 'The battle is the

Lord's, and He is the governor among the people'. They crossed a river short of the Yao settlement in the gorge between the two Chikala hills. Adams saw three men and fired. They saw no other Yao men all day. They burned the settlement and raided the gardens. Over 400 woman and children were brought in. They marched them to a small village called Mpola and arrived at dusk:

It rained piteously until 3 p.m. No food to be got. The goats that had been set aside for the people were stolen. Some of the Captives came in last night, but most this forenoon. Children cried. No fires could be lighted outside, and the huts were all filled before half were housed. How to get them disposed of so as to secure their liberty was now the difficulty. We gathered them and the chiefs together, and asked where they wished to stay. They could not make up their minds; how could they? They did not know the nature of the choices they had, to go with the English or with the Mang'anja. Some made choice and were put aside. It began to pour; all ran for shelter and confusion followed. At last those who declared for us were got together, and put into three huts. I wanted to see the rest have their choice with whom they would go, but at last came to the conclusion that if I pressed this point they would all be starved with hunger, and so there would be nothing left to contend about. Went away with the full belief that Nampeko would allot his friends to take such as they liked, who would then have them as slaves to pay debts with or such like ... I do not think I ever spent a more miserable day: wet through, urging the chiefs to do something but not succeeding, quieting the crying of the children, feeling for the hunger of our freed people, which I could ill abate by two or three fowls among 60 or 70 and, finally, doubting on the whole whether we had done much good by our fighting, as we had been the means of 400 women and children being severed from their relations ...

The Bishop arrived home with forty-eight new dependents, all of them old and wretched. Otherwise, he had achieved nothing. The expedition was a raid, differing from the Yao raids only in its scale. No second station was established at Nampeko's, and the Yao remained firmly in control of the Chikala hills. None of the missionaries ever went that way again.

With the arrival of forty-eight more women and children from Chikala there were more Yao people settled at Magomero than there were Mang'anja. For the first time, the missionaries began to learn something of the people they had been fighting.

They took it for granted that Africa was inhabited by 'tribes'. A tribe was less than a nation, both in scale and in the sophistication of its political systems, but it was still assumed to be a collection of people with a discrete language, a centralised and hierarchical system of government, fixed territorial boundaries and theoretically a common ancestor. Warfare between tribes was rather like the collision of different coloured balls on a snooker table. The balls moved around into new positions, but the number and size and colour were constant. Thus, in the Shire Highlands, in 1861, the problem was that the 'Yao' were moving into 'Mang'anja' territory, and the Mang'anja were the missionaries' clients.

With these assumptions, they became impatient with the Mang'anja for their lack of 'real patriotism'. The Mang'anja, Rowley explained, were agricultural people. They lived in villages dotted here and there over the country, each village having its own headman and caring only for itself. An invader had little difficulty in subduing the nation piecemeal. There were elements of truth in this. By the middle of the nineteenth century, the Mang'anja were not well organised for defence. But, as Rowley and his companions were already half aware, the real position was more complicated. There was a Mang'anja chief acknowledged as paramount by the people of the Highlands. This was Mankhokwe, whose capital on the Shire river the missionaries visited on their first arrival.

Mankhokwe was called *Lundu*, a title some of the chiefs were beginning to apply to the English. As applied to Mankhokwe it also indicated a shift in overlordship, for Mankhokwe was not the original *Lundu* of the Shire valley. Much of the history of the Mang'anja people remains obscure, but from oral testimony and Portuguese records broad outlines may be constructed. The original Lundu was a minor chief in the kingdom of the Maravi first described by Gaspar Bocarro in 1616. During the fourteenth century, Maravi people under their leader Karonga migrated from Luba territory and settled at the southern end of Lake Malawi. The settlement did not long maintain its stability. Undi was the first to break away, trading independently with the Portuguese at Tete and founding his own capital on the modern Mozambique–Zambia border, from which he dominated the triangle of land between the Zambesi and the Luangwa rivers. In breaking with Karonga, Undi took with him a chief called Kaphwiti who appears to have been Lundu's superior. Lundu then broke with Kaphwiti, moving into the Shire valley and establishing a capital on the west bank, from which he traded with the Portuguese at Sena. By the early seventeenth century, Lundu had established by conquest a kingdom extending from the Shire valley eastwards as far as the Indian Ocean. This alarmed both Karonga and the Portuguese who united to defeat him, and Lundu's later inability to protect his kingdom from incursions by the Portuguese in the lower Shire valley led to its decline. Rival chieftaincies emerged, including Mankhokwe's. By the beginning of the nineteenth century, Mankhokwe had asserted his authority so successfully as to carve out a kingdom of his own in which he ruled as *Lundu*, including the upper Shire valley and the Shire Highlands. Chiefs like Chisunzi, Kankhomba and Mbona were Mankhokwe's appointees or his 'children'. The lower half of the Shire valley was controlled by another chief called Tengani, who maintained a standing army to resist the Portuguese.

When Livingstone and his party first sailed up the Shire river in January 1859, he had encountered a blockade of the river established by Tengani to protect the valley. Four hundred armed men with spears and bows ordered him to stop. Livingstone was in no mood to accept further obstacles to navigation and he sailed on. He spent a night at Mankhokwe's village but under armed guard and in an atmosphere of great hostility and suspicion. Then, at the furthest point of navigation, he was welcomed by Chibisa who became his friend. Chibisa is a rather shadowy figure, looming on stage briefly as the man who welcomed Livingstone and dying at the hands of a Portuguese trader early in 1863. The obscurity of his background was part of the politics. His reasons for welcoming Livingstone were the same as his reasons for dealing with the Portuguese slavers – that is, he needed guns and ammunition. Typically, Livingstone at once wrote off Tengani and Mankhokwe as irrelevant to his purposes.

The story was repeated when the *Pioneer* brought the Universities' Mission up the Shire river in 1861. Despite the enormous amount of time they spent on this journey, the missionaries under Livingstone's conduct saw nothing whatsoever of Tengani, who controlled the river by which all their supplies would have to be transported. They visited Mankhokwe and heard him claim authority over the Highlands which were their destination. But they did not allow his suspicions that they 'wanted to rob him of his territory' to interfere with their plans in any way. They sailed on to Chibisa's and it was Chibisa who became their sponsor in the Highlands. In supporting them he was effectively laying claim to part of Mankhokwe's territory.

It was not until after they had abandoned Magomero that the missionaries came to understand this, realising too late that when they had complained of the disunity of the Mang'anja they had themselves been deeply implicated in undermining the authority of Mankhokwe, the paramount chief. At the time, they merely drew distinctions between the endless bickering of their friends and the apparent organisation and purposefulness of the Yao.

Then, after the battle at Chikala, they began to learn something about their enemy. The fact that the Yao, too, might be victims had already occurred to them. They had discovered within a fortnight of settling at Magomero that a number of the men and women they had released at Mbame's were actually Yao, including boys like Wakotane and Chinsoro, the Bishop's and Waller's servants, who were rapidly becoming their favourites. They learned, too, that the Yao were coming into the Shire Highlands as refugees, their own territory to the north-east having been invaded by Ngoni people from the extreme south-east corner of Africa, fleeing the aftermath of the wars of Shaka Zulu.

This, though, was a 'tribal' explanation, the scattering of the snooker balls. What surprised the missionaries was that the Yao were themselves divided into different groups, and that their wars against each other were at least as fierce as their struggles with the Mang'anja. When the Bishop had attacked the Chikala hills, his opponent was a chief called Malemia, who had settled there after driving off the Mang'anja Kalonjiri. Malemia was a bitter enemy of another Yao chief called Kawinga, who had already attacked him at Chikala, and the only effect of the Bishop's raid when Malemia's village was burned was to ensure that Kawinga became installed at Chikala – where his descendants are chiefs to the present day. Malemia fled to Zomba to his ally Mlumbe, the Yao chief the missionaries had attacked at Chirumba. Mlumbe and Malemia divided Zomba between them, this division once again, despite the missionaries' attack, becoming permanent.

Meanwhile, three further groups of Yao under chiefs Njowe, Nkanda and Kumpama were advancing into the Shire Highlands down the Shire valley and behind the back of Zomba mountain. These groups had not entered the Shire Highlands by way of Chikala and, contrary to the Bishop's assumption that a strike against Chikala was a strike against the 'Yao advance', they were affected by his action only in that Malemia's flight to Zomba drove them further south into the area between Chiradzulu mountain and the Shire. It was Kumpama, or Mpama as his descendants at Chiradzulu have become known, who had been settled for three years in the valley beyond Barwe's village. They were the only group who posed any direct threat to Magomero, and they were the only group the Bishop refused to fight.

Although they came as refugees, as they moved into the Shire Highlands the different groups of Yao people had certain advantages. Long before the coming of the slave trade the Yao had acted as middlemen in the trade between the coast and the peoples of the interior. The trade in slaves superimposed itself on a much older system of exchange, involving ivory, tobacco and beeswax traded for cloth and other luxury goods, the term 'Yao' becoming in fact very close to being a purely professional designation. It was easier for the Yao than for other peoples of the region to obtain guns and powder, and it was because the new Yao warlords were so well armed that the Mang'anja needed the missionaries' firepower.

A second advantage was that the Yao traders had always been men. Whereas Mang'anja men and women worked together in their fields, Yao men would be absent from their villages for unpredictably long periods and it was the women who took over the role of cultivators. A sexual division of labour had arisen within Yao society which, while not suited to the purely agricultural economy of the Shire Highlands in the days before the slave trade, was better adapted to the new culture of stockaded villages and towns which was the Africans' answer to the slave trade. While the men fought, defensively or in raiding for food or for slaves, the women cultivated. It was not true, for instance, that Malemia's followers at Chikala did not grow food. During and after the battle, Scudamore reported 'large green flourishing gardens all around', which were cultivated by captive women. Much of the enmity between Malemia and Kawinga had its origins in a competition for women whose labour was essential to the new economy.

In these circumstances, the missionaries' distinctions between Mang'anja and Yao had little relevance. As with their own stockaded settlement at Magomero, most villages or stockaded towns in the Shire Highlands contained, by 1861, a considerable ethnic mixture. Even Chigunda owned Yao 'slaves', and one of his villages near Machereni was populated by Nguru people from the east. As the political map of the Highlands was being redrawn, the relationship that came to matter was not that based on kin or 'tribe' but that between patron and client, the protector and the protected. It was because they understood this that Wakotane and Chinsoro had already become so popular with the missionaries who, with their guns and their regiment of women, fitted the new pattern in everything except ruthlessness.

Decades afterwards, a British colonial official recorded an African description of Malemia, the chief the Bishop had attacked at Chikala and who had settled at Zomba. Malemia, he was told,

was very good at looking after the boys. All of them used to go to his court to get food at about 12.00 noon and 5.00 p.m. Whether they were his own or not, provided they lived near the court. His wives cooked the food for these boys, sometimes numbering 200, bringing it with beer in baskets.

In broad terms, this would have been no bad description of the settlement at Magomero.

For Chigunda this turn of events was a disaster. Chigunda had persuaded the white men to settle at Magomero to protect him from the Yao. Somehow, without his permission, the peninsula had been turned into a Yao camp. Not only were the majority of the people living there Yao, but the political hierarchy, the patterns of production, the relations of men to women and of men and women to the land, were all new and disruptive. There was nothing Chigunda could do about it. The Mang'anja still needed the missionaries' guns.

The economic benefits had also ceased. From the end of October food became scarce. It would be January before the first green maize was available, or the grain called *sumbwe* which sprang from the roots of last year's sorghum. Meanwhile, people stopped bringing food to the stockade. Instead, William and Charles set out in search of food. The expeditions ranged further and further afield, taking them as far as the Shire valley in a wide sweep of some 150 km before their baskets were filled. Charles had on occasion to threaten people that their attitude was 'unfriendly to the English' before they would part with supplies. They became expeditions of extortion, the levying of tribute from a subject people. In the village of Mpasa, close to the Shire river, Charles and his carriers were driven away by an armed crowd shouting 'that the English had joined with the Ajawa against the Mang'anja and were attacking them'.

The problem was that the bonanza at Magomero during August and September had drawn in not just the surplus food of the Highlands. The high prices had tempted people to part with their stores, and many had nothing left until the new season arrived. The missionaries who had come to teach agriculture and trade had destroyed the economy. On the peninsula within the stockade, they cut their meat ration to one meal per day. Up the footpath in Chigunda's main village, a man died of starvation in mid-December.

Meanwhile, three new missionaries had arrived at Magomero. The first was Henry de Wint Burrup. Burrup had married the day before leaving England and his new wife was already following him to Magomero. Impatient at the delays in reaching central Africa, he had made the journey up the Zambesi and Shire rivers to Chibisa's alone in hired canoes and without guides – a feat which Livingstone never ceased to admire. The second new member was John Dickinson, a doctor, whose first action was to condemn Magomero as unhealthy. They devoted some days to clearing bush from the far bank of the river in the hope of creating breezes. Rowley, hard-headed as usual, built himself a hut on Nanyungwi hill and retired to live there. Richard Clark, the third arrival, was a shoemaker. He had come to make shoes from the tanned hides of the game the missionaries had expected to live on. Like Gamble, the incompetent carpenter, Clark became another odd-job man.

Barwe was still coming regularly to ask for help against the Yao. The story was that Kumpama's villages had been swamped by refugees from Chirumba and that groups under Kumpama and Njowe had begun raiding west of Chiradzulu mountain and towards Soche. But the Bishop was preoccupied with other problems. Miss Mackenzie, his sister, and Burrup's new wife were due to arrive shortly at the Zambesi mouth. Livingstone had undertaken to meet them and transport them to Chibisa's. Now in mid-November he wrote that he could bring the ladies no further up the Shire than the junction with the Ruo river, 75 km downstream. As usual when revising his plans to other people's disadvantage, Livingstone's letter was testy: 'you will see now the necessity I have so often referred to, of your having a steamer of your own'.

Examining the missionaries' predicament at this time it is hard to see that this was the most serious of their problems. They had lost the confidence of Chigunda. They were living with over two hundred dependents on a small unhealthy peninsula. They were at war with people who were taking over their diocese. Their supplies were running out and there was no food to be purchased. Yet none of these difficulties seemed to loom so large as those raised by Livingstone's letter. They had taken it for granted that all their problems lay to the north. This, suddenly, was a blow to the rear. The Shire was no longer navigable and Livingstone no longer at their disposal. Magomero might not be tenable for much longer.

The immediate task was to find out how to get from Magomero to the Ruo mouth, where the ladies were due by the first of January.

Procter and Scudamore were delegated to explore the route. They took with them Charles, a boy called Nkuto, and a guide and six Nguru carriers supplied by Sachima, one of Chigunda's headmen. Afterwards, there was controversy about the path they had taken. Livingstone claimed to have advised that they should simply keep Mount Thyolo on their right hand, which would indeed have been the correct route. But he also suggested they should find the Ruo valley and follow it downstream, guessing wrongly that the Ruo flowed out of Lake Chilwa. In the event, the party set out to the south-east across the Phalombe plain looking for the Ruo. They forded the Tuchila river and turned east under the southern face of Mulanje mountain. This was precisely the wrong direction. They were also heading towards trouble.

The population of the southern slopes of Mulanje had in the 1850s been swollen by refugees from the slave trade. Nominally, the area was ruled by a Mang'anja chief called Tombondira. Recently, however, an Nguru chief called Mangasanja, driven from his home by the Portuguese, had built a fortified village on the Ruo which, like Tengani's blockade of the Shire, had set limits to the slave trade. As Procter and his party approached the village they were asked if they were slavers. The bolts of cloth and the guns they were carrying made their denials unconvincing. Detaining the party until late afternoon, Mangasanja made plans to attack them at night. Warned by their guide and by the sight of women removing their possessions from nearby huts, they decided to leave at once. There were scuffles and skirmishes as they fought their way through the stockade's narrow gateway. As darkness fell Procter and Scudamore became separated from the others. It was two days before they got back to Magomero. They found Charles had arrived hours before them with the news that they were dead. Over the next few days all the party turned up except Nkuto and two of the carriers who had been kept prisoner. Mangasanja had also kept 140 precious yards of calico.

That night, Chigunda was troubled by a dream. Chibaba appeared to him and said: 'You see how the English are clearing away all about the village where I was chief, and how they have knocked down my hut and pulled it in pieces. I am grieved and angry and now ask you to build another that I may have a hut to live in.' Instructions were given that the *pombe* used at the ceremony was to be made of millet – Chibaba had told Kirk that millet beer was the best – and a warning was added: 'You see that the English have driven out the Ajawa, and in doing this they have rendered great service to the Mang'anja. But now take care lest they do not soon turn against the Mang'anja and drive them also out of the country.'

Next morning, Chigunda walked down to the clearing where the corner post of the Church of St Paul had been erected. He rebuilt the prayer hut and built a small fence around it. When he had finished, he assembled his people outside the stockade. Together, they marched between the straight lines of rectangular houses, and entered the enclosure surrounding the prayer hut, the women sitting to one side and the men to the other. His sister Mbudzi went into the hut carrying a pot of *pombe* and a basket of flour. While she poured out the flour and the beer, she prayed in a high-pitched voice:

> *Imva Mpambi*
> Listen, Mpambi
> *Adza mvula*
> Send us rain

To this, the people outside responded, *Imva Mpambi*. When the sacrifice was complete, Mbudzi fastened the door and lay down on the ground for several minutes, repeating the prayers and clapping. Then the whole village stood up, clapping, and the women danced around Chigunda where he sat. A jar of water was brought and placed before him. Mbudzi washed her arms and face and water was poured over her. Then all the women dipped their calabashes in the jar and threw water in the air.

Chigunda's people were reclaiming their village. They believed – it was something else Chibaba had said in the dream – that the English would depart before very long.

Reluctantly, for the fourth time, the missionaries prepared to fight. It took them a few days to assemble their latest army. Chigunda offered a 'few hundred men' who would be led by Zachurakamo. This worried the Bishop, who was not sure Chigunda could still be relied on. He preferred to trust his own people and the Kololo, fourteen of whom came up from the Shire. These, however, began to make terms. They wanted permission to marry and settle at Magomero. Caught in his own prevarications the Bishop temporised again, offering to speak with Livingstone 'if they behaved well'. Ten accepted this offer, joining the expedition. Four refused. Subsequently, while the Bishop was away fighting, they had second thoughts. They went raiding as far as the upper Shire valley and returned with twenty released slaves and 150 fathoms of cloth which they presented to Procter. 'Behaving well' had become a confusing concept.

53

The Bishop's force was a small one and twenty of Chigunda's men were needed. His suspicions were confirmed when, for the first time, Chigunda himself insisted on accompanying the expedition. Chigunda was asserting himself, though for what sudden purpose was unclear.

Two days before Christmas the Bishop and Burrup set out, first to 'punish' Mangasanja and then to meet their ladies at the Ruo. On the 25th, they stopped at the village of Chauka. Chigunda explained there was to be a *mirandu* at which Chipoka, the senior Mang'anja chief of the area, would make an appearance. The Bishop began to be impatient.

On the 27th, they were still at Chauka. The Bishop, with his mind on meeting his sister, could bear the delay no longer. He insisted against all objections on moving to Chipoka's – 'a perfect triumph', he wrote, 'of determination over obstinacy and indolence'. The following morning he took the Kololo and attacked Mangasanja. They found the village completely deserted. Mangasanja and his people had gone to Chipoka's to negotiate the return of the captives and the goods. Whereas in previous battles the Mang'anja had insisted on fighting while the Bishop tried to negotiate, it was now the Bishop who was interrupting negotiations by fighting. This explained Chigunda's presence. Mangasanja was not regarded as an enemy. Chigunda was trying to negotiate with him, using Chipoka's good offices and keeping the Bishop's army in the background as a threat.

Mangasanja's village was plundered and burned. Scudamore's valise was recovered, along with a pair of shoes, a bar of soap and two tins of meat. On the way back to Chipoka's they were ambushed and one man was fatally wounded.

Chipoka was outraged, first with Chigunda for failing to keep the English under control, and then with the Bishop. He absolutely forbade them to continue to the Ruo mouth, denying them guides and refusing to send messengers ahead. Chigunda left at once for Magomero. The Bishop refused to move. Now he proposed negotiating. The first of January came and went. At last, deeply frustrated by Chipoka's firmness, the Bishop and his party returned northwards. They reported to Rowley that they had upheld the English name and taught a tyrant a lesson. Nkuto turned up a few days later and then disappeared. The two carriers from Sachima's village remained at Mangasanja's where they were kept in slave sticks. Early the following March they escaped and returned home. Mangasanja kept the rolls of calico.

Meanwhile, the Bishop and Burrup spent one night only at Mago-mero and hurried on immediately for Chibisa's. They were both ill from exposure and diarrhoea. Incessant rain and swollen rivers kept them five nights on the road. At Chibisa's, they hired a canoe and set off downstream with three of the Kololo. They were now eight days late for their rendezvous. Towards dusk, they entered the wilderness of Elephant Marsh, a maze of waterways and shallows and sudden rapids. Twice the dangers of continuing made them stop and twice they were goaded by clouds of mosquitoes into travelling on. About ten o'clock the canoe grounded and sank. In rescuing it, they lost all their medicines. They reached the Ruo mouth to discover that they had just missed the *Pioneer* travelling downstream. The haste had been for nothing.

They remained where they were in a hut provided by the headman, teaching each other texts in New Testament Greek. The Bishop had been worried about Burrup's health, but it was he who suffered most from the journey. His mind went back to Livingstone's letter and, in a hand shaken by exhaustion and fever, he drafted an appeal to the boat clubs of Oxford and Cambridge Universities for a steamer to patrol the Shire. Its purpose would be to bring Christianity and Commerce to the river valley and to stop the slave trade. Ten days after their arrival, his speech became incoherent. On the 31st, on the headman's instructions, he was moved to another hut and died. He was buried the same evening, Burrup reciting in the twilight among the reeds as much of the burial service as he could remember.

There was nothing for Burrup to do but to return to Magomero. He spent three days trying to persuade the Kololo to force the canoe upstream through Elephant Marsh. At last they refused to go any further by water and continued along the right bank with Burrup staggering behind them. Mankhokwe treated them with great kind-ness, offering food although their cloth was finished. From Chibisa's Burrup was carried in a litter to Magomero, where he arrived on the 14th, a few minutes after the news had reached the missionaries of Bishop Mackenzie's death. He had 'shrunk to half his usual size, and his colour was that of a guinea'.

The following morning, the Kololo approached Procter who had been nominated by the Bishop to take charge in the event of his death. They wished to take their wives and settle at Chibisa's. The women were content to leave. It was obvious the mission settlement was doomed.

The Bishop's death was not the only cause of this conclusion. From the first day of 1862, when Procter wrote 'Hunger and Scarcity are among us', the community had begun to fail.

Through January, the famine intensified. Charles and William, Job and Adams were sent regularly in search of food. But the stored remains of last year's harvest had already been eaten or sold or raided, and it was only by forcing people to sell their goats and chickens to the English that they were able to bring home anything at all. Their own crops, those plots of wheat and barley and coffee and parsley and beetroot, had all come to nothing. The gardens planted by their own people and in Chigunda's villages were flourishing in the abundant rains. But it would be weeks before maize, millet and sorghum were harvested. Meanwhile, Chigunda explained to the white men who had come to teach him agriculture how to survive famine. By mid-January, the first crop of pumpkins would be available. By the end of January, they were able to eat *sumbwe*, a flour made from the grain which sprouted from the roots of last year's sorghum left in the ground as insurance. There were various kinds of wild bean available and the cobs of green maize could be eaten by the end of January. The missionaries were humble about such information, and also about the African habit of sharing whatever was available. All recorded in their journals instances of unselfishness over food. Meanwhile, for days at a time, Rowley had no food to distribute.

Famine was aggravated by disease. From mid-December there was an outbreak of amoebic dysentery. First they blamed the site which Dickinson had declared to be unhealthy. Then they blamed their diet of pumpkins and cucumbers. Only gradually did they realise that their water supply, the river flowing round the peninsula, was contaminated. In designing Magomero, with its square houses and straight lines, they had made no provision for sanitation. While Chigunda dined at their table in the Bishop's place, eating 'like a civilised creature using knife and fork dexterously', the deposits of over two hundred people were spreading infection. Magomero became a death camp. Between December and early April, over fifty women and children died of dysentery aggravated by malnutrition.

Death made the missionaries once more aware of their people as individuals. They were all distressed when Akoombe died. She and her child Chilondaga, whom Procter had cured of an ulcer, had been among those released at Mbame's. Then, following the attack on Chirumba, her mother Kinamwisa and her sisters Biya, Sengwa and

Chiko, all of whom had fled from Mulanje after the raid in which Akoombe had been captured, joined Akoombe and Chilondaga at Magomero. After the happiness of so dramatic a reunion, the family's grief affected them all. 'There is', wrote Waller, 'something very sad in the grief of her old mother Kinamwisa ... the old woman and the child now walk about so much alone.'

Their community dwindled in other ways. Ncheoka and Kabanda, two of the married men, disappeared one night. Five women ran away early in January to join the Kololo who had refused to fight at Mangasanja's, breaking their pots as a token of final departure. Nasimvagwe and Matuira, the latter 'a really nice and quiet boy' from Procter's class, disappeared and Nasimvagwe was brought back the next day by two men to whom he had offered himself as a slave. Twelve more boys followed their example, three of them going to work for the fishermen at Lake Chilwa. Kamvaino stole corn from one of Chigunda's men as a token that she wished to live with him and be under his protection. He didn't want her, and returned her to the missionaries. By late March, through deaths and departures, their numbers were down to approximately half.

Early in February, before the news reached them of the Bishop's death, they assembled the men together in their gardens across the river to make a proposal to them. In the past, they declared, the men had worked for them and been paid a daily food ration. Now they all had wives and huts and gardens of their own and it was time to put them on 'a superior footing'. In the future they should support themselves. If they worked for the missionaries they would be paid at the rate of one fathom of cloth for six days' work. This was generous pay – most of them had originally been sold for a fathom – and the men were delighted with this confirmation of their new status as husbands, householders and tenured farmers.

Afer the meeting Ndoka approached them with a petition. Ndoka and Gwasala had been among the earliest couples married during the week of weddings, Gwasala being a widow separated from her two-year-old child. Ndoka's news was that this child had been seen. She was in the possession of a man called Kankadi who had bought her near Soche's for two baskets of maize while the Bishop was attacking Mangasanja's. Gwasala had demanded her child back and been told she must offer another in exchange.

Kankadi was summoned and came armed and in aggressive mood. He would surrender the girl but only 'if the English bought her'. The missionaries took the matter to Chigunda. Their case was that

Kankadi had fought with them against the Yao and been a party to all the agreements against slave trading. To their amazement, Chigunda refused to intervene. He was still furious over what had happened at Mangasanja's. He had, he said, 'no authority' over Kankadi. He had 'joined himself to the English, and would not leave them, but all his people were going from him'. The missionaries were contemptuous – 'poor Chigunda ... a mouse of a man', wrote Rowley – but in fact it took courage to stand up to the missionaries. His response was of a piece with his new attitude to the English since his dream and the prayers to Chibaba.

Procter then assumed authority, passing judgement on a case heard in Chigunda's own village. Kankadi was told he must give up the child and pay a fine for breaking the agreement about slave trading. Kankadi was furious, relieving 'his hot wrath by fiercely plucking up the tufts of grass around him'. He denied breaking any agreement. He had promised not to sell slaves. There had been no law against buying them.

Was he right or wrong? The missionaries were adamant but uneasy. The position of domestic slaves in Chigunda's village was one they had consistently avoided. They waived the fine and offered to compensate Kankadi with a fathom of cloth. Then Waller intervened:

He pictured to him the sorrow of the poor mother, her heart yearning for her little one, and trembling with anxiety for fear it would not be returned to her; he told him of the sorrow desolating the hearts of many poor mothers in that land, through their children being sold from them. And while he spoke a better spirit came over the man; his face assumed a milder expression; he ceased to speak or behave insolently; and when Waller said: 'Supposing you had a child, and it was stolen, and sold away from you, would you not think it very cruel, very wicked of those who took it from you? Would not your heart feel as sorry as this poor mother's here?' an expression of pain passed over the man's features. He did not reply for some moments; he was much agitated; but at last he said and while he said it he was almost choking with emotion: 'It is true I should feel it. I should feel it here', laying his hand over his heart, 'and my heart tells me it is a cruel thing to take the child from the mother. Take the child. Give it to the mother; I will keep it no longer. I don't want anything for her, I give her up freely.' And the child was given to its mother.

It was the mission's most magical moment, an episode none of them ever forgot. Yet Kankadi, like Zachurakamo's wife on a previous occasion, had reasons for speaking with great feeling. His own wife

58

and child were in the possession of a chief near Soche. No one suggested trying to recover them for him.

Chigunda's predicament was a tragic one. In abandoning him, his people were acting decisively. For men to return temporarily to their own villages was not unusual, though it left Chigunda unprotected. For their wives to accompany them was drastic, and for families to leave their crops unripe in the fields was proof of repudiation.

There was nothing Chigunda could do about this. He could not expel the missionaries. The best he could do was avoid them. He lived outside the stockade and, as the dispute with Kankadi illustrated, he resolutely refused to take their part against any of his own people. From the time of his return from Mangasanja's he was unwell, the symptoms perhaps reflecting his dying authority as chief. But he refused Dickinson's medicines, preferring to be treated by a Mang'anja doctor. His tactic was to wait until the English went away, as Chibaba had promised they would.

Part of his problem was that to the world beyond Magomero the possibility of an alliance with the English still had its attractions. While Chigunda was ill in his hut the missionaries, who still awaited news of the Bishop and of Burrup, were once again being courted from all sides.

Their first visitors thrilled them. They woke one morning in January to find four men and a woman waiting to speak with them. They had come from Kumpama, the Yao chief settled beyond Barwe's, and their purpose was to seek peace. The Yao, they declared, were surrounded by Mang'anja who were continually harassing them, asserting 'that the land by them occupied was not theirs and that the crops they had planted belonged to the Mang'anja and the English'. They were also being attacked by the Kololo. Having failed to persuade the Bishop to allow them to settle at Magomero, the Kololo were establishing their own villages in the Shire valley. After the English fashion, and invoking the English name as anyone with a shirt and trousers seemed entitled to do, they were raiding the Yao for women and children, for food and animals, and for goods.

Excitedly, the missionaries sent at once for Chigunda. But Chigunda sat angrily in his hut and refused to come. This sobered them considerably and in the absence of the Bishop they 'thought it better not to be "Hail fellow well met" all at once'. Next morning they sent to Chigunda again. Reluctantly he appeared, bringing with him a headman of Barwe's called Kwawala, who interrupted Procter's account of their negotiations with the news that his mother's village had been burned the day before. Chigunda refused absolutely to allow any of Kumpama's people to settle. The missionaries decided that Chigunda was very difficult to deal with. That afternoon there were three more weddings. The Yao men who had been left with them by the Kololo in the new year were given wives and land for their huts and gardens. That evening Rowley's food store was raided and some dried fish was taken. The missionaries blamed Sinjere, one of Zachurakamo's relatives, and gave him a public flogging.

Their second visitor was Kankhomba, the senior chief of the Highlands Mang'anja after Chisunzi. He wanted the white men to make rain. Towards Lake Chilwa the rains had ceased and their crops were drying up in the fields. There had been plenty of rain, though, at Magomero. Kankhomba had brought one of his headmen, a lively man with long twisted hair, to make the request and he listened without seeming to care about the answer. It was, all the same, the most important petition he could have presented.

The provision of rain was at the very heart of the Mang'anja religious system. It was because he controlled the rain shrine at Mitande that Chisunzi was the senior chief of the Highlands. Set above Chisunzi was Mankhokwe, and set above Mankhokwe was a rain spirit called M'Bona. M'Bona's rain shrine had been for five centuries the official cult of the Lundu paramountcy. It was located at Khulubvi in the lower Shire, where M'Bona lived as a python with a woman supplied by the Lundu as his wife. A second shrine was located on Thyolo mountains and was under the control of Mankhokwe. For some years no wife had been supplied to M'Bona at Khulubvi. Before they left central Africa the missionaries were to witness an attempt by Mankhokwe to take over the Khulubvi shrine and the whole M'Bona cult by supplying a wife from his own village. Meanwhile, the cult languished.

In this situation, Kankhomba's invitation to the missionaries to make rain was no casual enquiry about the weather. It was a challenge to them to substantiate all that was implied by their actions, in fighting, in allocating land, in levying food as tribute, by demonstrating that, as the new overlords of the Highlands, they could control the Spirits of the Land. William was the only one of the mission party who understood this and his reply was a masterpiece of ambiguity. They had prayed for rain, and so had Chigunda, and plenty of rain had fallen. They would pray to Pambe for more rain, and perhaps he would send it.

Before they could respond, news of Bishop Mackenzie's death was brought to them by the Kololo. Reading the Bishop's last will and testament, Procter found himself the acting head of the mission. He made a number of swift decisions. He gave permission to the remaining Kololo to take their wives to Chibisa's. He resolved that in no circumstances would the mission engage in further fighting. He began speaking urgently to the women about *Pambe*. He called an assembly of all the people. The men, he announced, would be governed by the decisions of the previous meeting, though until fresh supplies of cloth arrived there would be no work for them. The women, except for the married and the sick, would have to fend for themselves among the Mang'anja. If they brought back husbands to Magomero, they would be welcomed and given land.

Before this blow had been absorbed by their community, Burrup too died. He had been lucid for only a few hours since his return, as he described the Bishop's last hours, and his death moved them profoundly. His young wife was somewhere to the south, approaching them at that very moment. They buried him in a bamboo coffin at the west end of the peninsula next to Chibiba's grave and close by the corner post of their own unbuilt church.

For the remaining missionaries Burrup's death defined their predicament. Procter's rapid decisions had been contradictory except from one perspective, that their duty was to survive until fresh instructions came from Cape Town or a new Bishop was appointed. Nothing should supersede their responsibility to keep the mission alive. Nothing therefore was done about Kumpama's diplomacy or about Kankhomba's request. No response was made to their third visitors, the chiefs of the Highland Mang'anja who, hearing of the Bishop's death and suspecting that the loyalty of the English was wavering, came to pay the necessary court.

Kalonjiri came asking for help against Malemia. Barwe came complaining of raids by Njowe. A chief came from beyond the Ruo asking for protection from raiders who were coming up from Quelimane. A man came as ambassador from Mamvula, the *Lundu* of the upper Shire valley to the north-west, asking again for help against the Yao. These were only the important requests. All petitions ran up against Procter's new policy of non-involvement.

For six months the English had held the balance of power in the Shire Highlands. With the mission bent only on survival there was a sudden vacuum. There was scope for someone of energy and purpose to assert himself, to begin behaving like Kawinga or Njowe or like the

Kololo establishing their power base in the Shire valley. Briefly, and impatiently, the initiative was seized by Zachurakamo.

His pretext was the death of a man in Chirara's village near Chiradzulu. The man had been struck by lightning and Chirara, who had made proposals to the man's mother, was accused of having ascended as a spirit into the sky and sent down the lightning. Though as a headman he was subject to Mbona, Chirara was also a relative of Chigunda, who claimed the right to hear his case. Chigunda found him guilty and his goods and crops were declared forfeit. Zachurakamo was sent to carry out the sentence. Arriving with his men at Chirara's he shouted that the English had come, and proceeded to plunder the whole village. When news of this reached Procter, he sent Clark and William to investigate. At another village called Kavarininga they interrupted a further raid. Zachurakamo and his men, with a group of women to carry off supplies, were plundering all the gardens in the neighbourhood. Clark made an armed intervention and confiscated Zachurakamo's gun.

Chigunda was furious. Storming into Procter's hut he demanded to know why his brother had been attacked. William, as Zachurakamo's old enemy described the raid, offering to bring Mbona for confirmation. The breach between mission and village was open and irreparable. Chigunda 'went away in a very dejected state but Zachurakamo thought the matter a joke and laughed openly'.

His career as a raider with English credentials was short-lived. Just as the initiative was passing to him, his ninth child died of 'atrophy'. All the issues became focussed by this tragedy. There was a trial and Zachurakamo as suspected *mfiti* had to submit to the poison ordeal. The *mwabvi* was, however, 'prepared by a friend' in a non-fatal form, emphasising his innocence. Zachurakamo had supporters and there were other explanations current of why disaster had come upon Chigunda's village. That night, Burrup's grave was dug open and his head removed. The missionaries never knew for what purpose it had been taken. In their extreme distress they guessed that it was to be used as a charm in fighting the Yao and they may just possibly have been right. Almost certainly, though, the grave's desecration was a blow against the mission. Chigunda's action in rebuilding Chibaba's prayer hut was no longer enough to pacify Zachurakamo's angry supporters. Their own act identified the missionaries as *afiti* and Burrup's skull gave them, in Mang'anja belief, the means of defeating the white men's malign influence.

Confirming Zachurakamo's status, his dead child was given a

lavish funeral lasting five days. The missionaries were allowed no part in it though they watched with emotion the sad columns filing to the graveyard. Public grief conformed well with their own mood. On the fourth day *nyau* dancers appeared from the river bed and ran wildly through the village dancing and chanting obscene songs. They wore elaborate masks symbolising the unity of the world of humans, animals and spirits. It was taboo for women or non-sympathisers to catch sight of them. The dancers forced people into taking sides, choosing between the missionaries with their Yao clients and those who practised the rites of Mang'anja religion. Circumstantial evidence makes it likely that Burrup's skull featured in their ceremonials. It was a powerful and frightening demonstration of the strength of Mang'anja religion.

Yet Zachurakamo was still feared as *mfiti* by some, including the women who took no part in *nyau*. Chigunda was still the legitimate chief. In any case, it was all happening too late. On the very day the *nyau* danced, the decisive battle for the Highlands was taking place.

The mission's end came swiftly. In March they were startled by a request for help from Mbona, 'a quarter whence we least expected it'. If Kumpama was raiding south of Chiradzulu, the missionaries were cut off. Their refusal all along to assist Barwe might prove their undoing.

Procter's first thought was to find a new site in the Highlands but closer to the Shire. With Dickinson and William he visited Mbona, who was keen for an alliance. Next day, they climbed the northern slopes of Chiradzulu, enjoying the views of the Highlands from Michiru in the west to Zomba and Chikala in the north to Mulanje in the south-east. Below them, not three miles off, was a smoking village burned by Kampama that very morning. All round them on the mountainside among the rocks was a portent of the future – the temporary huts where people took refuge during the day, going down at night to their huts and gardens below. Returning to Mbona's, the missionaries tried further south, investigating sites on Nguludi and Nkuwili hills. These were tempting for being so much closer to the Shire. Before they could decide, however, they were visited by their old friend Mbame. He, too, was being threatened. He asked for help and was refused and went away. His information further undermined their hopes, for if Mbame's village at the very edge of the escarpment was under attack there could be no security anywhere in the Highlands.

Mbame, Mbona and Barwe resolved to unite in an attack on Kumpama. The battle took place in mid-April, the morning after Burrup's grave was disturbed and while Chigunda's people were preoccupied with the death of Zachurakamo's child. It was the decisive battle for the Highlands and no one from Magomero took part. The attack was a failure. Kumpama called out to the retreating chiefs that he would be their enemy 'as long as I live'.

On 23 April, as they were finishing breakfast, Chigunda came into the Bishop's palace and told them quietly there was war at Barwe's. They went out together and stood on Nanyungwi hill. They could plainly see Barwe's village burning, and another towards Chiradzulu, and five more in an arc, some less than three miles distant. The refugees – women with baskets of maize on their heads, the old chief Chisamba looking distraught – were pouring into Masambala just across the river. Even then, Zachurakamo standing bitterly beside them tried to play a last card. It was a swift raid, he observed, because Kumpama was afraid the English would come out in pursuit. Adams and Johnson wanted to fight and were over-ruled. The experiment was over.

Eight of their Mang'anja women and children elected to stay with Chigunda. The remaining ninety-eight went with the missionaries to Chibisa's. They included all the married men who knew they had no chance of retaining their land after the English had gone. Even then, the missionaries had insufficient carriers and were forced to leave some goods behind.

They stayed at Chiradzulu the first night. Chigunda's people, including Zachurakamo who had helped them with their boxes, left them at dusk without saying goodbye and without waiting to be paid. The missionaries continued to Soche's, and then Procter went back to Magomero for the last few items. Their stockaded village was desolate. Some of the round huts had been appropriated but the square ones were empty and already partly destroyed. Procter lay on straw in his own hut eating essence of beef and thinking about Bishop Mackenzie.

They had achieved little. They had acquired a hundred dependents. A few of these had been taught the alphabet. Militarily, they had confined Kawinga to Chikala and Malemia to Zomba and had allowed Kumpama to seize Chiradzulu. They had denied the Kololo any foothold in the Highlands. Procter could not know that these divisions would still have force a century later. Otherwise, a few square huts of grass and mud, a grave surrounded by a bamboo fence and a redundant cotton gin were all that remained on the peninsula to mark their passage. Before he left the following morning, Chigunda asked him to fire a gun to give Kumpama the impression the English had returned.

Down at Chibisa's they built a new settlement on a site eighty feet above the Shire river. For just over a year they waited there for their new Bishop, intent upon surviving until he came. They lived quietly, almost 'out of the world' as Procter, the ex-country curate noted with relish, with 'none of the grand *mirandus* and visits of chiefs with presents that we used to have at Magomero'.

Relations with Livingstone were polite but increasingly strained. He had moved quickly after the Bishop's death to exculpate himself in a series of well-placed letters. After all he had said about the health of the Highlands he blamed the Bishop for not taking fever seriously. He blamed the missionaries for fighting and he blamed them for not holding on to their position. He blamed them for settling the people he had presented them with on the site he had chosen. He could not admit that their withdrawal was in any way linked with his own denial of the use of the *Pioneer*. But when the deaths of Bishop Mackenzie and Burrup were followed by the deaths at Chibisa's of Scudamore and Dickinson, the gap between Livingstone's Cambridge lecture and the realities the mission had encountered became too obvious to conceal.

Relations with the Kololo, too, were strained. As they built their own stockaded villages, the Kololo were far more successful than the missionaries in creating stability. By the 1870s, when they had used their guns to create a new kingdom from the ruins of Mang'anja power, the slave trade had been excluded from the Shire valley and replaced by trade, not in cotton but in ivory and oil seeds with agents of European companies. This transformation, though, was brought about by means the missionaries had repudiated. They complained bitterly to Livingstone that the Kololo were undermining their own work.

Occasionally, they had news of Magomero. In June, William was sent to collect the rest of their goods and returned with Zachurakamo. Chigunda was repairing the stockade. He slept each night in his old hut but did not dare to remain there in daytime and went everywhere with his gun. In August, Rowley made a final visit. He was accompanied by Rev. James Stewart, a minister of the Scottish Free Church who had come up river to investigate the prospects for establishing a mission. Already dismayed at the contrast between Livingstone's writings and central African realities, Stewart was in no mood to be anything but savage:

With difficulty we reached the other side of the Magomero stream on the single tree which overhangs the river and after scrambling up the bank, got within the stockade. The aspect of the place was not pleasing. The village was dirty, tumble-down and miserable looking. A few women, 7 in number, set up their *lilili*-ing and came round about Rowley in a way that disgusted me. One woman went round and round, very much as a cat does against one's legs. The children looked half-starved, the women as they really were, lazy and dirty. Of the buildings erected by the mission only three were standing. These were the Bishop's house, Procter's hut and that by Clark for the ladies. So little appreciation have the natives of the value of improvement that one of these houses is turned into ———! while they continue to live in their miserable dog kennels ...

Nothing was lying about except a cotton gin of the old form (saw) by Jameson, Ashton-under-Lyne. There has not been a pound of cotton to clean by it ...

Chicundo himself made his appearance shortly afterwards in a most extraordinary dress for an African, a loose woollen coat or shirt; above that a grey old Witney top-coat, and an old pork-pie hat on his head. He carried an old Tower musket, the barrel of which was polished bright.

Civilisation had come to Magomero with a vengeance!

With this description, contrasting so starkly and emblematically with John Kirk's of just three years earlier, Chibaba's village disappears from history. The next recorded visit to the site was almost forty years later when it, and the land for miles around, was uninhabited and covered with secondary forest.

By the end of 1862, the Yao chiefs were in firm possession of the Shire Highlands. Barwe was the only Mang'anja chief who attempted resistance, earning the missionaries' belated admiration. In November, Zachurakamo was killed making a further raid near Chiradzulu. The following month, an attack into the Highlands by Kawinga from his stockade at Chikala forced Chisunzi and Kankhomba to fly to Mlumbe for protection. Chigunda seems to have chosen the patronage of Kumpama instead. Nothing more is known of him. Perhaps, like Chisunzi and Kankhomba who, under the new regime, retained a remnant of their former power as subordinate chiefs and whose line continues to this day, Chigunda might have survived and even flourished under Kumpama. But then came the famine.

The fighting had left people ill-prepared for the months of shortage.

As the year turned, mass starvation spread through the Highlands and the Shire valley. Village after village died or was abandoned. By the end of February Rowley estimated 90 per cent of the Mang'anja had been killed by hunger. His figure is an adjective rather than a statistic, though it brings home forcibly the scale of the disaster, and it insists on too 'tribal' a description. Those who survived did so because they were able to secure the patronage of the new rulers – the Yao in the Highlands, the Nguru in control of Mulanje, the Kololo and the missionaries themselves in the Shire valley. They were not all by any means Yao or Nguru or Kololo, but it was sensible of them to begin calling themselves so. Those who died were the helpless, without protection or the means of raiding. 'Magumanya', the Mang'anja called the famine, meaning 'heap upon heap'. In June 1863, ten days before their new Bishop at last arrived, the missionaries were visited by Mbame's two sons. Mbame had been killed in February. Mbona was dead and Soche was in hiding. Magomero and every village in the neighbourhood had been burned.

The new Bishop was William George Tozer, and the first news he received as he stepped ashore at Chibisa's was that Scudamore and Dickinson had died and that Procter and Rowley were medically unfit to remain in the country. The Bishop had brought letters recalling Livingstone's Zambesi expedition.

He resolved to withdraw the mission as well. With four of the original members dead and two being invalided out of the country, with food unobtainable and the surviving population at war, and with Livingstone's steamer no longer available, his decision was hardly unreasonable. Bishop Tozer, though, wanted a complete disengagement and a fresh start elsewhere. He refused to accept responsibility for the mission's dependent men, women and children.

The argument that followed at Chibisa's was rancorous. Their new Bishop, the survivors noted bitterly, had no interest in their people, driving the curious out of his hut with such abruptness that the word passed round that he had a 'bad heart'. He was concerned only with accounts, taking an inventory of the mission's belongings that extended to candle wicks and pieces of string. It was like having the bailiffs in a house of bereavement. But Bishop Tozer was more than tactless. The heart of the matter was his judgement that Livingstone's release of the captives at Mbame's had been inexcusable, nothing less than 'highland robbery'. None of the people had been baptised and it was time to leave them to their own devices.

Procter, Rowley and Waller could accept none of this. Repudiation of their dependents was repudiation of all they had lived through. It made entirely useless the four deaths which had occurred. As a compromise, the Bishop agreed to set up a station on Morumbala mountain, close to the junction of the Shire with the Zambesi and in Portuguese territory. He would establish a school there with the twenty-five orphan boys. The rest would have to fend for themselves.

Waller had been of all the missionaries the one most passionately committed to the fight against slavery. Loading canoes with thirteen of the women and children, he followed the Bishop downstream to Morumbala. On the way, he received an ultimatum ordering him to abandon them. Instantly, he resigned from the mission. For the next five months, from September to January, while Bishop Tozer built a new settlement among the clouds on the summit of Morumbala mountain, Waller and his refugees lived at the landing stage awaiting a reprieve. Chinsoro and Chasika his wife joined him, with one or two others. But there was no contact between the two groups. Waller wrote various drafts of his letter of resignation and a brief history of the mission, and he translated the Lord's Prayer into Mang'anja. For the first time he got to know his people as individuals rather than as objects of compassion. With Chinsoro particularly he became close.

In January, Bishop Tozer gave up the experiment, resolving to launch the Universities' Mission afresh from the island of Zanzibar. He offered to take the boys with him. Six refused and were sent back to Chibisa's. Livingstone was outraged and demanded and obtained custody of them all. Packing them and Waller's people together in the *Pioneer*, he sailed with them from the Zambesi in February 1864. The Portuguese took especial pleasure in protesting about the export of slaves.

The party divided. Chuma and Wakotane voyaged with Livingstone in his second steamer, the *Lady Nyasa*, to Bombay where they were eventually placed by him in the mission school run by Dr Wilson. The remaining people, forty-two in all, accompanied Waller in the *Pioneer* to Cape Town. The plan was to place the boys in the new Zonnebloem College, which had been founded by Bishop Robert Gray in 1858 as part of his scheme for the evangelisation of central Africa which had also included his sponsorship of the Universities' Mission. For the women and girls, other places would be found.

In the dispute which had split the mission, Bishop Gray's sympathies were with Waller, and he began to devise a new plan, which came to nothing, for Waller to take holy orders and to return to central Africa. About the Magomero boys, however, he was dubious. Zonnebloem College was intended for the sons of chiefs who, as educated Christian gentlemen, would rapidly bring about the evangelisation of central Africa. He was reluctant to take responsibility for a bunch of homeless orphan boys. In the event, Waller spent weary weeks knocking on the doors of Cape Town's Anglican community trying to find places for his people as apprentices or as domestic servants at wages of £2 to £3 per year. Most of them disappeared into Cape Town's black proletariat.

One of the exceptions was Daoma, the little girl brought back to Magomero on Bishop Mackenzie's shoulders after the attack on Chirumba. Daoma was christened Ann and placed in St George's Orphanage in Cape Town. She grew up to be a teacher and corresponded regularly with Waller until her death in 1936, sending a wreath from Cape Town when Waller's wife died.

Chuma and Wakotane came back to the Shire Highlands among the servants and carriers recruited by Livingstone when he returned to Africa in 1866, commissioned to search for the source of the Nile. The party travelled south-west from Zanzibar to the eastern shores of Lake Malawi and reached Mponda's village at the south end of the lake in September. There Wakotane met his brother and learned that his father, who had sold him to the slavers, was dead. He decided to remain and to marry. Livingstone expressed misgivings but could hardly object. Chuma refused Wakotane's offer of a home at Mponda's. He travelled with Livingstone throughout his final years and was one of the famous group who carried his embalmed body 1,500 miles back to Zanzibar. Along with Susi, a former employee of the Zambesi Expedition, Chuma was brought to England and, under Waller's patronage, was presented with a bronze medal of the Royal Geographical Society. Suzi and Chuma assisted Waller to edit the two volumes of Livingstone's *Last Journals*.

Chinsoro and Sinjeri also returned to central Africa. In 1867 they were recruited in Cape Town by E. D. Young, a former member of the Zambesi Expedition, who had been commissioned to investigate rumours that Livingstone had been killed by Ngoni people west of Lake Malawi some time during 1866. Chinsoro and Sinjeri were 'invaluable to us during our travels', wrote Young afterwards in his account of an outstandingly successful expedition. 'The intelligence of the one could hardly be placed before the untiring zeal and hard work of the other.' Young's second in command was a former officer of the 17th Lancers called Henry Faulkner. Faulkner returned to the Shire in 1868 on a hunting expedition, re-employing Chinsoro in

Cape Town. It was a disastrous expedition, afflicted by smallpox and malaria, by constant quarrelling, three deaths and two desertions from a party of seven. In February 1869, Chinsoro set fire to several huts in the village where they had caught smallpox. He was court-martialled and summarily shot.

E. D. Young made a third visit to the Shire Highlands in 1875, conducting the pioneer members of two new Scottish missions which were being established as a memorial to Livingstone. He took with him Mbakwiti, one of the young men rescued at Mbame, and Lorenzo Johnson, the Jamaican cook, whom he met again at the Cape. Arriving at Chibisa's old village, they were met by Jessiwiranga, who wailed bitterly on learning that Rowley was not of the party. At Mponda's, Young was greeted by Wakotane who joined him for the remainder of his tour of inspection as he helped the new missionaries choose suitable locations. Back on the Shire, his task accomplished, he was disturbed in his tent one night by 'well known music'. Wakotane was singing 'one of the chants used by the missionaries sixteen years ago on the hills at Magomero':

> This night I lay me down to sleep
> I give my soul to Christ to keep;
> If I should die before I wake
> I pray to God my soul to take.

Up in the Highlands Bishop Mackenzie's achievements, in so far as they were remembered at all, were remembered differently. His battles had played a part in the division of the plateau between the different warring groups in 1861 and 1862. In 1894, an official of the new Protectorate of British Central Africa visited Chipoka's village near Mulanje, where he was given a lively account of Bishop Mackenzie's raid on Mangasanja by two old men who had been Mackenzie's guides. Two years later, in April 1896, the annual Military Sports Day at Zomba was attended by one thousand Africans and several chiefs. Among them was an old man called Mbalu, a Mang'anja headman from the shores of Lake Chilwa. Mbalu, probably confusing him with Bishop Mackenzie, claimed to have known Livingstone and to have fought with him against the Yao. 'Dottori Livingstone', he declared, 'was a very good man. He killed lots of people.'

The Lomwe villages | II |

1901–1915
'This place is wonderful'

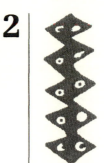

Early in the dry season of c.1901 a man called Njenjema was hunting in the waste land of scrub and *misuku* trees which stretched north from Chiradzulu. He was living temporarily in the territory of a Yao chief called Malika, one of Mpama's (Kumpama's) subordinate chiefs at Chiradzulu. His real home was across the border from British Central Africa in Mozambique, east of Lake Chilwa, an area newly conquered by the Portuguese. As the Portuguese had moved in levying taxes and compulsory labour, Njenjema, along with many thousands of others from the area, had moved across into British territory.

Njenjema was hunting game, but he was also looking for somewhere to settle. The area was inhabited only by animals – kudu, wild pig, zebra, lions, an occasional herd of elephants – but as he approached a river lined with mahogany trees he thought he had found what he was looking for. The river, even at the height of the dry season, flowed clear and strong and the soil looked fertile. He travelled upstream to the track linking the new colonial towns of Blantyre and Zomba and enquired about the land. He was directed to a man called Kalino, a Yao who had been appointed headman for the area. The land, part of a huge undeveloped estate extending from the Blantyre–Zomba road as far as the Phalombe river, belonged to a Major Bruce. Njenjema could build a village on the bank of the river on one condition – that he agreed to work for Major Bruce for two months in every year.

Njenjema and the people who had fled Mozambique with him were already working for Malika, cutting trees and clearing land as a condition for living in his territory. Major Bruce's offer conveyed through Kalino seemed reasonable and there was plenty of fertile well-watered land to choose from. If Kalino told Njenjema that Major

Bruce was the son of Livingstone's eldest daughter Agnes, the information would have meant nothing to him. Returning with a group of people carrying food given them by Malika, Njenjema began clearing away the bush and building a village 1½ km upstream from Nanyungwi hill. As the rains approached they planted crops from seeds and cuttings they had originally brought with them from Mozambique. When the crops were ready for harvesting, Njenjema sent for his friend Ntholowa to join him. Ntholowa was another refugee from Mozambique living under Malika. With a group of friends and clients he began clearing the land downstream from Njenjema's.

They stumbled upon a furnace which they knew to be a relic of the Mang'anja people who had once lived there. It was Zachurakamo's, evidently abandoned in a great hurry on a day when he had been working in his smithy. There were hoes and axe heads lying under the matted roots of the tall grass. Ntholowa used the axes to cut down trees which were forty years old.

After the withdrawal of the Zambesi expedition, Livingstone's reputation had reached bedrock. 'We were promised cotton, sugar, and indigo', declared *The Times*, 'and of course we got none. We were promised trade, and there is no trade.' He had returned to Africa in 1866 commissioned by the Royal Geographical Society to settle the dispute about the source of the Nile. As he disappeared, apparently and misleadingly indifferent to public opinion, his reputation revived. Between 1867 and 1871 no fewer than four search parties were despatched to investigate rumours of his death, culminating in Stanley's famous scoop. Early in 1874, his embalmed body disguised as a bale of cloth was delivered to the British consul in Zanzibar by a group of Africans including Chuma, one of the young men from Magomero. They had carried it for over eight months across 1,500 miles.

To a British public which, then as now, liked its pictures of Africa kept simple, this act of devotion confirmed all Livingstone had said. But the Africans handed over more than a corpse. They brought his journals with fresh information about the slave trade. They brought the image of Livingstone dying in a hut on his knees beside his bed like a Victorian child at prayer. It was an image to compel action. Within weeks a plan was announced to create 'an Industrial Mission Station at the southern end of Lake Nyasa, in connection with the Free and Reformed Churches of Scotland, as a Memorial to Dr

Fig. 4. Beauty and the Beast: imperialism to the rescue: from the Livingstone memorial volume, 1874

Livingstone … with the view of encouraging trade, suppressing slavery, disseminating the arts of industrial civilisation, and opening the southern interior of the Lake country to commerce'.

In fact, two missions were established, their forerunners travelling from Scotland together in 1875 under the conduct of E. D. Young, who had led the search expedition of 1867. The first was the Livingstonia mission, fathered by James Stewart, who had judged Magomero so savagely, but dominated by Robert Laws who came to personify the mission for half a century. Meanwhile, Henry Henderson, who had accompanied the party on behalf of the established Church of Scotland, chose a site for a second mission between Mbame's old village and Soche's. Work began on the settlement called Blantyre in October 1876. A third initiative, complementing the new missions, was the formation in 1878 of the African Lakes Company founded by John and Frederick Moir. Within a few years the company had established a chain of twelve trading stations extending from the new port of Inhamissengo in the Zambesi delta to the north of Lake Malawi.

In later years these efforts would read like a success story. The

75

names, the route, the steamers, the policies – everything seemed to vindicate Livingstone's vision. In fact, the early years of all three enterprises were precarious. Some things had become easier since the days of the Universities' Mission. The wars of the mid-1860s were over, with the Kololo firmly in control of the Shire valley and the different Yao chieftaincies established in the Highlands. Raids by Ngoni people based to the north posed an irregular threat. But there were no more famines like that of 1862–3 and there was no need for the missionaries to engage in fighting. The slave trade flourished still but by adopting a strict policy of non-intervention the missionaries found they could live with it, deploring it in their despatches but taking no action themselves.

Even so, they could not avoid Bishop Mackenzie's dilemmas. The question of Church and State presented itself in revised forms. Livingstonia was a Free Church mission and handled its dealings with the secular authorities – especially the Ngoni chiefs – at a level of personal diplomacy. The Blantyre Mission, however, had been planted by the established Church of Scotland, and the absence of a civil power was bewildering. At Blantyre, as at Magomero, the mission compound became the home of refugees. Despite their neutrality over the slave trade and their policy of educating the sons of chiefs, the missionaries were once again drawn into becoming 'chiefs' themselves. When, like Bishop Mackenzie, they assumed the power to punish offenders, matters got out of hand. There were acts of brutality and one man was flogged to death. A fresh start had to be made in 1881 with a new staff of missionaries.

The African Lakes Company experienced these problems from a different perspective. The opening of the Suez Canal in 1869 had made the east coast of Africa directly accessible to European trading houses. A new economy sprang up along much of the Mozambique coast based on the production by peasants of oil seeds for sale to French, Dutch and German companies. There were limits, though, to the areas which could be profitably exploited. The African Lakes Company was attempting to bring commerce to the Shire valley and beyond. Even though it enjoyed the advantage of using the Kololo chiefs as its middlemen, buying oil seeds which the chiefs had gathered as tribute from their subject peoples, the costs of transport cut into profits. It was only by trading in ivory and by extending its operations to the north of Lake Malawi that the ALC managed to remain in business. Ivory in central Africa was a commodity linked with powerful vested interests. The company came into violent conflict with Arab and Swahili traders.

In 1887, a brief but well-publicised war between the ALC and Mlozi, an Arab trader at the north end of Lake Malawi, produced demands for British intervention. But the real threat to British interests came from the Portuguese who, in the same year, published their famous 'rose-coloured map', indicating a belt of Portuguese territory across Africa from Mozambique to Angola and including Lake Malawi. In combating the Portuguese the missionaries had a powerful ally, for the plan to link Mozambique with Angola ran athwart Cecil Rhodes' vision of a block of British territory extending from the Cape to Cairo. Nevertheless, they took their own measures to protect their position.

Among these measures was a plan devised by John Buchanan, who had joined the Blantyre Mission in 1876 and who, after the scandals of the early years, left to become a planter. By 1884, he owned three estates on which he was experimenting with coffee, rubber and indigo, and he had begun to develop his vision of a Shire Highlands dominated by a plantation economy: 'I can see no reason', he wrote, 'why an estate of 200 acres under coffee in the Shire Highlands should not yield a clear profit of £2000 yearly.'

To increase British stakes in the area, he began to act as broker in a campaign to purchase land from the Yao chiefs. In 1889–90 the freehold title to just under one million acres of the Shire Highlands passed into European hands. Buchanan himself with his two brothers purchased 168,000 acres in various parts of Zomba, Blantyre, Chiradzulu and Thyolo. A British subject of German origin called Eugene Sharrer, who had begun operations in Africa as a trader on the lower Zambesi, secured the title for no less than 372,500 acres in separate estates in Zomba, Blantyre, Thyolo and Liwonde. The African Lake Company under the Moir brothers bought 55,000 acres in different parts of the Highlands and the Shire valley, together with massive blocks of land to the north. These purchases were formally registered with the British Consul who, from 1887 to 1891, was Buchanan himself in an acting capacity. Equally impressive were the other names Buchanan managed to mobilise in support as he made purchases on their behalf. Horace Waller, for instance, bought 5,000 acres in Chiradzulu as a coffee plantation. But Buchanan's biggest catch was the Edinburgh millionaire, Alexander Low Bruce.

Bruce was the husband of Livingstone's favourite daughter Agnes.

He had made his fortune as a manager and later a partner in Youngers Breweries, and had for some years supported African causes, contributing to the various Livingstone search expeditions. He was a founder member of the Royal Scottish Geographical Society and had become in 1888 a director of the Imperial British East Africa Company. In 1888 he had visited his wife's birthplace at Kuruman. It was natural that he should lend his name and purse to the campaign to take over central Africa and in February 1890 he allowed Buchanan to negotiate on his behalf the purchase of two estates. The first, 7,448 acres on the northern slopes of Mulanje mountain, was called Likulezi after the river which flowed through it. The second was a huge block of 169,000 acres which Buchanan purchased from the Yao chief Mpama, based at Chiradzulu. This estate was bisected by a river which the Europeans had come to call Namadzi (meaning 'the river'), on the banks of which lay the site of Chibaba's former village at Magomero.

Why did Mpama part with so much for so little? This transaction of 1890 was accomplished by Buchanan without the supporting threat of a colonial army. Why did the Yao chiefs surrender almost one million acres to the merest handful of British settlers?

Later, and especially after land shortages became an issue, this question would baffle Mpama's subjects, who could only conclude that he had been swindled. It would also baffle Justice Nunan who, in a memorable judgement in 1903 arising from a dispute between the superintendent of Native Affairs and the heirs of Buchanan Brothers, commented on the alienation of 'about a million acres':

In some cases, as in that of Mr Eugene Sharrer's 372,500 acres, vast tracts were confirmed to a single individual or corporation, in whose mortmain they have since remained. In all about one half of the Shire Highlands, including the very best land, was thus confirmed ... The chiefs, headmen and people appear to have surrendered the fee simple of their lands over these vast areas ... with a gaiété de coeur which must have endeared them to the traders in question. The 60,000 acres which are the subject of this judgement were sold for Fifty Pounds in trade goods – viz., for a quantity of cloth, coloured stuff, guns, powder, brass wire, beads, and other things – being at the rate of one fifth of a penny per acre. With equal cheerfulness and simplicity the natives refrained from specifying any conditions on which they might themselves be allowed to remain on the transferred land.

The usual explanation is that chiefs did not understand transactions in land which was communally owned and could no more be bartered than the air everyone breathed. Mpama can certainly be forgiven for not comprehending such matters as mortmain and fee simple. There are limits, though, to the value of explanations based on assumptions of naivety. The Yao chiefs may not have understood English law. But they knew it was possible to lose their country to an invader.

Two other suggestions may be more illuminating. The first is that Mpama, and other chiefs who made such deals, were still embroiled in the politics of the 1860s. The second is that most of the land involved was unpopulated and largely unused.

After the Yao takeover of the Shire Highlands in 1863 there was a long period of instability which overlapped with the British takeover in 1891. Those who by the circumstances of their expulsion from their homeland in Mozambique had raised themselves to positions of power as chiefs were compelled by the circumstances they had created in the Highlands to continue as rival warlords. They all spoke the same language and held most of their customs in common. But the mutual enmity of the most important transcended bonds of nationalism and culture. This was partly the result of feuds which had developed during the period of their migration. But it was also caused by intense competition for the Shire Highlands' remaining resources. Most of them continued to be involved in the slave trade. But the population had been decimated by war and famine in 1863 and the survivors were those who secured the protection of the victorious chiefs, whether Yao or Kololo. Apart from a small refugee population living in the reeds alongside Lake Chilwa or maintaining a purely nocturnal existence on Nchisi Island in the lake, there was nowhere in the Highlands for chiefs to obtain slaves except by raiding each other. There was little profit in this but it kept them on bad terms. The most important slavers – Makanjira and Mponda at the southern end of Lake Malawi, Kawinga at Chikala, and Matapwiri in the Fort Lister gap between Mulanje and Mchesa peak – drew their profits from controlling the trade routes between the interior and the east coast.

Similarly, although the new economic order required large numbers of 'slave' women to act as cultivators while the men raided and traded, women too were in short supply. Competition was intense and most of the chiefs maintained within their hilltop stockade enormous retinues of 'wives'. The wars between Mlumbe and Nkhata, for instance, or between Kawinga and Malemia, who is described as having 'a hundred wives or more', are attributed by oral

79

historians to quarrels over women who fled from one camp to another.

Had the Yao chiefs been left to themselves a rough balance of power might eventually have been established. Chikoja, one of Mpama's headmen, even lived for a while in the 1870s on the Namadzi river not far from Magomero. More of the Highland's plateau land might have been reoccupied but for raids by the Ngoni in 1880 and 1884.

Chikusi's Ngoni were the people whose incursions into northern Mozambique during their long anabasis from Zululand had first driven the different Yao groups into the Shire Highlands. Eventually, after crossing the southern end of Lake Malawi, the Ngoni had settled near Dedza mountain. They raided for food and for captives, marrying the women and incorporating the young men into their regiments but taking no part in the slave trade. Twice in the 1880s they struck southwards, crossing the Shire river and raiding the Highlands. In 1880 they followed Mpama's old route down the west side of Zomba mountain before sweeping into the Highlands and driving Mpama and his headmen, including Chikoja, to take refuge on Chiradzulu as Mpama himself had once driven the Mang'anja. Four years later, they reached the outskirts of Blantyre in a raid which British officials, collecting accounts a decade later, never ceased to admire for its speed and efficiency. John Moir of the ALC and Henry Henderson of the Blantyre Mission presented the Ngoni with cloth as tribute, ensuring the protection of the eight hundred people who had taken refuge in the ALC stockade.

Against this background, the ease with which Buchanan persuaded chiefs to part with such huge tracts of land in the late 1880s becomes a little more comprehensible. The Yao chiefs in their hostility towards each other and their fear of the Ngoni were ready, as Chigunda had been in July 1861, to accept any alliance which might protect them from immediate danger. As for the land itself, most of it was unoccupied. Apart from those hiding among the reeds or on the islands of Lake Chilwa, the majority of the population lived in fortified hilltop villages with the most powerful chiefs occupying the mountains – Malemia and Mlumbe on Mount Zomba, Kawinga in the Chikala hills, Kapeni on Mount Soche and Matapwiri and Ntiramanga across the plain at Mulanje. Mpama, occupying Chiradzulu, was reputed to have taken refuge for ten years among the crevices of the summit after the Ngoni raid of 1880.

In May 1897, a writer in the Protectorate's new monthly newspaper, *The Central African Planter*, belatedly reviewed Henry

Rowley's book about the Magomero mission. The writer was puzzled by Rowley's description of large Mang'anja villages in a district which 'up until lately has been without almost a single village and is pretty uniformly covered with trees'. Noting that most of these trees seemed to be between thirty and forty years old, he concluded that war and famine had destroyed a population which 'had found its subsistence from the fields which now form the bulk of our coffee plantations'.

With the exception of some small estates in the Blantyre area and the Shire valley, it was this largely unoccupied and uncultivated land which became alienated in the late 1880s. From then on the issue dominating the politics of colonial Nyasaland, at least in the southern region, was not the terms on which Africans could be driven from their ancestral lands but the terms on which they would be permitted to settle.

In 1889 after two years of inconclusive bickering with the Portuguese, Harry Johnston was despatched in a gunboat up the Shire river. By August, he was deep in the interior making treaties with chiefs and distributing Union Jacks commissioned hastily from the ladies of the Blantyre Mission. Meanwhile, the Portuguese were doing exactly the same. Two expeditions were sent to Shona territory and a third to the eastern shores of Lake Malawi, where chief Mponda was reported to keep two flags in a sack, English and Portuguese, for hoisting as diplomacy demanded. However, when Serpa Pinto was sent up the Shire in Johnston's wake with 700 armed men, the crisis came to a head. Lord Salisbury issued the famous Ultimatum of January 1890 and the Portuguese began a series of humiliating retreats. Matters had been made easier for Salisbury by an offer from Cecil Rhodes, whose British South Africa Company had just received its charter and who had purchased £20,000 of shares in the ALC, to contribute £10,000 annually to the costs of occupying the new Protectorate. Conceived by the missionaries and delivered by Rhodes, British Central Africa was born.

Rhodes' investment, though, was hardly an act of charity. If British Central Africa was to remain a Protectorate and not be swallowed by the Chartered Company, it would have to pay for itself. It needed an economy and Buchanan was the man with an idea.

Buchanan preached the virtues of coffee. His promise had been £2,000 per annum from 200 acres, and the planters began to move in. They were true disciples and they enlarged on the vision:

Gentlemen, we could offer to the home investor 25%, 15% if we want to make sure, but for a dead certainty we can offer 12%. Now for 10% men will soar to the skies and go deep to the bowels of the earth, but having found, proved and established a truth the next thing is to hammer it into the heads of the people.

This could well have been the moment for the big landowners to cash in their investments. In fact, fatally for the economic history of the Shire Highlands, very little land exchanged hands. Among Harry Johnston's first acts as commissioner was to investigate the transactions which had preceded his arrival. Though this exercise infuriated Rhodes it was essentially a minor adjustment of existing arrangements. Johnston is usually praised for having stood up to Rhodes' demands that he use his powers of confiscation to create a landless African proletariat whose labour would develop the territory. In fact, by rejecting this option and rejecting the alternative, that the alienated land should be returned to its original owners, Johnston inaugurated six full decades of economic stagnation. No further African land was alienated but the great estate holders, Buchanan, Sharrer and A. L. Bruce, were confirmed in their possession of far greater hectarages than any of them had the capital or labour to work. A final option, that they break up their holdings for resale as medium-sized estates, was effectively blocked by Johnston's policy of fixing an upset price of 5/- an acre for land in settled districts, and 2/6 in outlying districts, a rate five times that current in the Transvaal. In the event, the big proprietors employed managers to open up small plantations, leaving the bulk of their holdings unused.

Among those who arrived in the Protectorate were two men appointed in 1893 by Alexander Low Bruce to manage his new estates and to turn them into coffee plantations. It was almost the last action of his life. In November he died unexpectedly at the age of 54, bequeathing his African assets to his two sons, David Livingstone Bruce and Alexander Livingstone Bruce,

not on account of any pecuniary advantage ... but in the hope and expectation that they will take an interest in the opening up of Africa to Christianity, Commerce and Civilisation on the lines laid down by their grandfather the late David Livingstone.

The two men already despatched to central Africa were D. B. Ritchie, who was put in charge of the Likulezi estate, and William Jervis Livingstone, who took over management of the principal estate of 169,000 acres.

William Jervis Livingstone was twenty-eight years old. He was from the island of Lismore on the west coast of Scotland and was distantly related to David Livingstone. After his beheading by estate workers in the uprising of January 1915, his name and character passed, like David Livingstone's, into the mythology of Nyasaland. All sides found it convenient to accuse him of consistent brutality in his treatment of Africans and they had little difficulty in amassing abundant and convincing evidence. As early as 1901 he was convicted and fined £5 in the High Court on a charge of aggravated assault against Sousa, a chained prisoner in Zomba jail. Yet, as we shall see later, the accusations brought against his memory in 1915 were in part self-exculpatory. He arrived in 1893 with instructions to call the main estate Magomero.

Livingstone, Magomero: the names were a substantial moral investment, as the *Central African Planter* noted:

The plantation which Mr Livingstone is opening up at Namadzi is called Magomero. The name recalls memories of Dr Livingstone and the first attempt of the Universities Mission to get a footing in this land. Mr Livingstone, who is a distant relative of the great explorer, intends keeping the graves at Magomero in good order. That they have been neglected hitherto is not to our credit.

This new Magomero was a block of largely uninhabited land covered with forest and extending some 56 by 38 kilometres. Its headquarters were 13 km from Chibaba's old village, on the overgrown track linking Blantyre with Zomba. On a slight hill above the track, Livingstone built a brick planter's bungalow and cut out a curving road, lined with blue gum trees, to the small plantation of coffee bushes below. By 1895 he had planted 70,000 coffee seedlings, with Pride of India shade trees planted 30 feet by 30 throughout the clearing. This, by central African standards in the 1890s, was progressive farming. By the following year 200 acres had been planted. The coffee bushes were thriving and other planters had been attracted to Namadzi, which was becoming an established coffee area, rivalling Zomba, Blantyre and Mulanje. By May 1898, 1,040 acres were under coffee at Namadzi, 260 of them belonging to the A. L. Bruce Trust, and 180 acres were already bearing. The news that there had been frost at Magomero in August 1896 sufficient to produce ice in the buckets at the brickworks was no more than a temporary setback, a confirmation that pioneer settlers must expect difficulties. So, too, was the news that W. J. Livingstone was confined at the mission hospital at Domasi with fever.

In 1909, Nyasaland's Department of Agriculture looked back on the decade 1893–1903 when coffee had been the staple crop of European planters. The variety used was Arabica, reputedly descended from a single bush surviving of three brought from Edinburgh in 1878 by Jonathan Duncan, one of the early Blantyre missionaries. Plantations were opened regardless of soil and climate. Little attention was paid to planting out or to weeding and the planters' muddled attempts at method only made matters worse: 'practically the whole of the coffee estates were planted very thickly with shade trees of every description. It is wonderful that the plants gave a yield at all.' Pride of India, which W. J. Livingstone established so assiduously at Magomero in 1895, was worse than useless, giving the coffee 'not the least chance'. As a result, bushes began to die off after yielding the maiden crops over which such excited calculations had been made, and the succeeding smaller crops contained high percentages of empty berry.

W. J. Livingstone recovered from his spell in hospital but never made a success of coffee at Magomero. The meagre crop of two tons in 1898, down from an estimated twelve tons, was blamed on poor rains which prevented blossoms forming. In August of the same year, another freak frost killed 70,000 young plants and hailstorms did further damage in 1899. Ironically, only those plants under the shade trees survived. While his neighbours at Namadzi began to contemplate selling out, Livingstone turned his attention to other crops. Maize could be sold to the government or to government contractors to feed their labour forces. Chillies, too, was a crop with the potential for small but steady local sales. The estate as a whole, Livingstone found, was rich in wild rubber, especially along the Namadzi and Thondwe rivers. Waller had noted rubber vines in 1861 but had doubted their commercial possibilities. Gathered wild by Africans and traded at Magomero, rubber became for a period a second small export crop. Meanwhile, Livingstone had begun experimenting with cotton.

It was as coffee failed and as the chorus began to rise once more that cotton was the crop for the Shire Highlands that Njenjema and Ntholowa and their countrymen from Mozambique were allowed to clear the bush and build new villages, using the hoes and axes they found scattered near Zachurakamo's old furnace. As, forty years on, cotton growing came to Magomero, it seemed like a confirmation of the original vision, a late flowering of Victorian philanthropy. The first two cotton plantations were opened with labour provided by

Njenjema's and Ntholowa's people at Machereni, a little to the south-east, where the missionaries had once obtained their supplies of cassava and at Nasawa, not far from Bishop Mackenzie's village of the married people.

Yet the terms on which the dream was fulfilled brought oppression and violence and the death of W. J. Livingstone himself.

When the new planters of the Shire Highlands complained of their problems with coffee and cotton, it was not their own technical ignorance of which they were speaking. Their theme was labour.

In 1893, to the angry displeasure of Rhodes who was paying his salary, Harry Johnston had rejected the option of creating a landless African proletariat to work on the settlers' coffee plantations. All land not confirmed in its alienation by his Certificates of Claim became Crown Land to be used by the African population. But Johnston was also a firm believer that the future lay with plantations rather than with a peasant cash-cropping economy, and to create a flow of labour to the coffee plantations he introduced in August 1894 a hut tax of 3/- per year. The tax was to be paid in coin or, at the discretion of the Collector, in produce, and fell due on 31 December, the taxpayer's hut to be forefeit if the tax was unpaid by 1 March.

Hut tax involved a confirmation of sovereignty, the cashing in of all those 'treaties' of 1889. It also involved war. Between March and December 1895, the power of the Yao warlords was broken. First Kawinga was attacked in March and his fortified settlement on Chikala mountain captured. In September, Matapwiri and Ntiramanga were defeated at Mulanje and their chieftaincies plus a 'fine iron and brass bedspread' were added to the Protectorate. Finally, in November, Mponda's stockade was captured at the southern end of Lake Malawi. In a manner reminiscent of Bishop Mackenzie after the attacks on Chirumba and Chikala, the administration listed by sex and tribe the 379 slaves released. They included 212 women and 128 children, the majority of them Nyanja. Though Makanjira and Zarafi continued to operate as migrant warlords across the border in Mozambique for another five years, the balance of power in the Shire Highlands had shifted decisively.

Immediately, the change began to produce a shift in settlement patterns:

The defeat of the various Yao chiefs throughout the Shire Highlands has had the effect of rendering a residence on the plains around Mlanje no

85

longer a matter of perpetual danger to the natives and many villages have
therefore been vacated on the hillside of Mlanje and new ones built in the low
countries. The native ... much prefers the plains to the hillsides.

By 1904, settlement in the Mulanje district had advanced as far as the
Tuchila river and by 1912 the whole region was dotted with villages
up to the Phalombe river and the very borders of the Magomero estate.
Similarly in Zomba, Mlumbe's and Malemia's people moved down
from the plateau and by 1898 were cultivating land three miles from
the mountain's base. In Chiradzulu, as Mpama's and Malika's people
shifted their villages, they moved southwards, settling the land along
the Mbombwe river in the direction of Blantyre. The land to the
north-east, bordering the Magomero estate, remained uninhabited
until 1907 when the Mwanje river first began to be lined with new
villages.

The coffee planters' hopes of securing labour from this new source
proved illusory. Though the hut tax was successful in forcing Africans to deal in economic and usually monetary terms with the
British, as a means of mobilising labour it was an inefficient device. It
generated only one month of work per man per year, which allowed
no time for the development of particular labour skills, and it
produced a huge labour surplus in the dry season but virtually no
labour at all during the rains when the Africans were planting their
own crops at the very time when the settlers wanted to extend their
coffee plantations. Few of those Africans building their villages on
Crown Lands had much difficulty in raising their hut tax money by
other means. As Blantyre and Zomba expanded they became markets
for the sale of African-grown maize and vegetables.

With increasing desperation, the planters looked to the north of the
Protectorate, where the absence of markets forced Tonga and
Tumbuka and Ngoni peoples to look further afield for their tax
money. In the year W. J. Livingstone was planting his first coffee
bushes at Magomero, groups of Tonga and Ngoni men began travelling southwards in search of work. Many were prepared to stay on the
coffee plantations for periods of six to twelve months. Even so, the
planters were not satisfied. Labour contracts could not be enforced
and there were no penalties for absenteeism. The bulk of the workers
presented themselves in March and April when the rains were ended
and when the settlers had little use for them. Migrant workers had to
be housed but the planters had no wish to invest money in building
compounds. They also had to be fed. Not only was this a further
expense, it also undermined the local labour supply by expanding the

market for African-grown foodstuffs. Finally, the migrants demanded to be paid in money rather than calico, and wages crept up to 4/- to 6/- per month. In 1901, the administration tried to break this circle by introducing a Labour Certificate which could only be signed by a European employer and which had the effect of compelling Africans to pay a double rate of hut tax if they chose not to work for a European. But by this stage the Tonga, Tumbuka and Ngoni migrants had penetrated the far more lucrative labour markets of Southern Rhodesia and South Africa and were leaving Nyasaland in their thousands.

Salvation came from an unexpected source in the immigration of many thousands of people from Mozambique. This movement began in 1895 when, following the defeats of Kawinga, Matapwiri and Zarafi, a 'large influx of natives found its way into the Zomba District where', as the *Gazette* noted, 'they are peaceably settled in full assurance of freedom and immunity from slave-raiding'. Some were slaves freed from the warlord's stockades while others came from the country between Lake Chilwa and the Namuli hills. The British called them 'Anguru', though the people moving into Zomba District in 1895 spoke mainly Lomwe, Mpotola and Mihavani. During the days of the slave trade they had taken refuge for a generation in tiny hilltop settlements, their groups living in relative isolation. But the defeat of the Yao chiefs brought them down in search of land and across the border into British Central Africa. By May 1897, the *Gazette* noted that 1,000 'Anguru' were working in the Shire Highlands compared to 9,000 Ngoni and 2,000 Tonga. A year later, when Ngoni labour was scarce, the deficit was filled by 'the large influx of Anguru which has taken place this year'.

In 1899, this movement became a mass flight when the Portuguese colonial government, itself anxious to develop a plantation economy in Zambesia, introduced a new Labour Code for Mozambique. The code reversed the policies of earlier liberal regimes by stating that all male Africans between fourteen and sixty years of age were legally obliged to work. Africans in their thousands crossed the border into British Central Africa. They were greeted by the Resident at Mulanje, who handed out one-year tax-exemption certificates to the new settlers.

What made them so valuable was their vulnerability. As immigrants they lacked the right to settle. In particular, they lacked land. By being offered land in return for their labour they could be turned into a captive work force. Two groups took advantage of their vulnerability, the established Yao chiefs and headmen and the European planters.

As the 'Anguru' came across the border as individuals or in family groups, they settled first under the protection of chiefs and headmen in Mulanje district. Some moved on after a year or two to chiefs in Chiradzulu. Their arrival coincided with the broad movement of the population back to the lower ground. To clear the plains for resettlement by cutting down the trees which had grown since the 1860s required labour and it was the immigrants who supplied it. The Yao chiefs rewarded them with land on which to build their villages and with gifts of food which the immigrants called by the Portuguese word *ganyao*, meaning 'bonus'. In Mulanje they cleared land and cultivated cotton under the supervision of the chiefs and headmen. Cotton became the major cash crop for Mulanje district and the Resident was empowered to suspend the Labour Certificate for chiefs who produced requisite amounts, a system abandoned only when the rise of the Mulanje tea industry created a demand for plantation labour. In Zomba and Chiradzulu districts, once the land had been cleared, labour under the *ganyao* system was used to produce maize and vegetables for sale to the swelling populations of Zomba and Blantyre.

On the whole, the administration approved. The new settlements along the Tuchila river led to accusations of domestic slavery and one important Yao headman called Kada was imprisoned in 1909. On the other hand, the chiefs were very successful in getting cotton and foodstuffs produced for sale and useful in supplying labour to the administration. The concensus was that although the immigrants 'were kept in a certain degree of mild subjection and occasionally perform a little menial labour for the protection of the chiefs under whom they serve, there is no serious interference with their rights and duties'. This is probably fair comment, for although the immigrants were vulnerable they were not, at the most local levels, altogether without alternatives. They could choose between districts. Within districts, they could choose between individual chiefs and headmen – with consequences of lasting significance for, as we shall see, the chiefs who came to prominence in the colonial period were precisely those who attracted the largest number of settlers. Finally, the immigrants could also choose to settle on the private estates. With half the Shire Highlands under their direct control, it was the planters who had most land to offer.

To describe the terms on which immigrants were allowed to settle on their estates, the settlers used the Mang'anja word *thangata*. The word means 'help', and was originally used to describe help provided freely and reciprocally by kinsmen or neighbours in building huts or clearing or harvesting fields. The people of Chibaba's village would have practised *thangata* in this form, when the job to be done needed more workers than the household could provide. After the Yao invasions had imposed a new economy on the Shire Highlands, there was a shift in the word's meaning. One of the African witnesses to the Commission of Enquiry into the 1915 rising described the *thangata* of the pre-colonial period in images of such powerful nostalgia that the Commissioners were momentarily silenced:

In the old days it was a good thing. The chief would kill fowls and goats, and make a lot of food, and prepare everything ready. And then he would take a small boy and tell him to beat the drum and tell him to say that the chief wants thangata tomorrow. And everyone would turn out to thangata. And when they came, the chief would offer them beer and say, 'Now come to the garden and so give me your labour'. And when they went to the garden and started hoeing [sic]. I cannot say what time. They had no way of keeping time, but I should say it would be about 6.30 to 7.00 a.m. when they started working away till midday. And then food and beer came. And after that they marched to the Chief's village in peace and with no signs of grief. And they all sat down around the chief's courtyard. And all the food was brought. And after feasting away, they began to dance. And the chief said, 'Now you have done very well and helped me – go in peace', and that is what is known by the natives as thangata.

'Those must have been happy days,' commented the Chairman before, mindful of his position, he lectured the witness about Ngoni raids.

In the hands of the planters *thangata* was modified further. The 'Anguru' who chose to settle on their estates became tenants, their rental being commuted for paid labour. In strictly legal terms, this promised to be as inefficient a way of mobilising labour as the hut tax had proved. According to the legislation of 1904 which was devised to regulate the system, *thangata* workers were each to be provided with eight acres of land, the 'rent' on this land being one month's labour in lieu of hut tax plus one month's *thangata* labour paid at the current rate of the tax. In theory, then, the planter was required to provide eight acres in return for two months' labour annually. To obtain a permanent labour force of 1,000 men he would need to settle 6,000 families on 48,000 acres. The attractions of the system lay in the hidden advantages to the planters. Labour was supervised by the

Fig. 5 Alexander Livingstone Bruce at Magomero, 1908

planters themselves or their *capitaos*. A month's hut-tax labour could be stretched to six or eight weeks by withholding the necessary signature from the tax certificate. *Thangata* agreements were verbal and informal, so that most planters had little difficulty in extending the requirement to four or five months. Unlike hut-tax labour, *thangata* labour could be levied in the rainy season. The immigrants were in no position to bargain. If they refused to work, or if they attempted, like other Africans, to seek work in South Africa or Southern Rhodesia, they lost their right to reside in British Central Africa. Despite the nominal restrictions of the Lands Ordinance of 1904, therefore, the planters encouraged people to settle.

In his testimony to the Commission of Enquiry after W. J. Livingstone's death, Major A. L. Bruce explained how his Magomero estate had been populated. In the early 1890s, there had been no more than 40-odd huts on the whole 169,000 acres. The first Yao village had been settled in 1898 and from then on W. J. Livingstone, his agent, had followed the policy of appointing Yao veterans from the King's African Rifles as headmen of new villages and paying them to attract 'Anguru' immigrants. Between 1900 and 1914, 4,926 new huts had been built. Each hut-holder – the married men, the single women –

performed two months' labour in lieu of tax and two to three months' *thangata* labour. The *thangata* system had thus provided him with a permanent labour force of over 3,000 workers per month for eight working months each year.

Among these 4,296 new hut-holders, Njenjema settled with his followers on the land beside the Namadzi river which had once been occupied by Chigunda's people. They lived off the maize and millet they had earned working at Malika's and as the rains approached they planted crops from seeds and cuttings brought from Mozambique – sorghum, bush and finger-millet, pigeon peas and, of course, cassava. No *thangata* labour was demanded of them in the first year. As soon as their first crops were ready for harvesting, Njenjema sent for Ntholowa to join him. Ntholowa had also been working for Malika and now he built a village upstream from Nanyungwi hill, discovering Zachurakamo's old furnace in the process. While they cleared the land, using the abandoned hoes and axes, they were fed partly by what they brought from Chiradzulu and partly by Njenjema.

Over the next two or three years – oral testimony is imprecise about dates – four more villages were established. First came Nasawa and Komiha who, like Njenjema, had been living with Malika, and then Mpawa and Nazombe, who had spent some time with the Yao chief Somba at Soche. Nasawa built his village on a small tributary of the Namadzi stream where a shallow swampy depression promised to make good dry-season gardens, Mpawa occupied the horseshoe-shaped peninsula of the old mission site with Nazombe his neighbour, and Komiha settled 2 km further downstream towards Machereni. Nominally, each of the new villages was subject to Kalino. Apart from checking that, from the second year of their settlement onwards, they understood their *thangata* obligations, Kalino left them very much to themselves.

Meanwhile, across the river two further villages were being built. The first was Mpotola and was established in the same year as Nasawa. Like Kalino, Mpotola was one of the Yao chiefs appointed by W. J. Livingstone. He was Muslim and the people who settled with him came from backgrounds unconnected by language or family. Some were Mihavani-speakers from Mozambique and some were Nyanja and Ngoni people who had come to Chiradzulu from Nyasaland's central region looking for work. Mpotola was a tiny artificial settlement of people who had nowhere else to attach themselves to, and after eleven years it contained only eighteen huts. The second

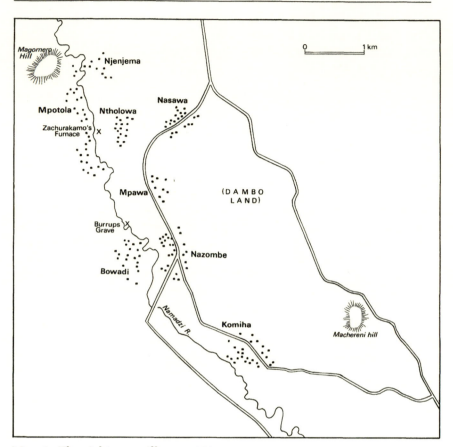

Map 2. The eight new villages c.1904

new village on the west bank was settled downstream the following year under Mpotola's authority. Originally called Maliko at Mpotola's insistence, it afterwards became known as Bowadi, taking the name of the man who became headman after the Chilembwe rising. Like the people settling in the six villages on the east bank, Bowadi and his people were Mihavani-speaking refugees from Mozambique. They had spent two years settled under Chief Likoswe near Maravi mountain.

By 1903, then, eight new villages had been established on the land occupied forty years earlier by Chigunda's people. Those on the east bank accepted Njenjema's pre-eminence and those on the west bank Mpotola's. How closely their village boundaries coincided with those of the former Mang'anja settlement is uncertain since the missionaries never drew a detailed map of Chigunda's twelve villages. But some correspondences may be deduced from their descriptions of the area. The original Magomero peninsula and the land immediately east of it, where Chigunda had a house outside the missionaries' stockade, was cleared and settled by Mpawa, with Nazombe half a kilometre to the south. Upstream from Mpawa, Ntholowa built his village around Zachurakamo's furnace and forge while Chigunda's former 'Anguru' village downstream towards Machereni became the site of the new village of Komiha. Across the river, where Zachurakamo's wife had quarrelled with the missionaries and where his nephew was killed by Sesaho's gun, Bowadi settled in the village they called Maliko. Upstream and opposite Ntholowa, Mpotola's village was on the site the missionaries had known as Masambala. Nasawa appears to have been built on land unoccupied in Chigunda's time though it was under his control. It was there that Dr Mellor isolated the missionaries' smallpox cases. Of the eight new villages, then, only Njenjema on the east bank across the river from the bald hill which became known as Magomero cannot be linked directly with the patterns of settlement in Chigunda's time. Perhaps Sachima lived there, the headman who supplied carriers for the expedition against Mangasanja.

No population figures for the new villages are available until a dozen years after they were settled, and the numbers are of huts rather than of people. Thus, Mpotola had eighteen huts and Maliko just eleven. But Njenjema with fifty and Ntholowa and Nasawa with fifty-six each were the three largest villages on the whole Magomero estate and were sizeable villages by Nyasaland's standards. Mpawa was a little smaller with forty and while Nazombe had twenty-

Fig. 6 'Anguru' women at Magomero, 1908

six and Komiha thirty-four. This makes a total of 291 huts on the eight square kilometres where Chigunda governed some 150 homesteads.

Translating these figures into actual men, women and children involves more guesswork than one would like to admit. By 1914, the mechanics of hut tax were forcing people throughout Nyasaland to live three or more adults to a hut, whereas in Chigunda's day all men and most women had their own huts within the family homestead. This suggests an adult population in Chigunda's day of perhaps 500, and in the eight new villages perhaps half as much again. But these figures need qualifying. People in the new *thangata* villages were not so closely related as to tolerate living three adults to a hut. Perhaps as many as half the women were widows or spinsters who lived on their own or as 'slave' wives in their own huts. Bearing in mind, too, the number of dependents the missionaries had acquired at Mbame, Chirumba and Chikala, the population of the new villages was probably very similar to that when Chigunda and Bishop Mackenzie were co-proprietors at Magomero.

But there were two important differences. Chigunda's villages had straddled the river which flowed through them. It was this that gave the horseshoe-shaped peninsula its special importance as the home and burial ground of the chiefs. From 1893, however, the Namadzi river marked a boundary between two administrative districts, namely Blantyre (later Chiradzulu) and Zomba. People in Mpotola's villages would from time to time find themselves living under different regulations to those affecting the villages under Njenjema. Though in their day-to-day affairs people ignored this boundary, they could not always evade its bureaucratic implications. Secondly, Chigunda's villages had been largely homogeneous, his people bound together by a strong sense of kinship. This was not entirely true. There were Yao people living under his protection, and a number of 'slave' wives, and a whole 'Anguru' village towards Machereni. But these were exceptions thrown up by the turmoil of the times. The new villages, by contrast, resembled far more closely the disparate group brought together by the missionaries.

They had come as refugees and they considered themselves lucky. They had chosen the sites for their villages themselves. They had far more land to cultivate than had been given them by Malika or Likoswe, and far more than they had had within living memory back in Mozambique, where the slave trade had driven them to take refuge in the hills. The soil varied from red clay on the slightly higher ground on either side of the river to black sticky cotton-based soil on the river banks themselves. Each of the villages controlled a *dambo* or marshy depression for use as a dry-season garden. They shared a perennial stream, an average rainfall of between 35 and 40 inches, and unlimited supplies of firewood and of poles and grass for house building. There was also an abundance of game – buffalo, sable, kudu, water and reed buck, even elephant – so that, unlike the missionaries, they had plenty of meat. Even in later years, when the consequences of settling on Major Bruce's land had become all too clear, they never regretted their decision, and they would look back to the golden age when they first built their villages with a nostalgia far greater than anything they felt for their original homes in Mozambique.

Who were the people who came and built the eight villages? One point that is clear is that although comparative large villages were established in a surprisingly short time, the original inhabitants were not kinsmen. The picture of whole villages departing *en masse* from Mozambique led by patriarchal headmen wielding flywhisks is seductive but quite false. Though thousands crossed the border, the migrations in most instances involved 'just my grandfather, grandmother and his close relatives. In those days they moved together as families and no more.' Most people say their grandparents were left behind. Mpawa, for instance, travelled accompanied only by his wife. The people who eventually settled under him, or in the neighbouring villages of Njenjema, Ntholowa, Nasawa, Nazombe, Komiha or Maliko, came from a variety of different places across the border. Though none was as diverse as Mpotola's, where three languages were spoken, they were all composed of separate groups of refugees largely unknown to each other as they set out.

Like most of the people who settled on A. L. Bruce's 169,000 acres before the 1915 uprising, the present inhabitants of the eight villages give as their original home the area east of Lake Chilwa. 'Our grandparents left Mangulu because of the war' is the commonest statement. Others refer to Portuguese labour policies or the famine of 1900 as causes of their migration without being able to identify their home villages. Njenjema's people do not know where their ancestors are buried. Ntholowa claims to have come from Menembo. This is in the valley of the Lurio river, some 160 km north-east of Magomero. Mpawa claims as his most important ancestor M'miso, who lived at Mulumbo. Mulumbo is 70 km upstream from Menembo in the direction of Magomero. The people who settled at Maliko came from three separate villages near Pikuni, 20 km south-east of Mulumbo. Other families speak of their grandmothers coming from Amaramba or from M'nyamwelo. An old women in Komiha remembers a song sung by her mother about their journey:

> Mother, mother
> > *ee*
> Mother, I have travelled, mother
> I'm tired
> > *A – hee*
> I have crossed Malema
> I have crossed Malema
> Mother, eya
> > *A – hee*

Mother, I have travelled, mother
Mother, I have travelled, mother
I'm tired
   A – hee

Malema is a river rising in the Namuli hills and flowing north into the Ligonha river. It is some 200 km from Magomero. In short, even the villages with apparently homogeneous populations drew their first inhabitants from an area of some thirty thousand square kilometres.

The question is further complicated by the fact that this area had itself become, from the mid-nineteenth century onwards, heavily populated with refugees fleeing slave traders operating in the river valleys towards the east coast. The names given as places of origin – Menembo by Ntholowa, Mulumbo by Mpawa, Pikuni by the people of Maliko – are actually the names not of villages but of mountains. As in the Shire Highlands at the same period, so in the mountainous territory east of Lake Chilwa though on a fragmented scale due to the number of hills, people took refuge from the slavers in fortified or inaccessible settlements. At Mpotola, a young man performed in 1982 a stick dance whose words, preserved over four generations, vividly illustrate the insecurity of that period:

Sister, my younger sister, my mother, sister, my mother
   Oye eee
   kum-kum-kum-kum-kum
Light the fire, sister, my younger sister, my mother,
   Oyo eee
Light the fire, sister, mother,
Light the fire, sister, mother,
   Yo-ho eee
Light the fire, mother, sister, my mother,
Mother is feeling cold oyio
Sister, my younger sister, my mother
   Oyo hee
War has come
War has come
War has come and it has taken my child
I cannot see him anywhere, my younger sister, my mother
   Oyo eee
Be attentive, mother
Be attentive, mother
Be attentive, mother, war has come and it has taken my child
I cannot see him anywhere, my younger sister, my mother,
   Oyo eee

Long before the migrants set out on their separate journeys, their patterns of settlement and kinship had already been disrupted. It is not surprising, therefore, that even people travelling from the same villages often separated and made their new homes far from each other.

What made it possible for so many families to settle together in such large villages so quickly? Language was clearly a factor of enormous importance. Though they came from places more than 100 km apart, most of them – except in Mpotola's – could understand Mihavani. Mihavani is the language of the region east and north-east of Lake Chilwa, but it is mutually intelligible with Lomwe, which is spoken in the Namuli hills and the Lubella river valley, and with other languages to the south and north. Nor should the role of Malika, the Yao chief at Chiradzulu under whom so many of them lived for a short period, be underestimated. Malika, like Likoswe and Somba in Blantyre districts, was anxious both to boost his own political importance and to produce cash crops for the Blantyre and Limbe markets, and he encouraged immigrants to settle. It was under Malika that many of the people who ultimately settled on the Namadzi were brought together for the first time. They arrived as refugees but by the time they moved on two or three years later they had begun to form new relationships.

There was a third factor easing the process of settlement. Like most other peoples of central Africa, the villagers were identified not only by their personal and family names, but also by the names of their clans. Mr Nantoka, for example, the oldest man in Mpawa who was brought there as an infant, is also addressed by his clan name Mbewe. Mbewe, along with Mwale, Nkhoma, Dzimbiri, Banda and Phiri, have long been the commonest clan names in the villages, though Gama, Ngondo, Chanza and Chisale also occur. These clan names are Nyanja and Yao in origin and none appears to be Mihavani, though people will claim they are translations of Mihavani equivalents. In Chigunda's days, most people took the name of their mother's clan, the exceptions being the children of 'slave' wives who, by definition, had no kin. In the new villages, significantly, people have from the beginning taken the clan names of their fathers. Given that they normally grow up in their mother's home village under the special authority of the male members of her family, clan names become an important link with their father's lineage.

Over a wide area of central Africa the clan names are the same or have the same meaning in different languages. People will speak of their clans as having existed before 'tribes' or language differences. 'In the past', it is argued, 'they must have lived together.' The Mbewe 'were one people at one time but later they moved to different places'. As a result, fellow clansmen will treat each other as brothers and sisters even if they cannot speak each other's language. If a Lomwe Mbewe meets a Nyanja Mbewe, 'he is your relative'. What this belief made possible to immigrants travelling in small family groups was easy integration in their new homes. The 'Anguru' presenting themselves to Yao or Mang'anja headmen in Mulanje or Chiradzulu districts made use of their clan names as a claim on hospitality. There is some evidence that people sometimes changed their clan names *en route* to make their credentials more appealing – a process made simpler by a considerable degree of vagueness among the immigrants of just what exactly were the Yao or Nyanja equivalents of their own clan names. There was scope for creative confusion in securing a host. Similarly, the different families settling in the new villages along the Namadzi river were, by using or manipulating their clan names in dubious translations, able to claim they were 'relatives' even though many of them had never previously met.

This flexibility in managing their relationships did not prevent splits occurring after their settlement. Ten kilometres north of Njenjema is the village of Makalani, whose headmen came originally from the valley of the Lugenda river beyond the Mangoche mountains. After living in Mulanje and Chiradzulu, Makalani settled with Njenjema until a quarrel arose over the allocation of land and he and his followers moved to build their own village. Similarly, Balakasi and his people, who now live close to Nchema, the senior chief of the area west of the Namadzi, once belonged to Mpotola's. It was Nchema himself who tempted them away, arguing 'You are my relative, come and stay with me'. There were probably more of these splits, the memory of which is preserved only in the histories of the villages which moved on elsewhere. They happened, though, in the earliest years of the settlement. What is most striking is how quickly disparate peoples joined together to form cohesive communities. Part of the reason lay in their origins. They soon found urgent contemporary reasons for uniting together.

As far as A. L. Bruce was concerned, the new villages were fundamentally labour camps. In a region where labour was competitive it was highly convenient to have settled on the estate workers who built their own houses and provided their own food, who were disciplined by fellow-African Yao chiefs, who, given the rights of the landlords, were largely unprotected by government legislation, and who, by the very terms of their settlement had forfeited the option of looking for better pay elsewhere.

To the villagers, however, their deal with the landlord was essentially a means of securing land. Nothing was, and is, more important to rural Africans than adequate land with wood and water, and the *thangata* system did not at first seem especially onerous. As explained to them by Kalino and Mpotola it did not seem more demanding than the labour they had already provided for Malika or Likoswe at Chiradzulu and Blantyre or indeed, than the labour they provided for each other when building their villages.

In the first year of their settlement they paid no tax and performed no *thangata* and for the next couple of years there was very little for them to do. Only one plantation was so far established, the coffee plantation at Magomero, and that was already in decline. During the two months in which tax and *thangata* were claimed of them, the men walked the 14 km to Magomero, arriving at 6 a.m. when Liwonde, the head *capitao* of the estate took a roll call. They were then divided into gangs of twenty to thirty men and given fixed tasks to perform. For coffee picking they had to fill a basket of 40 lb. For clearing land, hoeing and ridging, or for weeding the coffee or maize plantations, they had fixed distances to cover. The tasks occupied them until midday, when they would walk home to help their wives in the village gardens. Apart from this two-months' labour, levied between November and March, the rest of their time was their own, and some seem not to have been required to work at all. So little work was available, in fact, given the number of immigrants already settling on the estate, that hut tax had to be levied in millet, grown in the village gardens and handed over directly to the collectors from Zomba and Blantyre districts.

In the early years the deal seemed a good one. There was, however, a complication which became increasingly tortuous as the demands of the *thangata* system intensified. In theory it was the men of the villages who had secured land by contracting their labour to A. L. Bruce. According to the 1904 legislation they became tenants, with the right to a house and to eight acres of land on which to settle their families. In devising this law, the British seemed to have assumed that men were family heads and property holders and that this was in no way incompatible with their going out to work. Forty-three years earlier, Bishop Mackenzie had assumed the same thing when he overrode Mang'anja custom by giving land to the married men.

In fact, the pattern adopted in the villages was a mute defiance of British law. As the land was cleared and the villages were built, Njenjema, Ntholowa and the other chiefs divided the land between the different families. Following the custom they had brought with them from Mozambique, this meant that land was distributed to the female heads of the lineages. In practice it was distributed to the women, including the large number of unattached women who had to be accommodated. With a population so recently brought together, it must have been difficult to apply the rules consistently. Men who objected to the arrangements could hardly in the circumstances be disciplined and some of the early splits in the villages were over the issue of land distribution. What helped the pattern become established was the absence of the men at Magomero fulfilling their *thangata* and hut-tax obligations. It was the women who made decisions about planting the village gardens. Later, as the *thangata* system intensified, it came to be unquestioned that the villages 'belonged to the women'. Despite the legislation under which they had settled, the men gained access to land through their marriage and lost that access on divorce. Even in the selection of chiefs the women had the principal voice and the successor, though usually a man, had to be a maternal brother or nephew of the deceased.

It would be wrong to see these arrangements as a 'system', determining people's actions and incapable of being adapted to individual circumstances. There is an element of fiction in the description of any customs, a wish to read order into diversity. Just as the new settlers had been creative about their lineages and clans, so different marriage arrangements could always be made if they suited the parties concerned. In any case, a man from Mpawa marrying into Ntholowa was only moving a couple of miles upstream and retained strong connections with his birthplace. If village matters became increasingly the concern of women, this was as much a consequence of the intensification of the *thangata* system as it was of any inflexibility about their own traditions. Nevertheless, for a picture of what life was like in the villages before the 1915 uprising, we must return to the older women for their memories of their mothers and grandmothers.

The road which nowadays turns south-west from the Young Pioneer base at Nasawa, passing through Nasawa village and along the fringe of Ntholowa before straightening through the centre of Mpawa and on downhill to Komiha, was not cleared until the 1920s. At the beginning, the houses were built not alongside the road but in separate homesteads linked by a network of footpaths. At the centre of each village, close by the chief's own hut, was a *bwalo* or meeting place, an arena of cleared and beaten earth protected by shade trees from the afternoon sun. Ntholowa and Njenjema made use of trees already established when they arrived. Ntholowa's shade tree is a *kachere* tree, a gnarled but cheerful tree with bright green leaves which filter rather than shut out the sun and which is full of birdlife. Njenjema's colossal *nthundu* tree, by contrast, is a dark wet giant, impenetrable and forbidding, and the chief's house and all the others in the village have now been moved some 200 m uphill, the *bwalo* being scarcely used. At Mpotola and Mpawa, the arena is surrounded by blue gums and jacarandas with, in Mpawa's case, a single sweet-smelling Pride of India, planted by the first chiefs, whose gravestones are close by, and today well-established and beautiful.

The first houses were in a mixture of styles. Most of them were round, with bamboo frames smeared with mud and roofs thatched with long grass fastened at the crown. But rectangular huts, as encountered at Malika's, were already becoming fashionable, and had the considerable advantage of being larger and easily subdivided. This was important because although the immigrants would have preferred to build family compounds composed of several round huts each inhabited by a single adult with the whole group surrounded by a grass fence, the combination of hut tax and *thangata* made such arrangements prohibitively expensive. Only unattached women stuck to the old round houses. Hut building was a communal activity, the owner brewing millet beer to reward the helpers. The framework was built by the men who also did the thatching, while the women mixed the mud for smearing on the walls and floors.

As soon as the houses were built people began working on their gardens. Fires were lit under the larger trees and kept burning slowly until they collapsed, and controlled fires were also used in clearing grass and scrub. The newcomers were aware that the Mang'anja had cultivated this land before them and they poured libations of millet beer to quiet any restless spirits. Then, while the men divided their time between Magomero and their villages, the women set about planting the gardens with seeds and cuttings they had brought with them.

As the rainy season approached in November, the day began at first light. Akite Chiunda of Mpotola can remember her grandmother Che

Simani, who came from Mulanje and settled with the first Mpotola, starting the day by splashing her face with water from the clay waterpot and then lighting a fire, rolling a bamboo stick between dry twigs until the first smoulderings could be blown into flame. She would tell Akite to boil beans or pumpkins while she departed for the gardens carrying her hoe. Che Lakalaka, her husband, would have already left during darkness for Magomero. Akite had other duties, such as refilling the waterpot at the river, and towards mid-morning she would take the cooked food to her grandmother in the fields. About three acres was cleared altogether, though it took many weeks to cultivate such a large area single-handed. Cassava was the first crop to be planted, the thick stumps being thrust into holes made with a stick in the bare soil. As the staple crop, cassava had the enormous advantage of requiring no further attention and of being able to withstand almost any weather conditions. *Nandolo* or pigeon peas, which grew into a head-high bush, would be grown in the same way from seeds planted in holes in the bare ground. Then, using a hoe, Che Simani gathered soil and trash into low mounds, about one metre in diameter, and sowed them with several different crops which, as they grew, would support each other. It was a system which provided both ground cover and drainage. Millet was the most important grain crop but sorghum and maize were also grown, maize being a crop they had cultivated for the first time at Malika's. Pumpkins, sweet potatoes, and several varieties of beans and peas would also be planted on the mounds.

During the rainy season Che Simani stayed in her fields until late afternoon with Akite helping her and Che Lakalaka, too, if his task at Magomero had been finished early enough. Only then would she return to domestic tasks. There was firewood to be collected from the bush and perhaps further trips to the river for water. Some tasks were carried over from previous days. If her stock of millet or cassava flour was low, she would take some to the river bank with her mortar and pound it to a coarse flour. Then, washing it carefully to separate the husks, she would soak the flour in a large clay pot for a week before draining it and grinding it between two stones to a fine white powder which was spread on reed mats to dry. This flour, boiled in water, was used to make *nsima*, an unsweetened porridge which was the main ingredient of the day's main meal in the early evening. In addition to *nsima*, which was served on flat baskets called *nsengwa*. Che Simani would cook a relish of pumpkin leaves or pigeon peas or occasionally she would kill one of her chickens. All food was boiled or roasted

Fig. 7. Basket making, 1908

directly over the wood fire, and no oil was used for cooking. Coming as she did from Mulanje, Che Simani was especially fond of *nsima* made from rice flour which was hard to obtain at Magomero, though rice was grown at Lake Chilwa. Occasionally, she would take a basket of flour to Blantyre to sell it to buy small luxuries – rice flour, an extra hoe, or a piece of black *biriwita* cloth.

For most of the women money was a rarity. Their hut tax was paid in millet and there were no local markets. Almost everything they possessed was made locally or had been brought with them. They owned and needed to own astonishingly little. Within the house a home-made reed mat served as bedding and a grass handbrush kept the floor clean. Most of the women made their own cooking utensils –

a stirring stick, a set of carved wooden spoons, a collection of gourds for water. Clay plates for the relish and clay cooking pots were made by mixing red soil and water and stamping it to a thick paste, when it could be shaped by hand and baked over a wood fire. Larger clay pots used to store water or for soaking flour were more demanding. Alice William of Bowadi remembers her grandmother as an expert who made pots for the whole village. Baskets of various sizes for storing flour and the *nsengwa* for serving *nsima* were usually woven by the men. All food was eaten in the fingers.

For transactions outside the villages, millet was used as currency. As in the days of Chigunda's village, there were some items which could only be obtained by exchange. Most of the women arrived wearing bark cloth which they called *chiondo*, their only concession to personal decoration being the wearing of *chipini* or nose rings and bangles called *thangala*. A few of the older women still wore *pelele*, the old-fashioned lip ring which had been popular back in Mozambique. But a coarse, hard-wearing black cloth called *biriwita* became available very early, first from W. J. Livingstone who used it briefly as payment for field labour, and then from an Indian trader called Karim who established a store at Magomero, downhill from Livingstone's house. Karim sold cloth in return for millet. He also sold salt, no longer brought by African traders from Lake Chilwa but imported from the Mozambique coast, where the salt pans had been taken over by the same plantation companies – Companhia da Zambesia, Companhia do Boror – whose labour policies had driven the 'Anguru' over the border.

Finally, supplying the third indispensable item obtained by exchange, Karim sold hoes. Back in Mozambique, the Mihavani had themselves been iron workers before the slave trade had disrupted their homelands. They recognised Zachurakamo's furnace as soon as they saw it, and in Njenjema there was for a short time a blacksmith called Che Namaponya, who specialised in hoes for sale in the villages. But hoes were available cheaply at Karim's and Che Namaponya soon went out of business. There was no room for special skills within the *thangata* system and soon all men, except chiefs and *capitaos*, were reduced to the level of field labourers.

Very gradually, this economy expanded. As W. J. Livingstone's operations grew, hut tax came to be paid by men with their labour and more millet was released for trading at Karim's or, following Che Simani's lead, at Blantyre market or at the newer markets which were inroduced at Njuli or at Mwanje near Chiradzulu. The villagers bought fish from traders from Lake Chilwa and they established small flocks of chickens and goats and pigeons. They also obtained money, supplementing the trickle of currency flowing back from the men's *thangata* wages, and used this to widen the circle of exchange. Different kinds of cloth came on the market – a white one called *mulekano*, and patterned prints named *satana* and *chita* and *matekenya*, selling at 3d a yard. An African tailor established himself with a sewing machine on the veranda of Karim's store and did good business hemming the new cloths to prevent them fraying at the edges.

This, though, was the extent of expansion. With their husbands absent for longer periods as new plantations were opened, there was a limit to the surpluses women alone could produce. Even when planting had been completed in early January, there was weeding to be done and the cultivation season was a long one. The first green cobs of maize for roasting on the fire were available in February but the main maize crop was harvested in April or May. Sorghum and millet followed in June, the sprays of millet being dried on reed mats spread in the sun or on the thatched roofs of the huts, making vivid red and purple splashes of colour. Cassava leaves or pumpkin leaves could be picked and cooked as a relish throughout the season, but the cassava itself was lifted in July and the stumpy roots dried in the sun before storage. Alternatively, they could be left in the ground like sweet potatoes to be eaten on demand. *Nandolo*, or pigeon peas, were ready in August and September and were stored in their pods in baskets. The season of staple crops thus extended from November to September and although the work lessened as the season advanced and as the men were released from their *thangata* work, there was never much time to relax.

In the weeks before the next rainy season began, new houses were built and old ones repaired. It was a time for beer parties, and for the initiation of young people, and for the negotiation of marriages. It was also a time for celebrating *chopa*.

Chopa was a festival they had brought with them from Mozambique and was the biggest of all their occasions. It was held in October or early November but in different villages irregularly as the chiefs decided. At Mpawa's, for example, *chopa* would be danced every three years or so, following a dream in which M'miso spoke to Mpawa demanding to be honoured, as the dead Chibaba had appeared to Chigunda on the same site in December 1861. A message was sent to all people in any way connected with M'miso – people originally from Mulumbo, people who had lived with them at Soche, people related by birth or marriage, and anyone else inclined to do M'miso honour. Several hundred people, as far away as Zomba, Blantyre, Thyolo and Mulanje, would immediately start brewing millet beer. On the day of the ceremony, drums broadcast a second invitation and the beer would be brought to Mpawa and all mixed together in the same clay pots. Among its other meanings, *chopa* was a declaration of unity.

Mpawa, like Chigunda, would say prayers to M'miso, digging a small hole under the *mpoza* tree behind his house and pouring in a mixture of beer and flour. Then the dance would begin in mid-morning, continuing until dusk. First the closest relatives would dance while the rest watched in a circle and gradually everyone would take their turn. *Chopa* is a ceremony of great violence. To an immense battery of drumming, the men danced in procession in an inner circle, wielding spears and axes and sometimes even with venomous snakes draped round their necks, while the women dancing in an outer circle carried green-leaved branches. As the dance got wilder, the men's threats became more dangerous, and the women's task of pacification more demanding. For its opposition of male to female, violence to gentleness, hunting to planting, dust to the rains, *chopa* drew for its symbolism on the Lomwe creation myth, which tells how the first man and woman came out of a cave in the Namuli hills where their footprints can still be seen on a flat rock, and brought dissension to a harmonious world by the discovery of fire.

Mpawa himself would join the dance, his flywhisk, the symbol of chieftaincy, being passed around from dancer to dancer and back to him. Meanwhile, one of the young men stood on the roof of Mpawa's house calling out the names of all the different chiefs present, and each in turn came forward with his people and received their share of the millet beer. There was also food – *nsima* made from millet or cassava flour and a mixture of relishes including goat meat. All this continued until nightfall, and many of the people would spend the night at the village before setting off home the following day. Essentially, *chopa* was 'a dance of worship, a dance for calling the rain. After people offer flour to their ancestors they dance *chopa* and the rain falls.'

Chopa was the only dance which the villagers brought with them from Mozambique which is still performed. Others, like *kandodo* or *nkahula*, have died out and are remembered only by the very oldest people. There are, however, a few songs which old women will perform for an insistent visitor. They sing in the language only they and their husbands can remember, the original Mihavani which they spoke in Mozambique, and the music is in the old style which can still be heard across the border. Performed as songs, with a lead singer and a chorus but without any dancing or instrumental accompaniment, they have a delightful sweetness. Like the spirited descriptions of *chopa*, they provide insight into early days of the settlements on the Namadzi, despite *thangata* and the danger of arrests over hut tax:

> When I tell my husband, let's marry
>   *ee let's marry, ee let's marry*
> When I tell my husband, let's marry
>   *ee let's marry, ee let's marry*
> We should go up and down the hill
>   *ee up and down the hill, ee up and down the hill*
> Take the moon and give me
>   *ee give me, ee give me*
> I do not mean the moon I mean
>   give me your heart
> e – e – ya, e – e
>   *This place is wonderful*
>   *This place is wonderful*
> When I am caught, bail me out
>   to ferment beer
> e – e – ya, e – e
>   *This place is wonderful*
>   *This place is wonderful*
> When my husband has not commanded me
>   I do not pluck and eat
> e – e – ya, e – e
>   *This place is wonderful*
>   *This place is wonderful*

Meanwhile, 13 km away at Magomero, W. J. Livingstone was continuing his experiments with cotton.

In 1903, W. J. Livingstone sent to Alan Kidney of the ALC samples of Egyptian cotton grown at Magomero. Kidney valued it at 6d per lb., enough for profit, the fibre being 1¼ inches average and the colour good. The news was greeted enthusiastically by a planter community desperate for a crop to replace coffee. Early that same year, the Chamber of Agriculture and Commerce had met with Commissioner Alfred Sharpe to be told by him that 'ever since he had been in the country they had been trying to get some paying exportable product'. Coffee had failed, tobacco could not meet American competition and the prospects for cotton were 'not sanguine'. Now Sharpe had a letter from South Africa asking whether the Protectorate would contract to export its labour. Ten thousand workers sent to the gold mines of the Witwatersrand would bring £120,000 into British Central Africa. This would benefit commerce. It would also balance Sharpe's budget.

The threat galvanised the planters and cotton was their theme. The writings of David Livingstone were dusted down and extracts reprinted in the Protectorate's two newspapers. Once again the message rang out that British Central Africa was a cotton field 400 miles long. All that was needed was a variety of cotton which could be cultivated profitably. Inevitably, fatefully, it was W. J. Livingstone who provided the answer. Cotton was his greatest success, representing during his lifetime his one claim to minor distinction.

Experimenting with American Upland varieties and with Egyptian Abassi, W. J. Livingstone had, by 1905, succeeded in producing a cotton with good lustre and a standard 1½ inch fibre. A hybrid was developed which he named Nyasaland Upland and by 1908 Livingstone had 1,000 acres of the estate under cotton, producing a crop which he sold for 9¾d per lb., some 1½d more than first-quality American Upland. The achievement was celebrated in a letter to A. L. Bruce from their Liverpool cotton broker:

You can take it from me as a commercial man engaged in the selling of your cotton that it is undoubtedly the finest result out of Africa and not only is it suitable for American purposes but it is superior to any American ... I understand you are getting 300 lbs. of lint per acre: this is fully 50% better than America can do, as the price is 3d to 3½d higher than the general run of American cotton. Nothing better could be desired, and Lancashire would absorb half a million bales of it if it were produced.

The excitement seemed justified when Magomero cotton reached 1/2d per lb.

It was Nyasaland Upland which made cotton a paying proposition in the years preceding World War I. Most planters used W. J. Livingstone's seed and it was distributed by the British Cotton Growers' Association to African growers for cultivation as a cash crop. At Likulezi, where cotton was grown on the A. L. Bruce Trust's other estate, Ritchie made extra profits for the trust by processing at the Likulezi ginnery raw cotton bought from African growers who were themselves employing the *ganyao* labour of immigrants from Mozambique. Ritchie was joined by an assistant called John Meikle from

Fig. 8. A. L. Bruce in his *machila*

Leith, and on the main Magomero estate where W. J. Livingstone opened fifteen new cotton plantations additional European staff were appointed almost annually. A. J. Storey, who later became an auctioneer, worked as an accountant at Magomero until in 1908 A. L. Bruce himself arrived to handle the estate's financial affairs. Duncan MacCormick who, like W. J. Livingstone, came from the Western Isles, assisted Livingstone in managing the plantations. J. T. Roach, an Australian, was appointed engineer to maintain the ginnery. John Robertson, another Scotsman, was appointed section manager at Mwanje, with especial responsibility for cattle breeding, and a prize bull, 'Baron of Magomero', was purchased. Robertson eventually was allowed an assistant of his own in the appointment of Robert Fergusson in 1913. Finally, a Miss Prain of Edinburgh was appointed to open a dispensary at Magomero, intended to cater particularly for the African women and children.

Miss Prain had been appointed under the terms of the will of Mrs Agnes Bruce who died in 1912. Her death and the apparent prosperity of Magomero under the new regime of cotton led to a change in the ownership of the estate. David Livingstone Bruce and Alexander Livingstone Bruce purchased the A. L. Bruce Trust's interest in the

110

Magomero and Likulezi estates and on 2 May 1913, six weeks after the centenary of David Livingstone's birth, a new company called A. L. Bruce Estates Ltd. was incorporated, with a share capital of £54,000. The bulk of the shares were held by D. L. and A. L. Bruce and by their sister Agnes Blackwood Bruce, but D. B. Ritchie and W. J. Livingstone purchased 500 each. A new estate, the Kada estate at Mulanje, was bought for £1,000. Likulezi and Magomero between them were valued in the company's statement of assets at £41,220 12s 6d.

Cotton brought to the Magomero estate the full rigours of *thangata*. In the rush to expand, new plantations were opened up at the rate of two per year. Their locations were mainly determined by the labour available. People from Ntholowa, Mpawa, Nazombe and Komiha at first worked exclusively at Machereni, while the villagers from Chipale came down to Nasawa until the Chipale plantation was itself opened in 1908. Similarly, the plantations at Mwanje and Old Chimwalira were located within walking distance of the villages on the west side of the Namadzi, including Mpotola and Maliko. Others still of the new plantations, such as Chanda or Thondwe to the north or Chiradzulu in the south-west, were deliberately sited on the border of the estate in order to attract workers from neighbouring Crown Land areas. This was soon felt to have been a mistake. Hut-tax labour from Crown Land areas was not so easily controlled and the rates of pay were liable to discovery by the Collectors. It was better to be self-sufficient in labour, and from about 1910 this was achieved under the *thangata* system. A. L. Bruce was able to boast by 1915 that every plantation was serviced by its own villages and that no one had to walk more than five or six miles to work.

The plantations themselves were not large. The biggest was 500 acres and the total acreage under cotton in 1914 was 5,000. With 4,926 huts on the whole estate, each representing two months' labour per year (one for hut tax, one as *thangata*), W. J. Livingstone should have had plenty of labour available without ever needing to break the law. Everything at Magomero, however, was done by hand. There were no traction engines, no steam ploughs such as had been in use for two decades on the Zambesi, no machinery of any description. Oxen were used to transport the ginned cotton to the railhead at Luchenza, but oxen were not used in the fields. Land was cleared with hoes and axes and the controlled use of fire in exactly the manner that land had been cleared for building the labourers'

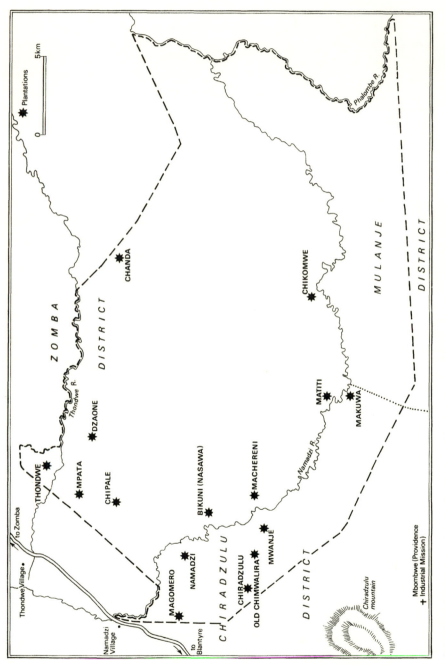

Map 3. Magomero estate in January 1915, showing cotton and tobacco plantations

villages. Sowing was by hand, thinning the cotton plants was by hand, weeding and mounding the cotton was by hand, picking off pests was by hand, and harvesting was done with the workers filling plaited grass baskets they had earlier manufactured themselves by hand. Even transport to the ginnery was by human portage. Only in the ginnery itself were mechanical methods employed. W. J. Livingstone soon discovered, moreover, that the exceptionally high yields celebrated by the Liverpool brokers were obtained only on freshly cleared fields. No fertilisers were used. More labour was used to clear more bush each year to maintain productivity. It was exactly the method used in the villages, except that the Africans rotated their crops in the full knowledge of what they were doing, and not as part of a process of wasteful experiment.

The consequence was that, as each new plantation was opened, simple arithmetic forced upwards the period for which labour was levied until almost five thousand people were working for fully six months in the year. First, the facility of paying hut tax in millet was withdrawn, and tax was levied in labour at a rate of 1/6d per month. This was illegal, the ordinance having fixed a minimum monthly wage to correspond with the current rate of tax, but the A. L. Bruce Trust was beyond legal constraint. Magomero's 169,000 acres spread into three administrative districts – Zomba, Blantyre and Mulanje – and no resident, for whom Bruce's brick house was a welcome turning point on district *ulendos* by *machila* (litter) or bicycle, felt in any position to intervene. Secondly, the period of *thangata* labour was extended to three or four months per year for each hut-holder on the estate. Thirdly, the obligation to pay tax and do *thangata* was enforced against *ambeta* or unmarried women, large numbers of whom had joined the village settlements. This was perfectly legal since the women were hut-holders and cultivated gardens. But the imposition was bitterly resented since, unlike the married men whose wives kept them supplied with food, the *ambeta* had no means of sustaining themselves adequately during their six months' tax and *thangata*. Fourthly, and again illegally, *thangata* was enforced against children.

In imposing these demands W. J. Livingstone depended on two groups of men. Ultimately, it was the responsibility of the Yao chiefs – Kalino with his six villages, Malinda with five, Mwalimu with twenty – to ensure that people fulfilled their *thangata* obligations. They were assisted, however, by rangers, who toured the villages with the roll books, checking up on absentees. The rangers' methods

Fig. 9. Carrying cotton to Magomero

were crudely simple. Defaulters were beaten with truncheons or a rhinoceros-hide whip and their huts were burned. No one, as the law then required, was simply evicted. A dance song, still popular at Ntholowa, records a ranger's visit:

> Ranger *capitao*
>   *e – e – e*
> Write me on the paper
>   *e – e – e*
> Ranger *capitao*
>   *e – e – e*
> I will die but I don't know when
>   *e – e – e*

W. J. Livingstone also had the support of district residents in Blantyre and Zomba, whose arrangements with A. L. Bruce after 1908 were a model of bureaucratic irresponsibility. Bruce was empowered to

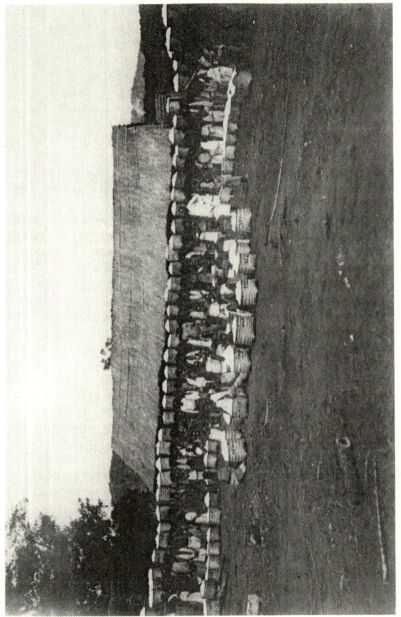

Fig. 10. Outside the warehouse

issue 'vouchers', exchangeable at district tax offices, to workers who had fulfilled tax requirments. He was thus excused from signing the official Labour Certificates which recorded how many days' work had actually been demanded. On 15 February each year, the administration's police toured the estates checking that everyone liable to hut tax possessed a *boma* (administrative centre) receipt. Defaulters were at once driven out to work. Bruce then wrote a cheque for the full amount of tax outstanding, and had a completely free hand in exacting the labour he wished. In November 1913, sub-resident Cruise at the new Chiradzulu *boma* became impatient with such chicanery and handed Bruce the tax receipts for him to distribute himself. For this he was reprimanded by superiors anxious to keep their fictions intact.

On the separate plantations, labour was organised as it had originally been at Magomero. The records were kept by head *capitaos* who took a roll call at 6 a.m. and divided the workers into gangs of approximately fifty each, working under the supervision of assistant *capitaos*. Tasks were set by the head *capitaos* in accordance with schedules set by W. J. Livingstone himself. Clearing the land, hoeing it into ridges, planting the cotton five or six seeds to a hole, thinning out the seedlings, and weeding and mounding the cotton plants, were all men's tasks. The cotton was planted in rows 100 to 120 yards long and a 'task', such as ridging or mounding, would consist of three or four rows depending on the type of soil. By starting at 6 a.m., most men would complete their task by noon or 1 p.m., depending on the weather or on their state of health. The unmarried women might also be assigned tasks of weeding, but their usual job was to remove pests such as boll worms – a job also done by the children – and to pick cotton at the rate of two baskets per task. Women and children would often be kept in the fields until 4 p.m. Once the cotton was picked, it was carried by the women to the ginnery. The main ginnery was at Magomero but there were others at Mwanje and Chipale. Packing the ginned cotton in June to August was not a job which could be arranged by tasks. Men and women worked from 6 a.m. to 4 p.m. daily under strict supervision and workers faced a walk to their home villages of anything up to five miles. No food was served in the fields and no official provision was made for them to have time to consume their own food, though individual *capitaos* permitted this so long as W. J. Livingstone himself was not present.

If a task was not completed because darkness fell or the weather

Fig. 11. Spading cotton

intervened or through personal disability, the whole day was forfeit. No fractions were allowed. Each month was assessed as twenty-eight days (legally, it should have been twenty-six) and a 'month' might easily extend over five or six weeks. There was no ticket system as on neighbouring estates, by which a worker was issued with a ticket each day as proof that he had finished his task, twenty-six such tickets being exchangeable for a hut tax receipt. Livingstone's *capitaos* simply ticked the roll books. If work fell behind schedule, they casually omitted to do so. 'People often worked for five weeks,' confessed Mwalimu later, 'and got nothing in the book. I did it because I was afraid of Bwana.'

Payment was by W. J. Livingstone himself and was equally casual. Legally, workers should have been paid for *thangata* labour at the current rate of hut tax. In fact, W. J. Livingstone paid them with rolls of tobacco – 'It didn't matter whether you smoked or not' – or with cash handed out apparently at whim. Fellow planter Capt. Thorburn of Thondwe described seeing workers 'come up with pay in their

117

Fig. 12. Inside the ginnery, with William Jervis Livingstone

Fig. 13. Loading cotton for the railhead at Luchenza

119

hand saying "is that all you are going to pay me?", and Mr Living-stone has taken a shilling back for complaining'. The workers' own memories are equally explicit. Livingstone 'used to throw 3d through the window and sometimes you couldn't find it. If you found it you had to run away or you'd be beaten.'

As these memories make clear, and as is obvious from the broader context, it was impossible for a handful of Europeans, even assisted by their African collaborators, to impose such a rigid labour disci-pline on so many workers. The theory was oppressive and the practice was brutal, but the brutality was arbitrary and unsystematic. In the villages 'Listonia' rapidly became *Mkango*, a figure of terror. As he toured the estate, first in a *machila* ('The Bwana's *machila* is not heavy', boasted the carriers in rhythm), later on a donkey or a bicycle, the sound of his approach drove people into hiding. Stories about him, emphasising gratuitous violence and occasional sexual abuse, are like the rumours which spread through Chigunda's village about the missionaries – rumours factually improbable yet vivid in their crystalisation of attitudes and essential truths. 'Listonia', it is said, used to attend village funerals, beating the corpse with his walking stick to ensure that the man was really dead and was not just evading *thangata*.

Inevitably, among people who had fled Mozambique to escape such exploitation, discontent multiplied. They could not emigrate a second time. They valued their new homes, and anyway there was nowhere else for them to go. They had, however, an alternative. Njenjema, the first chief to settle, Bowadi from across the river, Baison Chiunda, who was Mpotola's nephew and probable heir, and Norman Kasiye from Mpotola who had become one of Livingstone's *capitaos*, together with men from all the eight villages, took their complaints about 'Listonia' to a mission which had been established at Mbombwe, 9 km south of Chiradzulu *boma*. The mission was called the Providence Industrial Mission and its head was a fellow African called John Chilembwe.

John Chilembwe was born at Sangano hill, 8 km east of Chiradzulu mountain, some time in the 1870s, possibly 1871. There are different accounts of his parentage but all versions agree that his father was Yao and hence one of the group which had conquered the area under Mpama, and that his mother was Mang'anja, one of those who attached themselves to the conquerors after defeat and famine in 1862–3. She would have been old enough to have remembered the missionaries at Magomero, and her status is given in some traditions as that of a 'slave' wife. Some time during Chilembwe's childhood, possibly during the Ngoni raid of 1884, the family moved to Chilimoni, a village just across the Mudi river from the Blantyre Mission where Blantyre city now stands. At the Chilimoni branch of the mission school, Chilembwe was educated up to standard three, leaving school at about the age of twenty with a rudimentary command of English but without yet having become a Christian.

Early in 1893, he became associated with Joseph Booth, a Baptist missionary who had arrived the previous year to set up the Zambesi Industrial Mission. Booth's message was fiercely radical. He wrote home about the hypocrisy of 'elegantly robed men' preaching to labourers working a seven-day week for 5d worth of calico, and in his preaching and daily conversation with Africans he urged them to 'Rise up and save your country' from Europeans 'who are cheating the natives and robbing their land'. In February 1893, John Chilembwe wrote to Booth, asking, 'You please carry me for God. I like to be your cook boy', and from then on Chilembwe became Booth's interpreter, auxiliary preacher, and the guardian and nurse of Booth's two children.

Meanwhile, Booth had quarrelled with no less than three different missionary organisations and he began to draw up plans for a new Christian enterprise. The movement was to be called the African Christian Union and its slogan was 'Africa for the Africans'. Its aim was 'to equip and develop Industrial Mission Stations worked by competent Native Christians or others of the African race' and 'to promote the formation of Companies on a Christian basis', devoted to cultivating tea, coffee, cocoa and sugar, or to mining or industrial enterprises, the shareholders taking 'a moderate rate of interest only'. An appeal was to be made to European governments to return alienated land, to the American government for 'a substantial monetary grant' as compensation for 250 years of slavery, and to the vast community of black Christians in the West Indies and the United States for moral and practical support. The schedule was drawn up in January 1897 and John Chilembwe was one of four signatories. Immediately he and Booth left for America to propagate the movement. Fund-raising was difficult, particularly for a white and black man travelling together, and they separated, Booth handing Chilembwe over to the care of Dr L. G. Jordan, secretary of the Negro National Baptist Convention. Through Jordan's influence, Chilembwe spent two years at the Virginia Theological Seminary and

Fig. 14. John Chilembwe with his family

College at Lynchburg, where the influence of Booth's radicalism was reinforced by arguments in America about Negro advancement.

Back in British Central Africa in 1900, 'as a full-blown, round-collared, long-coated "Reverend" of the regulation type' (in Booth's description), Chilembwe wrote to the *Central African Times* giving notice of the formation of the Ajawa Providence Industrial Mission (later Providence Industrial Mission). In his uncertain English, he described himself as follows:

He has a school at Chiradzulu, containing with one hundred young people he is getting on well with his teaching as he believes that by giving the children of Africa good training they will be able to possess an indomitable spirits and firm dependence upon God's helping and sustaining hand.

It was a new voice in central Africa, the inevitable product of forty years of mission activity from Bishop Mackenzie onwards. Yet it was a difficult voice to accommodate. The difficulty lay not just in his association with Booth, who was deported in 1905, nor in the unusual credentials of his A.B. and B.D. degrees from the Virginia seminary. Chilembwe's challenge was to a colonial system which already discriminated against African advancement – socially, politically and commercially.

Chilembwe began by purchasing land at Mbombwe – 93 acres for £25 18s – and, like all missionaries before him, erecting a thatched church and schoolhouse. Over the next two years he was joined by two Negro missionaries from America, the Rev. Landon N. Cheek and Miss Emma DeLany, and cheques began to flow from American sources. By 1905, they were able to report seventy-one names on the roll call and with experimental plots of cotton, coffee, tea, chillies and rubber they had taken the first steps to becoming self-supporting on the 'industrial' model. By 1910, Chilembwe had 800 church members plus 625 pupils, and by 1912 the number of schoolchildren had risen to 906 distributed between the main school at Mbombwe and six branches in neighbouring villages. He was also well advanced with constructing to his own design a large and impressive church.

It was obvious that Chilembwe had a real following, not only in Chiradzulu district itself but also among the emerging group of mission-educated Africans who in 1909 founded the Native Industrial Union, a black equivalent of the Chamber of Agriculture and Commerce, and at once made Chilembwe chairman. He began to gather around him a small but influential business community. In August 1912, the sub-Resident at Chiradzulu *boma* was asked to supply details and obliged with a list. There were what he called the Gordon brothers, in fact Gordon and Hugh Mathaka in part-ownership with Duncan Njilima. Gordon Mathaka had been one of Booth's earliest converts and had been taken by him on a missionary trip to Zululand in 1896. Now he and his brother owned an estate of 250 acres and were employing fifty workers. Their most recent crop was three tons of maize and just over four tons of tobacco, and they also owned several trading stores in north-eastern Rhodesia. There was Duncan Njilima himself, farming with his own brothers on 30 acres next door to the Mathaka brothers at Nsoni. Njilima's two sons had already gone to America with the Rev. Landon Cheek. He was in some difficulties, his cotton crop having failed, and there were complaints that his labour force of twenty had not been paid. He owned, however, a solid brick house as evidence of earlier success and he had a ton of tobacco currently for sale. There was John Chilembwe farming 93 acres at Mbombwe. His cotton too had failed but he was selling foodstuffs locally. Chilembwe was 'not a very trustworthy person' and there was evidence of some resentment at his mission that the fifty workers had to take employment elsewhere for one month annually in order to get their Labour Certificates signed by a European. There was John Gray (Kufa), 'probably one of the best natives of this class', farming 140 acres at Nsoni. Kufa employed twenty-seven people and had cultivated 27 acres of cotton, 12 acres of maize and 50 acres of tobacco. He also had cattle, sheep, goats and an orchard of fruit trees. These were the most important of the group, though there were others including retired *capitaos*, and Gomani, an Ngoni headman, who was causing trouble by demanding *thangata* labour from settlers on his land.

There were three links between Chilembwe's community at Mbombwe and the workers on the Magomero estate. The first was John Gray Kufa. Kufa, who was originally from the Zambesi delta, had been trained at the Blantyre Mission as one of their first African evangelists. In 1896, he was given the responsibility of establishing a branch of the Blantyre Mission at Mulumbo, the original home in Mozambique of Mpawa and several of his people. Kufa built a church and maintained a school and he acted as interpreter for Portuguese officials laying claim to Mulumbo in 1900. That year, the new mission was withdrawn. Kufa went to live at Nsoni where he opened his small estate. As immigrants from Mozambique streamed across the border, many people from Mulumbo settled near Kufa at Nsoni where their descendants live to this day. Later, Kufa was trained as a dispenser and travelled widely inoculating people in an anti-smallpox campaign. When, under the terms of Agnes Bruce's will, a dispensary was established at Magomero, Kufa was employed as Miss Prain's assistant.

If John Gray Kufa was already well known to many of the immigrants both on and off the Magomero estate, Chief Malika of Chiradzulu was one of their earliest patrons in the Protectorate. Many of them had settled first under his protection before moving on to A. L. Bruce Estates. Malika was sympathetic to Chilembwe's work from the outset, and there is even a story that he invited the Rev. Landon Cheek to lead a revolt against British rule. One of Chilembwe's new schools, opened in September 1908 at Chingole, was established on Malika's invitation in his principal village. This was in sharp contrast to the attitudes of other Yao chiefs who resented Chilembwe's influence and who, as Muslims, objected to his Christian proselytising. Kadewere, for example, complained bitterly that 'John Chilembwe's people never respected me at all', and he burned Chilembwe's school in Ndunde village. Like Nkalo and Onga, neighbouring Muslim chiefs, Kadewere made a show of building a brick mosque instead.

The main links between the Magomero estate and the PIM, however, were Bruce's *capitaos* and ginnery workers. W. J. Livingstone had evolved a system by which workers were settled in villages in the control of Yao chiefs appointed by himself. Most of these chiefs were Muslims. They maintained schools for teaching Swahili and held classes on the Koran on the verandas of their houses. There was even a mosque at Mkanje. Some of them, like Ndala and Mwalimu, also worked as *capitaos* earning five shillings per month. To supervise plantation work, however, and to keep labour records, W. J. Livingstone needed *capitaos* who were literate in English. Similarly, for his ginnery workers and for other full-time labour, W. J. Livingstone needed a small but semi-skilled labour force of a kind not easily to be found among King's African Rifles veterans or 'Anguru' immigrants. Most of his specialist workers came from the Scottish mission schools.

The very names of these men declare their religion. Wilson Zimba was head *capitao* at Chiradzulu and storekeeper at Magomero. There was John Makande, *capitao* at Zaone, Herbert Kobiri at Mpata, Moses at Chikomwe, Malcolm at Makua and Robert at Magomero. Johnston Latis or Zilongolola and his brother Jonathan Maniwa, Henry Kolimbo, otherwise called Jumbe, Morris Chibwana, Norman

Kasiye, the *capitao* from Mpotola's, and Moffat Kanchanda, named after David Livingstone's father-in-law, were also employed at different periods. Isaac Maliro was the *capitao* in charge of child labour and Beaton Nsamwa was put in charge of groups of old men. Similarly in the ginnery, James Samuti, John Cameron and Fred Maganga worked as factory hands or cotton checkers, while across the road, Tom Kolomana, Nelson Storo and Abraham Botoman Seyani, together with Kettleo or Lupiya Zalela and Archie Makina, were in charge of the ox-waggons.

Not all these people were members of Chilembwe's congregation but most of them had visited Mbombwe at one time or another. Fifteen of them, including Wilson Zimba, Johnston Zilongolola, Fred Maganga and James Samuti, were on John Chilembwe's roll of Baptised Believers.

A striking feature of oral testimony is the extent to which these Christian skilled workers, including the *capitaos*, had the sympathy and respect of the villagers. Elsewhere in plantation systems in southern Africa, *capitaos* have long been the targets of bitter and scurrilous work-songs. Other 'Anguru' people who remained in Mozambique, and who worked on the plantations near Quelimane or along the Zambesi river, turned their protest over forced labour against the *capitaos* whom they ridiculed and insulted as the very agents of colonialism. By contrast, songs from the Magomero estate, including some sung to the same tunes as those across the border, direct their ridicule not at the *capitaos* but against fellow-workers who are not pulling their weight:

> Your mother's cunt
> > *Shirker, your mother's cunt,*
> > Shirker ...

These three lines would be sung repeatedly in derision when anyone left the field ahead of others. New workers would be taunted as being unlikely to stand the pace:

> A lot of these people
> Are *marepo:*
> > *They just come to watch*

— *marepo* being a kind of heron which stands for hours on one leg. There are many of these songs, sung in the fields by work gangs as the rhythmic accompaniment to labour and repeated many times, a chain of such songs often lasting for as long as an hour. Where the *capitao* is mentioned as in the following song,

> The *capitao*
> Yells at us
>   *The Bwana says nothing*

the old men are careful to insist that the reference was exclusively to Liwonde, senior *capitao* at Magomero and a Muslim. Liwonde later testified to W. J. Livingstone's great kindness, insisting he saw no reason 'to rise against my master'.

What these pre-1915 songs help to illustrate is how natural it was for men from the new villages, Christian or otherwise, to see in John Chilembwe a fitting spokesman for their complaints. Though their *capitaos* were better paid and worked as the front line of the labour system, they came as the confrontation developed to seem the villagers' best allies. The rising itself can be viewed from different angles – as nationalism versus colonialism, as Christianity versus Islam, as a petit-bourgeois struggle with feudalism, as a peasant uprising against oppression. Both sides subsequently found it expedient to explain all that had happened as a personal feud between Chilembwe and W. J. Livingstone.

In fact the two men met only once, when Chilembwe was hunting game on the Magomero estate and his shots attracted attention. Livingstone gave two versions of the encounter, differing in emphasis. To C. J. Carmichael, his fellow-planter from the Nachambo estate, he claimed 'he was given a severe talking to which John Chilembwe did not like'. Kathy Livingstone recalled her husband telling her that 'seeing a well-dressed native' he asked who he was: 'Chilembwe replied, "I am an educated gentleman", and my husband much amused at the answer, passed on without interfering with him.' Though partly contradictory, both accounts reveal something of the characters and issues involved.

Behind the legends which have accumulated around W. J. Livingstone's name, the man himself is obscured. His intense anxiety to make a success of cotton planting, the main cause of the abuses on the Magomero estate, is itself revealing. For, despite his ancestry and the peculiarly potent name he carried in Livingstone's Nyasaland, his personal position was uncertain. He had no money of his own and he depended entirely on his employers, who wanted results. He comes alive in three brief descriptions, each of them suggesting vulnerability. The first is an account by A. C. J. Wallace-Ross, a fellow cotton planter from Njuli, who travelled with Livingstone to Nyasaland in 1911. One night on deck, Livingstone asked him confidentially about attitudes in the Gold Coast to 'assaults on natives'. During his leave, 'the late Mrs Bruce heard that he had been fined by the Boma for an assault having been made on a native, and she said to him that if it again occurred he would be dismissed'.

The second is a comment by A. L. Bruce himself that 'Livingstone told me things that I thought were not necessary to be told, but I thought that he was so earnest about his work that I listened to him . . . He used to say, "Oh, I am getting old", and said he had been out in the country for 22 years.'

The third is the universal judgement of the planter community that his marriage in 1908 to Katherine Maclachan, a schoolteacher from Lismore, matured him considerably.

After his death in the uprising and his condemnation by the official Commission of Enquiry, Kathy Livingstone wrote a passionate defence of her husband:

I can see him now a few days before his death bending over a man who had been cruelly stabbed and brought to our verandah, staunching his wounds and supporting him while he gave him food to eat from his own table. I can see him that same week getting up at dawn, to carry into Zomba on his bicycle a native who had been bitten by a snake. I can see him during a year of famine passing many sleepless nights not knowing where to find food to feed not only the workers but their dependents. On this occasion, after having spent some hundreds of pounds of the Trust's funds, buying rice at 5d a lb., and groundnuts at 14s a ton, he approached the government for the purchase of rice and maize. They could not supply him although loads of rice were lying at Fort Johnston and maize was being eaten by weevil at Mlanje. I can see him coming into my store and taking some bags of rice which I had bought for my boys. I remonstrated saying we could not afford to be so charitable and he replied, 'Well! we cannot see these poor wretches hungry so long as we have a little food to give them.' Not only did he feed men on the Estate he fed many who came from Boma and other lands for he had not the heart to turn them away.

This loving portrait is one-sided, but there is nothing inherently improbable about it. For W. J. Livingstone, like his fellow-planters though in larger terms than anyone else, had to perform two irreconcilable roles. He was the salaried manager of a plantation company, responsible for producing an export crop which would bring profit to the owners and shareholders. He had to do this without sufficient capital, with an unwilling underpaid labour force, and with tropical agriculture still at the stage of experiment. At the same time, he was something between a Scottish laird and a paramount chief. He distributed to the peasantry enormous tracts of fertile land, and he demanded their labour in return according to the custom some of them called *thangata*. This set up among his subjects expectations he was powerless to fulfil. There is evidence that he tried. He did distribute food during the semi-famines of 1911–13, though mainly to the Yao chiefs and plantation *capitaos*, and he allowed himself to be used as chief in settling matrimonial disputes and arbitrating on land issues. Magomero 'as far as the natives were concerned was rather like a *boma*: they tried all their cases there.' But when the rush to expand cotton production led him to impose a regime of forced labour he was caught between two constituencies, between an employer and shareholders anxious for profit and villagers anxious for protection.

To this contradiction must be added two further points. The first is that despite the scale of his responsibilities he occupied a lowish position in settler society. There were sharp divisions of class within the Protectorate's white community between the administrators (public school and army), the missionaries (mainly Protestant non-conformist of a variety of backgrounds), and the planters (mainly Scotsmen of a 'fine independence of character' who were 'almost invariably "agin the Government"'). In Kathy Livingstone's passionate letter with its random argument and shaky grammar, she casts herself and her husband as victims of an English upper-class officialdom which has closed ranks against all outsiders. The second point is that W. J. Livingstone was clearly not the man to cope with such problems. Others in colonial Nyasaland, neighbouring planters such as A. F. Barron of the Makoka estate or R. W. Wallace of Thondwe, found the twin role of capitalist-planter and feudal lord thoroughly congenial and helped to set patterns for making money and exercising authority which have endured in Malawi to the present day. W. J. Livingstone was far too uncertain, impulsive, quick-tempered, uncalculating, hasty even in his generosity, for such a role. He could also be downright brutal.

The administration knew that something was badly wrong. The assault on Sousa in Zomba jail in 1900 had not been completely forgotten, and the arrangements for collecting hut tax on the Magomero estate, so carefully recorded for constant reference in the district book, provided an undercurrent of worry. Anxiety, too, underlay the studied statement in the Blantyre district book in 1910 of what the administration understood by *thangata* on the Magomero estate – 'a verbal agreement to the effect that each hut owner shall work for one month during the rainy season for his government hut tax and shall, if and when called upon to do so, work for a second month for pay during the rainy season'. In February 1911, there was a boundary dispute on the south-west border of the estate near Mwanje, when engineer J. T. Roach, acting for W. J. Livingstone tried to incorporate Khoromana village and 800 yards of land in the Magomero estate. Roach was manhandled and had his arm twisted. An official lands survey the following year upheld Khoromana's protest. 'Livingstone', warned the Blantyre resident, 'may want a bit of watching ... [he] is the type of man who will resent the boundary business going against him and he may try to take it out of the natives concerned.' No action was taken, however. The estates were private property and their owner was an unofficial member of the Legislative Council.

In any case, they were all too busy watching John Chilembwe.

Chilembwe had been distrusted from the start. As an associate of Joseph Booth, and as a representative of American Negro interests, he was clearly very much more than an ordinary village evangelist of the independent church variety. He preached a gospel of emancipation but in a confusing, and perhaps initially confused, manner which drew on two conflicting traditions. One element looked back to Booth's political radicalism. The message 'Africa for Africans' sprang from a working-class non-conformist denunciation of colonial society. Specifically, Chilembwe retained of Booth's doctrines his anger that Africans should be used to fight white men's wars and his anger over land alienation. At the same time, Chilembwe was profoundly influenced by American Negro notions of emancipation. Translated into colonial terms, this meant that Africans should be allowed to own land, employ labour, engage in commerce and practise religion on the same terms as the whites. The structures of colonial society were not to be overthrown but expanded to include Africans. The whites had set standards to which the Africans would raise themselves.

It is hard to say which of the two messages caused most offence. Official doctrine, building on David Livingstone and the nineteenth-century philanthropic tradition, was that colonialism had eliminated the slave trade and opened up legitimate commerce. Chilembwe, following Joseph Booth, was the first to proclaim the alternative doctrine, that the new society was based on expropriation and deep racial injustice. Yet white settler society seems to have been less worried by this than by Chilembwe's notions of African advancement – by his activities as a planter and employer, by his relations with

130

African businessmen and his industrial training schemes, in short by his assault on the paternalism of planter, administrator and missionary which left no scope for African initiative. Most irritating of all seems to have been Chilembwe's habit of dressing himself in three-piece dark suits, complete with bow tie, and his mixed-race wife Ida in silk stockings and high-waisted empire gowns with leg of mutton sleeves. These fashions caught on among his congregation, proclaiming the arrival of a new class. Photographs of the vast new church at Mbombwe in 1913 show several hundred African men and women suited and gowned for the occasion in disturbing mimicry of their rulers.

It was in his dealings with A. L. Bruce Estates that Chilembwe brought the two sides of his gospel together. In 1910 he made a hunting trip to Mozambique, where he preached to members of John Gray Kufa's old congregation and discussed the possibility of opening a church there. It was perhaps as a result of this illegal expedition that he had his gun licence withdrawn in 1911. About the same time, Wilson Zimba, the *capitao* at Chiradzulu plantation, approached A. L. Bruce in person, explaining that he 'had children and wanted them educated'. Bruce agreed that a school hut could be built at Magomero and that he would pay a teacher 4/- a month if one could be found. The teacher was supplied by Chilembwe and the arrangement lasted for six months as a 'school for the children of *capitaos*', until W. J. Livingstone discovered Chilembwe was involved and closed it down.

By this stage, Chilembwe was deeply concerned about the problems of the Mozambican immigrants who were bringing their complaints about *thangata* to him. Late in 1912, the sub-Resident at Chiradzulu reported incredulously that Chilembwe, as part of his regular discussions at Mbombwe of commercial schemes, had devised a plan for cotton growing in Mozambique. Bruce 'had been sent a copy of the minutes in which the meeting had decided that he should give them £50 for the project'. No other details are available, but the scheme was perhaps intended to provide a means by which the immigrants could return home instead of growing cotton for A. L. Bruce. Shortly after this, a deputation of some two hundred estate workers, led by Zilongolola, visited W. J. Livingstone at the estate office one Saturday afternoon asking permission to build a church. Bruce overheard the commotion and came down the hill from his house to give his personal refusal, insisting 'Do you understand? I do not like John Chilembwe. You are not to build this church.'

The deputation dispersed and at Namwani's village on the west bank of the Namadzi river 4 km downstream from the old Universities' Mission site they built a tiny church of mud and thatch. Zilongolola, who was Chief Namwani's nephew, was preacher and Moffat Kanchanda was one of the elders. The worshippers came from the Mwanje and Machereni plantations and included all the Christian workers. Others attended from the villages along the Namadzi.

In November 1913 they were discovered. W. J. Livingstone was outraged one Sunday afternoon to hear that they were holding a service and sent Fergusson and MacCormick to prevent them. The church was pulled down and the whole congregation taken under arrest to Mwanje. When 'Listonia' arrived, he beat them and expelled them from the estates. All the 'capitaos attending John Chilembwe's church' were instantly sacked. One hundred of those sacked and expelled marched at once to Chiradzulu boma to complain to sub-resident Cruise, and even the unsympathetic chief Kadewere noticed that 'blood was seen rushing from their heads'. Cruise sent for W. J. Livingstone and was satisfied with his explanation. He made a careful note in the district book: John Chilembwe's 'mission requires careful supervision and should not be allowed to spread'.

This episode, as much as anything else, explains what followed. From then onwards, the situation on the Magomero Estate seems to have focussed Chilembwe's thinking. It was by no means the only issue to concern him. He had incurred debts in building his vast church and had added to them by borrowing money to buy food during the shortages of 1913. Worried about these, he was worried too that his health was failing and he seems to have been especially anxious about his eyesight. Perhaps he was also influenced by the Watch Tower prophecy that the world would end in October 1914. The point has been much debated with its implication that he was losing his grip on reality. Contradicting this suggestion was the horrified realism of his protest to the *Nyasaland Times* in November 1914 about casualties at Karonga in an engagement between the King's African Rifles and German forces. 'Let the rich men, bankers, titled men, storekeepers, farmers and landlords go to war and get shot,' he wrote in the authentic accents of Joseph Booth. 'Instead the poor Africans . . . are invited to die for a cause which is not their own.' The letter was censored and plans were made to arrest and deport Chilembwe. These concerns need emphasis because when the uprising came in January 1915 Chilembwe attempted to give it a national dimension. There were planned attacks on Blantyre and, through links with branches of the Church of Christ, on Zomba and on Ncheu in the Central Region as well as at Mwanje and Magomero on the Bruce Estates.

It was the situation on the Magomero estate, however, that brought together the different strands in Chilembwe's thinking. Magomero with its single block of 169,000 acres was the most graphic example in the whole Protectorate of land alienation, while no other employer had in recent years practised the *thangata* system so rigorously or on such a scale. At the same time, Bruce's ban on schools and churches for his African employees, which the *boma* had upheld, illustrated vividly the obstacles to African advancement. If 'Listonia' were the enemy, then the English and the American, the radical and the progressive side of Chilembwe's thinking were reconciled. Was he influenced, too, by the celebrations in 1913 of David Livingstone's centenary with the proclamation yet again of the 'Livingstone' inheritance? Did the two Livingstones merge in his consciousness? Was it part of his anger that Major Alexander Livingstone Bruce was one of the officers at Karonga? The choice was not in the end between a local and a national uprising: an attack on Magomero could seem like an attack on the whole colonial system. He began to baptise hundreds of tenants from the Bruce Estates. They heard him teaching that W. J. Livingstone was anti-Christ.

The most damning evidence against W. J. Livingstone comes from fellow-planter A. C. J. Wallace-Ross of Njuli, who in two vignettes summed up the atmosphere on the Magomero estate in the months before the uprising. In February 1914, Wallace-Ross rode with Livingstone and MacCormick round some of the plantations, comparing their cotton with his own. The party inspected the cotton at Nasawa and then turned back towards Magomero, crossing the Namadzi at Njenjema:

We came across a boy sitting on a tree singing. This boy had around him some dozen or more cattle and everyone knows that in February there is plenty of grass, but Mr Livingstone did not seem to think that the cattle were being given the benefit of their outing. Some of the beasts were eating and some were lying down. Mr Livingstone said to Mr McCormack [sic] 'That boy wants a thrashing, go and give him one.' Mr McCormack got off his donkey and the boy ran away, and in running fell over a stone or something, and I saw Mr McCormack stand over the boy and beat him. I remarked to Mr Living-

Fig. 15. Baptism at the Providence Industrial Mission, with David Kaduya standing to the right

stone that the boy did not deserve that treatment. He said that there was too much 'Boma' about me. I told Mr Livingstone that when I got a licking, I liked to be told what I was getting a beating for.

On the other occasion, Wallace-Ross stayed overnight at Magomero in Livingstone's brick house at the top of the hill:

About half past 5 o'clock we went for a walk down to the ginnery, which is about 300 or 400 yards away from his house. As we went out of the house to go there, there were four Anguru labourers evidently wanting him, because they followed us, and when we went a little way I called his attention to the fact that they were following us, and he turned round and asked what they wanted, and they said 'Posho' (rations). He said something to them in the manner of choke off. It might have been 'Choka!' (clear off!) However, the boys did not go but followed us, and when we went out of the ginnery they were still there, and they were still following us. I said, 'These boys are still following us – why don't you give them *posho*?' He said they didn't require *posho*, because these people come with enough food for a week. We went on into the house and it was almost dark, and the boys were still there ...

Meanwhile, A. J. Storey, ex-accountant of A. L. Bruce Estates, was catching up on a long-postponed duty. Late in 1914, perhaps influenced himself by intimations of Armageddon, Storey visited the Universities' Mission site and set up a white cross. The inscription *In Memory of Henry de Wint Birrup Priest Died February 22 1962* was incorrectly spelt and the position chosen was some 200 m from Burrup's actual grave. Five blue-gum trees were planted, three at the head and two at the foot of the stone. Mpawa's people believed it to be the grave of a European hunter who had been killed by an elephant.

On the afternoon of Friday, 22 January, Chilembwe announced that the 'time has come at last to fight against our oppressors'. The war was to begin on the Saturday evening

There were to be three initial attacks. The first and most important was to be on the headquarters of the African Lakes Company in Blantyre, where Chilembwe hoped to seize rifles and ammunition. Three separate groups of fighters would converge on Blantyre. One, under the command of David Kaduya and Stephen Mkulitchi, would leave from Mbombwe. They would meet up at Limbe with a second force led by John Gray Kufa from his followers at Nsoni. Together, they would march to Blantyre where the third group, assembled by Duncan Njilima from houseboys and *capitaos* employed in Blantyre would be waiting for them.

The second attack, led by Zilongolola and Yotam Lifeyu was to be

on the Europeans in charge of the Mwanje plantation on the Magomero estate. The third attack would be on the headquarters at
Magomero itself and was to be led by Wilson Zimba. Magomero was
the headquarters of the Namadzi division of the Nyasaland Volunteer
Reserve and they were hoping to capture rifles. But the main purpose
of the two attacks on Bruce Estates was to kill all male Europeans.
William Jervis Livingstone was to be killed and his head brought back
to Mbombwe.

Chilembwe had further orders. None of the European ladies was to
be harmed in any way, nor any of the children. There was to be no
looting. No Africans, even those resisting, were to be killed. The
comparison with Bishop Mackenzie's preparations for his attacks on
the Yao is irresistible. Like the English clergymen, Chilembwe was
trying to use war to advance the work of his mission. Finally,
completing the preparations, two letters were despatched announc-
ing the rising and asking for support. Filipo Chinyama in Ncheu and
Stephen Kadewere in Zomba were to launch simultaneous attacks
and give it a national dimension.

On Saturday evening, David Kaduya and Stephen Mkulitchi
marched their small army to Limbe. With them were Garden and
Petrolo Makuwa from Maliko's village, along with Bowadi and a man
known only as 'Charlie'. They waited in vain for John Gray Kufa to
appear with his contingent from Nsoni. As his actions sixteen years
earlier in Mozambique had demonstrated, Kufa had little taste for
fighting and they never saw him again. Continuing to Blantyre in the
darkness of a cloudy and rainy night, they met Duncan Njilima and
his men. The attack on the main store of the African Lakes Company
was made at about 2.30 a.m. Five rifles were taken but the watchman
began shouting 'Nkondo!' In threatening him with a rifle they shot
him and the gunfire attracted attention. In the ensuing flight, four
men were captured, including James Chimpele, John Chilembwe's
cousin. The identity of the attackers and the direction from which
they had come were soon established.

Meanwhile, Zilongolola and Yotam Lifeyu had assembled their
men at Mwanje. With them was Namwani, headman of the village
where the church had been built, and many of the people who had
been arrested for worshipping there in November 1913 – including
people from Njenjema, Ntholowa, Nazombe and the other villages on
the Namadzi. Their aim was to kill two men – Fergusson who had
helped destroy the church and Robertson who ran the Mwanje
sub-section. At about 8 o'clock, one of them knocked on the door of

Robertson's house. As he answered it, a spear was thrust through his arm. Fergusson ran over to investigate but was speared and staggered into the Robertsons' house mortally wounded. The attackers then set fire to the house. Helped by their servant Bakiri, Robertson and his wife escaped to the cotton fields where they hid for a couple of hours. Bakiri himself was killed as they made their escape and Fergusson's body was left in the blazing house. Zilongolola seems to have assumed that the Robertsons were dead too and the attackers left for Mbombwe.

Wilson Zimba had spent the Saturday morning touring the plantations and summoning people to a meeting of his own at Chilumpha's village, far from observation, where the Mwanje river flows into the Namadzi. He passed on Chilembwe's orders that all European men at Magomero were to be killed, and as Abraham Seyani, the waggon driver at Magomero, later testified, a 'lot of the Christians went along with Wilson'. By 7 p.m., the largest army of the night was hidden on the north side of the small hill on which the Magomero houses were built. Kathy Livingstone's servant Hinges was present and most of the ginnery workers and other semi-skilled or skilled workers of the Estate. They had as their targets W. J. Livingstone, Duncan MacCormick and the engineer J. T. Roach. Livingstone and Kathy were at home with their five-year-old daughter and infant son, together with their weekend guest Mrs Agnes MacDonald, wife of a customs' official at Chiromo. MacCormick lived next door and the Roach family in another house some distance away. Roach himself had gone to Blantyre but his wife and three children were at Magomero, and Mrs Roach's sister, Mrs Emily Stanton, was a visitor.

At 8.50 p.m., Mrs Livingstone was about to get into her bath. She noticed the cat was still inside and called her husband, who was playing with his baby son on the bed, to put it out. As he did so, Wilson Zimba and five or six others, including James Samuti, broke in, wounding him with a spear. He grabbed his service rifle by the muzzle and tried to beat them off as blood ran down his right side. Then he collapsed. MacCormick, who had been summoned by the servant, staggered in with a spear wound through his heart. As he lay dying, one of the attackers, later identified as Solomon Kavea, cut off Livingstone's head, drenching the five-year-old Maria Nyasa with her father's blood. Abraham Chimbia carried the head away.

Mrs Macdonald was meanwhile being helped by Kamwana her servant through the window in her nightdress. Under his care she escaped into the darkness. Kathy Livingstone returned to the bedroom where her baby lay unharmed. Picking him up, she began an argument with the attackers which was to continue for most of the night. 'I asked the men in that ghastly room why they had killed my husband. The reply was "because we are killing all the white men".'

These events took just over half an hour. At 9.30 p.m., the excited attackers broke into Roachs' house shouting 'Osaphana dona' ('no killing of the Madam'), and were outraged to find J. T. Roach absent. Two rifles were taken and a thousand rounds of ammunition from the NVR stores, but Roach's pistol and a further thousand rounds were not noticed. In their disappointment, Wilson Zimba's army for the first time that night broke discipline and began to smash windows and furniture. Mrs Roach and Mrs Stanton and the Roachs' three children were taken outside to join Mrs Livingstone, her son on her back and her daughter by her side. Kathy Livingstone told them she had 'sent for the big guns to Zomba'. They repeated that they were now going on to Nachambo estate to kill Carmichael before returning to Chiradzulu. 'I told them they would meet the big guns on the way', and several of the men ran away at this down the road to the ginnery and had to be brought back by their leaders. The attack on Nachambo was abandoned, and the party set off through the night.

They made first for the house of Jonathan Maniwa at Chiradzulu plantation. On the way, the men assured the ladies that all the European men in Blantyre had already been killed. Later in their exultation the men developed this theme; 'twenty million natives, as they expressed it, were killing all the white men in Africa'. They reached Jonathan's house at about 1 a.m. As they stopped for the night, the Robertsons were passing on their way from Mwanje to the Namiwawa estate where they raised the alarm. Mrs MacDonald, too, was finding her way to safety at Carmichael's Nachambo estate. From there a message was sent overnight to Zomba.

On the Sunday morning, as the three ladies and their children continued their trek towards Mombwe, John Chilembwe held his morning service at the customary Scottish time of 11 a.m. Chilembwe preached triumph, with W. J. Livingstone's head displayed on a pole as his evidence:

I was told that the kingdom of God was at hand. John Chilembwe said this in his large church. I heard these words John Chilembwe said 'tembenukani mitima in January' [change your heart in January]. I know that all John Chilembwe's Christians go to heaven to stay with God. David Kaduya said the same, and that God would come and collect the Christians ... John Chilembwe said, 'You will hear the bugles sounding.'

138

Afterwards, the elders remained behind for a church meeting and a War Roll of 175 names was compiled. It included the name of Baison Chiunda (written as A. Chiunda), and several Kasiyes, one of whom was probably Norman Kasiye from Mpotola. A decision was taken to send the women and children away from Mbombwe to their home villages. Chilembwe himself prepared a retreat, in a cave on Chilimankhwanje hill 8 km to the south.

During that hot tense Sunday, the ladies and their escorts moved slowly southwards from village to village. At 5 o'clock they reached Stephen Mkulitchi's house near Sangano hill, still 8 km from Mbombwe. A meeting of David Kaduya's men was held in one of the nearby huts. When it broke up, with armed groups going off in different directions, a letter was given to Kathy Livingstone telling them to proceed to the *boma* 3 km away. They were to carry the message that 'the chiefs of all the tribes have agreed to kill all the white men as they have cruelly robbed us of our motherland'. They slept the night in Stephen Mkulitchi's house. Next morning a *machila* arrived for Kathy Livingstone and the baby and they set off for the *boma*. They had travelled only a few yards when the carriers whispered '*Askari!*', and ran off. It was Captain Triscott, with a contingent of KAR Reserves from Zomba.

While the ladies were escorted to safety, Triscott set off in pursuit. As his column crossed the Mbombwe river, it was ambushed from a maize field by Kaduya's men, making use of their captured rifles. Triscott was forced to withdraw in confusion, but Kaduya received a leg wound. He was taken to the cave on Chilimankhwanje, Charlie from Maliko's village acting as one of his bearers.

In Blantyre, the four men captured on Sunday morning were given a summary trial. At 4.30 on the Monday afternoon they were executed by firing squad in front of a huge crowd of Africans assembled for the purpose. That same day, Chilembwe's two letters – to Filipo Chinyama in Ncheu and Stephen Kadewere in Zomba – were finally delivered, and each man attempted hastily to coordinate local insurrections. Kadewere had the support of local members of the Church of Christ, including Chief Makwangwala of Kimu village, another of Bruce's former *capitaos*. His task was hopeless – the Zomba authorities knew about the rising before he did – and *askari* from Zomba *boma* quickly intervened. Filipo Chinyama was initially more successful and he put together a force of two to three hundred spearsmen who marched on Ncheu *boma* in an attempt to capture the armoury. Resident Cardew, however, was also forewarned. With the help of local village headmen and a levy of Ngoni warriors, he defended the *boma* and began hunting down Chinyama's followers.

At 3.30 a.m. on Tuesday, Chilembwe's men made their final attack. Zilongolola and Wallace Kampingo set fire to the Catholic Mission station at Nguludi. Father Swelsen, the priest in charge was badly beaten and a little orphan girl perished in the flames. The effect was to drive the whole white population of the Shire Highlands into fortified camps in Blantyre, Zomba and Mulanje.

Triscott's army, however, was still active. On Tuesday morning a second attack was made on Mbombwe, this time from the west. They found the mission undefended and deserted, Kaduya's men still guarding the approach from the north. There were cups of tea still warm in Chilembwe's house and a much-thumbed manual of military tactics was on the table.

On the outskirts of the mission village, they found the head of W. J. Livingstone.

The uprising was over: the reprisals began. Reserves of the King's African Rifles, divisions of the Nyasaland Volunteer Reserve, *askari* from the four *bomas* of Blantyre, Chiradzulu, Zomba and Mulanje, and the Yao chiefs of Chiradzulu and Zomba all began rounding up suspects with an enthusiastic lack of discrimination. A. L. Bruce himself hurried back from Karonga and arrested people like James Samuti, even going so far as to take written statements in his house at Magomero, all of which were subsequently upheld in court. The prospect of rewards produced a large crop of informers – such as Kapelimoto from Mpotola, who handed John Kachilumbo to the authorities and was afterwards given £2. One man, an African Muslim tailor called Gide, was arrested by Indian traders. To make an arrest was a declaration of loyalty to the administration and no one who did so found himself subsequently in trouble.

Obvious targets were the African planters and traders of Chiradzulu district. The Mikalongwe Volunteers were active at Nsoni, burning and looting houses and property belonging to Hugh Mathaka and John Gray Kufa who was arrested on the 28th. At Duncan Njilima's, they found

a fine brick building with verandah, etc. . . . . We went through the house and everything was taken out – tables, chairs, chest of drawers, fine tin boxes, a bath, a sewing machine, in fact everything under the sun, silk dresses, boxes of books, pictures, etc. . . . . My assistant bagged a fine new ladies cycle, a Swift, which had never been ridden, valued at £12:10 ... We have some swell natives in Central Africa.

Triscott's capture of Mbombwe on Tuesday morning had produced two documents crucial in identifying 'Chilembwe-ites' –the War Roll with its 175 names and a roll of Baptised Believers, listing 1,160 church members. In adding to these lists of suspects, the authorities were guided by two further considerations. The first was that as well as being 'Christians of John Chilembwe', the majority of those who took part in the rising were 'Anguru'. To be 'Anguru' was to be arrested and, as the earliest lists of suspects demonstrate, people rapidly switched to calling themselves Yao. The second consideration was that as Chilembwe's followers withdrew from Chilimankhwanje they made for the Mozambique border. The Magomero estate and the Phalombe plain became a hunting ground.

From the afternoon of Sunday 24th, the villages along the Namadzi had been deserted. The men who had joined the rising had not yet returned home, but rumours spread like wildfire. Some said 'the war of the Germans had come to Magomero'. Some 'had seen Listonia's head' and were terrified. People took to the bush for safety, hiding in the wooden thickets of Nanyungwi hill or Machereni and coming back to the villages only at nightfall. Then, on Wednesday 27th, the terror began in earnest. In the week which followed, 'a huge number of huts' were burned by the military. People began to make their own arrests in a desperate attempt to acquit themselves. 'I was arrested by Anguru villagers', testified a Nyanja man from Phalombe, 'who said they were told by their chief to arrest all strangers.' Anyone travelling was suspect:

I went to Machilingas to see my brothers there with my wife so I was coming back at night and I came to Bombwe's village and there people seized me and tied me up. I was with my cloth and they took it off. I don't know where my wife has gone, perhaps she has been eaten by hyenas. I don't know anything about the war.

It was no protection to remain at home while the Volunteer Reserve burned villages. Yet to run away was proof of guilt. 'The accused had no explanation of why he ran away' was charged repeatedly at the subsequent trials in Zomba: fifty-one cases, taken at a sitting, were charged with fleeing from the *askari* hunting John Chilembwe and each man got six months' imprisonment.

Any village found empty was immediately set alight. Thus Njen-

Fig. 16. Chilembwe's supporters arrested

jema, Ntholowa, Nasawa, Mpawa, Nazombe, Komiha and Maliko were all burned to the ground during that week. Ironically, since it was the home of Baison Chiunda, the chief's nephew, and of Norman Kasiye, Mpotola's village was not burned. Mpotola, as one of W.J. Livingstone's appointed headmen, was assumed to have been loyal.

Gradually the hunt became more selective. The burning of villages would interfere with tax collection, and the seizure by the Mikalongwe Volunteers of John Gray Kufa's cattle and the burning of his property before he had been put on trial had worrying legal implications. Reports that the 'Anguru' were massively departing for Mozambique also caused disquiet among the planters. Martin Wisikesi, the son of Wisikesi Nthitiwa, who was one of the few men from Maliko to join the attack on Magomero rather than march with David Kaduya to Blantyre, remembers his father's account from his childhood:

When the rising was over people were called back from their hiding places, because some hid in the hills – these were told to come back, because they said if a person was caught hiding in the bush he would be killed. And so people went back to their homes and the Christians were arrested.

Most of the arrests at this stage, as people rebuilt their houses and rescued their crops, were made by Muslim *askari* or village headmen or by informers seeking official rewards. 'We were arrested in our village by Yao because we were Christians,' was one of the commonest statements at the subsequent court hearings. The Magomero story has no sharper irony than this manhunt for Christians around the Rev. Henry de Wint Burrup's newly-marked, wrongly-marked grave.

Some of those captured were given summary trials and executed immediately. Hinges was court-martialled and shot at his own village less than a kilometre from W.J. Livingstone's house. Stephen Mkulitchi was shot hiding near Lake Chilwa. David Kaduya was caught with his *machila* men, still including Charlie, south of Chikomwe hill. He was taken to Chikoja's village near Chikomwe plantation, and shot in front of the workers. Charlie was luckier, being arrested and taken to Zomba prison. After several of the most prominent of the rising's leaders, including Wilson Zimba, Stephen Mkulitchi and John Gray Kufa had been hanged in Blantyre in mid-February, the lesser cases, involving some 1,000 people, were treated more leniently and by stricter standards of evidence. Charlie was found not guilty and allowed to return home. So, too, were Njenjema, Jauma

Fig. 17. Executions, 1915

Muralinje from Ntholowa, Bowadi from Maliko, Kitty and Mariko from Mpotola, and Baison Chiunda, whose initial conviction was quashed by Judge Casson who was not satisfied that the 'A. Chiunda' on the War Roll was indeed Baison Chiunda. Casson is remembered to this day in the villages as the man who stopped the reign of terror. Altogether, 547 of these lesser cases were dismissed. Norman Kasiye, however, was found guilty and jailed, as were Wisikesi Nthitiwa, and Garden and Petrolo Makuwa, who each got two years.

   Not everyone was captured. A group of the most important leaders escaped to Mozambique. These included Chief Namwani in whose village the church had been built, and his nephew Zilongolola and

Jonathan Maniwa. Ex-*capitaos* Fred Maganga, John Cameron, Archie Makina, Nelson Storo and Kettleo settled with them in two villages, one at Mulumbo and one near the other Chiradzulu hill south-east of Lake Chilwa. They had returned, decorated with Christian names, to the areas of their original homes. For sixteen months, the Nyasaland government raged about the danger they posed, as men with guns wanted for murder. The wives of several of the prisoners jailed in Zomba and Blantyre went to join them. Eventually, after the Portuguese had been threatened with gunboat diplomacy, the men were arrested and jailed in Lourenço Marques.

John Chilembwe himself never reached the border. Moving from village to village with his brother Morris, he was tracked on 2 February to a village near Migowi. It was his boots that had given him away to the *askari* who were tracking him. The following morning, they picked up the trail again across the Migowi stream. They killed Morris, shooting him through the head. The party split in two, one group intending to cut off Morris' head as identification while the others pursued John Chilembwe. They caught up with him after a mile:

Private Naluso fired and we saw that he had wounded him as he turned round and round and then stood still, and Sergeant Useni fired and hit him again. He stood still and I fired with Morris's gun and hit him through the head and he fell dead.

Morris' rifle turned out to be one of those taken from Magomero. John Chilembwe was wearing a dark blue coat, a striped pyjama jacket, a coloured shirt and grey flannel trousers. His spectacles and pince-nez had fallen off when he was shot and the right lens of each was missing.

The corpse was taken to A. L. Bruce's Likulezi estate and kept in D. B. Ritchie's house until dusk. Then it was taken in a cart to Mulanje *boma* and after formal identification was buried without ceremony in an unmarked grave.

3 | 1915–1945
'My children's market is the graveyard'

As survivors from the villages rescued the first green maize cobs from their gardens and repaired the charred skeletons of their huts in February and March 1915, it seemed that John Chilembwe's rising had not been a complete failure. The Christians were being hunted down and some of them felt 'deceived' by Chilembwe. But 'Listonia' was dead, and gone too was his brand of casual brutality. A. L. Bruce Estates depended on their labour and Major Bruce himself, for all his strident bravado in the Legislative Council, was anxious to return to a regime of paternalism. He had been chastened by the violence of the uprising, both by its physical horror and its symbolic force – he was David Livingstone's grandson and a Livingstone had been killed with overtones of ritual. He was to be further chastened by his severe reprimand at the Commission of Enquiry in June–July 1915 over irregularities in the Labour Roll books which 'could not be used to repudiate native allegations about cheating'.

From the Chilembwe rising onwards, wages on the Bruce Estates were paid at the official rate of 4/- (later 5/-) per month. Tasks were allocated reasonably and, though no ticket system was introduced, a month's work meant the requisite twenty-six days. As gains, these were very limited. The period of tax-plus *thangata* labour remained a full six months. The harshness of W. J. Livingstone's regime was modified to a dull attrition which was to endure for thirty years, periodically returning as violence when personalities changed and when the colonial economy shrank. But in that dry season of 1915, the people felt they were better off than they had been twelve months earlier.

In the villages there were political upheavals. Although Njenjema had been treated by the Magistrates' Court as a minor offender and acquitted, he was never forgiven by Major Bruce, who reduced him to the rank of village headman. The new post of group village headman was given to Ntholowa, who assumed responsibility for the villages on the eastern bank of the Namadzi. 'The one which we found and whom we know here as the head of us all is Njenjema', was still being said in 1980, 'but because of being clever Ntholowa has tended to eclipse him.'

On the west bank, when the first Mpotola died in 1916, Baison Chiunda was elected as his successor. Respect for him as a leading follower of Chilembwe had been reinforced by his acquittal in the High Court by Judge Casson. At about the same time, Bowadi, who had also been acquitted of involvement in the rising, took over as village headman from Maliko. In Mpawa's, there appears to have been a kind of *coup d'état*. Mpawa II, an elderly and cautious man who had come with the first Mpawa from Mozambique, was removed through popular dissatisfaction and a new headman brought in from Masanjala village, in Chiradzulu district close to Chilembwe's mission. His name was Hazwell Mkwamba and he was to remain village headman as Mpawa III until 1970. Within a couple of years of the uprising, half the villages were governed by Chilembwe sympathisers.

In returning and rebuilding their villages, the people had reaffirmed their original decision to settle on the banks of the Namadzi river. In the last resort, fertile well-watered gardens were more important than *thangata*. This belief was soon confirmed by developments across the estate border on Crown Land areas in Chiradzulu district.

In April 1915, Wade, the new sub-resident at Chiradzulu, reported that the Yao chiefs were very cooperative in providing labour to repair the district roads. It was decided to seize the opportunity of the chiefs' compliance and to proceed, years in advance of elsewhere in the Shire Highlands, with the implementation of parts of the 1912 District Administration (Native) Ordinance (DANO). This ordinance provided for the appointment in each administrative area of principal headmen and subordinate village headmen to whom would be delegated minor responsibilities in the general conduct and welfare of village life and in keeping the resident informed about births, deaths, crimes, disputes and disturbances and immigration. DANO represented, in short, a first step towards Indirect Rule.

Before it could be implemented, however, the 'villages' had to be created. Complaints from Chiradzulu district had noted that houses were 'scattered in twos and threes all about the place'. It was decided that houses should be 'concentrated' into settlements of not less than twenty: this figure, at a time when hut tax kept housing to a minimum and when there were on average 2·81 persons to a hut, meant that each 'village' would contain just under 60 people. A particular point was made of explaining to villagers that the scheme 'is in no way connected to the late rising'. Technically, Wade was right. DANO had been passed in 1912. But it was hardly surprising no one in Chiradzulu believed him.

Then in August 1915, Wade was instructed to find 1,000 men for *tenga-tenga* or carrier service to transport war goods to Fort Johnston. It struck him as an impossible demand and the suggestion that he ask the chiefs seemed wildly optimistic. To his delight they furnished 900 men in two days and offered more. That same month, the 'Anguru' began moving away from Chiradzulu district, back to Mulanje or on into Zomba districts or on to the Magomero estate. In November, there was an incident. Chief Nkalo requested the use of *askari* to help with hut concentration. Later that morning, Wade received a scribbled note, 'We have war here. They want to beat us. Now they're taking knives and sticks.' Wade's response in flogging Liveliwa, the headman of the village involved, was officially approved: 'in time of war and within a year of the Chilembwe rising it is doubly desirable to come down instantly and heavily on any such nonsense such as you describe'. By the end of the year, Wade had despatched 2,300 *tenga-tenga* carriers, the vast majority immigrants from Mozambique and, the chiefs being 'cooperative', he provided 800 more in January 1916.

Meanwhile, some of the widows and sons of John Chilembwe's followers had begun to resettle at Mbombwe. They included Gordon Matoga and Silas Mtala, Chilembwe's uncle and brother-in-law, together with Allan Chimpele, whose father had been captured and shot in Blantyre, and Duncan Njilima's two sons. Rumours began to connect them with Zilongolola and his camp of 'Chilembwe-ites' across the border at Mulumbo. There were said to be regular communications between the two groups, with some women electing to join the rebel *capitaos* in Mozambique. There was even talk of a second rising.

On the last night of February 1916 news again spread that 'spearsmen had been seen hiding'. At Magomero, the European staff spent the night blockaded in the main office. Wade was suddenly frightened. He arrested four people on a charge of 'being Christians' and then had to let them go because they were breaking no law. If trouble comes again to the district, he reported, it will be from

discharged *capitaos*, houseboys, mission teachers, etc., returned emigrants to South Africa, professional criminals and generally natives who have become dissatisfied with the state of life in which they were born, but are not prepared to improve it by honest industry.

Within months of the rising, conditions on A. L. Bruce Estates, where there were no schools, no mission teachers and no labour migration, were coming to seem like a model for the whole district.

As a result, despite the continuance of the *thangata* system, people in the villages on the Namadzi saw little to tempt them to shift to Crown Land areas. No one was forcing them to move their huts and none of them was eligible for carrier service. Once the initial manhunt for Christians had subsided, therefore, it became for the duration of World War I preferable to live as tenants on the private estates. The irony that this should be so in the immediate aftermath of the Chilembwe rising was not lost on the administration. Wade was asked to explain why the 'Anguru' were leaving his district. Since policy demanded he absolve the chiefs from blame, Wade attributed it to a 'vague nomadic instinct' combined with an 'aversion to living in properly controlled and supervised villages'. The report gave him trouble. Reading it over, he struck out 'supervised' and replaced it with 'settled'.

There was a final reason why conditions for tenants on A. L. Bruce Estates seemed tolerable in the aftermath of the rising. The company could afford to pay wages regularly. For the first time, it was making substantial profits.

Before his death, W. J. Livingstone had performed one final service for his employers. He had introduced to the estates the cultivation of tobacco. By 1914, 500 acres had been planted and the results were promising. He was not in any sense a pioneer as he had been with cotton. Tobacco had claims to being the oldest of all cash crops in the Shire Highlands and the variety introduced in the years before World War I had affinities with the tobacco Zachurakamo had been growing on the Magomero peninsula before the missionaries arrived. Zachurakamo's tobacco had been sun-cured, the leaves being plucked and left to mature in the sun until they were rolled into ropes and traded by length. The new crop was dark-fired tobacco, a type probably similar to that seen by Walter Raleigh in the Guyanas. Planted in October in well-watered nursery gardens, it was transplanted in December to ridged fields and harvested in March. The leaves were cured by suspending them from horizontal bamboo poles over smouldering fires in covered barns – a process requiring hard work and skill in producing a 'lemony' leaf, not too brittle and not attracting mould. This tobacco was purchased by the Imperial Tobacco Company, which in 1908 had opened a factory in Limbe. It was a tobacco heavy in nicotine, entering the market for plugs, twists and rolls for chewing rather than smoking, a market available to producers in Nyasaland because of a shift by tobacco growers in the southern states of America towards the light Virginia tobaccos popular with cigarette and pipe smokers.

In 1919, Lloyd George's introduction of imperial preference made it possible for Nyasaland growers to compete with the United States in the production of Virginia tobacco. This was a bright-leafed tobacco with a lower nicotine content, cured by being hung in large brick barns where hot air was blown over the leaves from metal flues connected with wood fires. Under Major Sanderson, manager of the Magomero estate from the end of World War I, flue-cured tobacco took over from cotton as the principal crop. Production expanded to 3,000 acres in 1920 and to 8,000 acres in 1925, on no less than 31 different plantations. Some cotton was still grown and there was a small plantation of chillies at Magomero itself. But tobacco had become the latest saviour of A. L. Bruce Estates, as prices jumped in 1919 from 4d to 1/2d per pound.

The company's performance since its incorporation in 1913 had been highly satisfactory. Although the initial share capital of £54,000 had to be supplemented in 1915 by the raising of £18,000 of debentures at 6 per cent interest, average profit for the first six years of operation was £8,318, representing a return of 15·4 per cent. It was a figure to match the wildest dreams of the planters of the 1890s. The company had no difficulty in paying wages at the official rates, in fixing 'task' fairly and in operating a twenty-six day month. Major Sanderson was never under the kind of pressure W. J. Livingstone had experienced in expanding cotton production.

It is difficult to chart exactly when the villagers' feelings that the Chilembwe rising had brought them real benefits first began to recede. The ending of *tenga-tenga* in 1918 removed one advantage of living on estate land. In the closing months of 1918, an epidemic of Spanish influenza swept the country, killing many thousands of people,

Fig. 18. Curing shed for flue-cured tobacco, with boiler and fireplaces

including the sad figure of John Chilembwe's widow Ida. It was followed in May by an outbreak of smallpox and in December by poor rains, causing food shortages in 1920. That year, nine villages from Chiradzulu district moved en *bloc* to new sites on the Magomero estate in the valley of the Mwanje river. Land and water remained necessities and the *thangata* 'deal' could still seem acceptable.

In December 1921 this feeling was confirmed when, for the first time since the villagers had settled in Nyasaland, the season's rains failed completely. The famine of 1922 is remembered as a landmark. For two months while their gardens withered they lived off the stored remains of 1921's harvest and made emergency gardens of sorghum and cassava in the *dambos* and along the river bank. Not until early February did any substantial showers fall. This was enough to save the estate's tobacco crop, so that the company was in profit on the year. But it was too late to ensure a full year's supply of food in the villages. By May, people were living off pounded cassava leaves. By August, men were making the long trek to Mulanje where the rains never failed completely and where dried cassava could be earned for *ganyao* labour. There was also a variety of famine foods available – banana roots to be pounded and dried to make flour and tubers and roots and grass seeds which could be gathered in the bush. In

151

surviving the 1922 famine, however, the villages had two special advantages. With their *thangata* wages men could buy imported maize, which the government put on sale at the high price of 1d for 2 lb. Secondly, the Namadzi river never once dried up and still contained flowing water as late as the first week in November.

The 1922 famine confirmed what the rebuilding of their villages in 1915 had reaffirmed, that their original decision to settle on the banks of the Namadzi river was a wise one. Set against this conviction, however, was a slowly growing awareness of fresh grievances. In 1917, a new Native Rents (Private Estates) Ordinance had made it illegal for any landlord to 'exact from any native residing upon his estate any service in lieu of rent'. Landlords, however, retained the right to charge a rent, fixed initially at 6/- by the Governor in Council, and the right to make written contracts with their tenants commuting that rent to labour under the terms of the Employment of Natives Ordinance of 1909, which governed all labour contracts. Tenants who defaulted on their rent could be evicted at six months' notice.

The intention was clearly to reform the *thangata* system, preventing the abuses that had been highlighted at the Commission of Enquiry. At once, a deputation of planters led by Major Bruce demanded to see the Zomba resident. They threatened to evict all their tenants unless they were given a free hand in enforcing *thangata*. It was the planters' first use of a weapon which was to be effective for three decades. Horrified by visions that they would have to settle thousands of Africans on Crown Land at six months' notice, the administration capitulated. The Chiradzulu and Zomba residents spent three days at Magomero signing on labour, but no mention was made of the new ordinance. The fiction was preserved that *thangata* involved two months' paid labour during the rainy season, and no tenant was offered the alternative of paying his rent in cash.

Earlier, the shift from coffee to cotton had increased W. J. Livingstone's need for labour. Tobacco expanded the estates' working year to a full ten months, from October when the tobacco nurseries were prepared, to early August when the grading and packing were finally completed. With new plantations being opened every year, with fresh land for the old plantations being cleared every other year, and with all estate labour still being done entirely by hand, there was no shortage of work. In practice, all hut-owners continued to spend six months each year performing their combined hut tax and *thangata* obligations.

What made these circumstances especially galling was the emergence of a new contrast with Chiradzulu district. In April 1916, exactly one year after he had begun the process of hut concentration, sub-resident Wade had noted that tobacco was being cultivated as a cash crop in Chikoja's villages, emulating 'the enterprise of their neighbours on Mr Hinde's land'. 'Mr Hinde' was R. S. Hynde, manager of the Blantyre and East Africa Company and proprietor of the *Nyasaland Times*, who had taken over John Buchanan's old role as the champion of the Protectorate's agricultural economy. Within a year, the dark-fired tobacco he had introduced as a tenant crop on his company's Chiradzulu estate was being grown as a cash crop not only in Chikoja's but in Kanyenda's and Mpama's villages as well. No reliable production figures are available until the mid-1920s, but descriptions of the crop make it clear this was a development of great importance, not only for Chiradzulu district but for the Protectorate as a whole. If the stimulus came from Hynde, however, it was the redistribution of power in Chiradzulu district which provided the opportunity. Hut concentration involved a change in land use, with the newly appointed headmen responsible for its distribution. The labour of immigrant 'Anguru' was available on *ganyao* terms. The long-overdue abolition of the Labour Certificate in 1918 provided chiefs and headmen, who were responsible for tax collection, with the perfect means of mobilising labour on their own behalf. By April 1919, the district was overrun with European buyers prepared to pay one shilling per pound for fire-cured tobacco and offering advances to individual growers to build brick barns for curing.

From the perspective of tenants on the Magomero estate, Chiradzulu district looked suddenly like a land of opportunity. In 1919, with dark-fired tobacco fetching up to 1/- per lb, a man selling 150 lb of tobacco could earn five times the gross wages over six months of a worker on A. L. Bruce Estates. After hut tax was deducted, the ratio of profit was 6:1. These differentials became less marked as prices fell gradually and as the Native Tobacco Board, instituted in 1926, imposed a monopoly of purchase at prices intended to discriminate against African growers. Even so, it remained more profitable to cultivate dark-fired tobacco on Crown Land than to grow flue-cured tobacco for A. L. Bruce.

Crown Land settlers had other advantages. They could emigrate to Southern Rhodesia or South Africa, securing the capital to improve their farming methods, or to set up as the proprietors of the tea shops or groceries, or to purchase the tools to become skilled workmen such as carpenters or blacksmiths. By contrast, A. L. Bruce's tenants found themselves trapped in an increasingly stagnant backwater. The company justified its enormous land holdings by taking for granted the superiority of European methods. Capitalised at £54,000, it invested in housing for its European staff, in a couple of small ginneries and a tobacco grading shed. There was no money for anything else – for agricultural machinery to relieve the burden of *thangata*, for irrigation equipment for dry-season cultivation or for perennial crops, for fertilisers to replenish the soil, or for roads to open up the vast eastern half of the estate. Yet faced with official hints that it should part with some of its holdings to settlers with capital, the company was adamant in its refusal. Not an acre of the Magomero estate changed hands until 1949.

There was a flurry of optimism in August 1919 when it appeared that the northern extension to the Shire Highlands railway would be routed across the Magomero estate, bisecting it exactly from south to north. This 'eastern route' for the railway, extending from Luchenza along the east side of Zomba mountain and on to the shores of Lake Malawi, was approved by the Crown Agents because it was shorter, involved easier gradients, crossed fewer rivers and served a much larger population than the alternative 'western route' which followed the Shire valley. However, one of the directors of the Shire Highlands Railway Company was Libert Oury, who also sat on the board of the British Central Africa Company. When the railway was built in 1922, its route had shifted west of Zomba mountain, following the line of British Central Africa Company estates.

From this disappointment onwards, for the next two decades, A. L. Bruce Estates Ltd. declined. As early as 1920 the profits on tobacco were not sufficient to cover expenses in Edinburgh and from 1925 the company went into permanent deficit. Over the next fifteen years the accumulated losses reached £72,455, with the reserve fund established from earlier profits exhausted. It is difficult to understand A. L. Bruce's motives in meeting these expenses from his own pocket. Something survived of David Livingstone himself in his stubborn inability to accept the most obvious evidence of failure. This failure was not just recorded in the company's balance sheets. It was visible in the increasingly sterile soil, in the deforested hillsides, and above all in the poverty of the villages. With *thangata* consuming the bulk of their labour, there was no way the Africans could improve their condition. For three decades, trapped by the Livingstone inheritance, the villages stagnated.

At some stage during the years following World War I, attitudes in the villages towards the Chilembwe rising were transformed. As the benefits receded, John Chilembwe's preoccupations with education, business and African advancement were made meaningless by the levelling drudgery of the *thangata* system. A story began to circulate, becoming eventually the commonest explanation in the villages of why the rising had occurred and why W. J. Livingstone became its chief victim:

He went to John Chilembwe who had a bell for his church. Listonia advised John to burn the bell so that it can be ringing very hard and very loud.

Once the bell was burnt, the bell never rang as it used to do before. Then John said, 'What's wrong, we have been tricked. Why did you say that if I once burn my bell it will be sounding very loud so that it would be heard as far as Zomba. Let's go where Listonia lives!'

People gathered and went to Listonia's place at Magomero. They entered this house and said, 'You have annoyed us, why did you tell us to burn the bell?' They killed him, cut his head off, and forced his wife to carry it.

There was, indeed, a big case. Even the government was highly concerned. The government tried to control both ends (Listonia's and John's). The people said, 'The Europeans should leave.' There was no peace. In the end, the government helped the Europeans and killed Chilembwe.

It is a tantalising story, so far removed in its explanations and emphases from ordinary accounts of the rising as to challenge the historian's most basic assumptions. Yet in all the villages the old people know this story and give it their assent.

Chilembwe did have a bell for his church at Mbombwe – a witness at the Commission of Enquiry claimed he had been in trouble for smuggling it from America. 'Listonia' had, as we have seen, burned down one of Chilembwe's churches. These elements became the basis of a myth which stresses the personal nature of Chilembwe's grievance, the remoteness of his enthusiasms from the lives of ordinary villagers, and the concern of a colonial government forced reluctantly into taking sides by the violent nature of a 'case' so big it had to be referred to the highest authority available.

R. S. Hynde had told the Commission of Enquiry, 'this country is agricultural and there is no room for highly educated natives'. For different reasons and by a different route the villagers came to the same conclusion. Mr Dines Mandawala of Mpotola was twelve years old at the ringing and just old enough to remember its excitement. He wanted to go to school himself, 'but my parents refused because they said I will learn war at school'. Even when schools were opened by the Blantyre Mission at Mpotola and at nearby Chimwalira they were ignored by the local villagers, who could see no connection between their curriculum of the 'three Rs' and the circumstances in which they lived, though similar schools in Chiradzulu were packed.

By the same token, very few of the incidents of the Chilembwe rising can be learned by questioning the older people in the villages. Even those whose fathers were involved can give only the sketchiest of accounts. The records in the Malawi National Archives, which survived a fire in the Secretariat in 1919, are more informative than the people whose parents actually took part. When men like Norman Kasiye, Wisikesi Nthitiwa, and Garden and Petrolo Makuwa returned home after their imprisonment they were not held in any special regard. Emily Makuwa of Bowadi, for instance, knows that her father Garden was involved in the attack on the African Lakes Company building in Blantyre because he was sent to jail. But that is the extent of her knowledge and she has never heard of John Gray Kufa. Her son learned about John Chilembwe's rising at school and did not know until I told him that his own grandfather took part.

The same point can be made with different emphasis. The villages, as was noted earlier, were 'owned' by the women to whom the chiefs distributed the land, and who did most of the cultivating. This was partly because it was the custom the people had brought with them from Mozambique and partly the result of tax and *thangata*, which took the men (and the unmarried women) away from the villages during the cultivation season. The Chilembwe rising, however, was an all-male affair. Its causes lay in problems experienced primarily by men, and men were the only participants. Some versions claim that the women were not even informed until the morning after the attacks. In the aftermath of the rising, the imprisonment of some of the men, the flight of others to Mozambique and the continuance of the *thangata* system left the villages once again largely in the possession of the married women. The accounts of the Chilembwe rising which have persisted in the villages emphasise the disturbance to harmony and hierarchy and do their best to minimise conflict. They are women's accounts.

Ida Thamanga is a sixty-year-old widow. She was born at Mpawa and, apart from a brief residence in Mulanje where her husband worked as a watchman for a tea estate, she has lived all her life in the village. Her family came originally from Mkhwapa in M'Nyamweri in Mozambique. It was her father and mother, Thamanga and his wife, who made the journey into Nyasaland, settling first at Machado in Zomba district. Towards the end of World War I, they shifted to A. L. Bruce Estates to avoid the *tenga-tenga* recruiting parties. They asked Mpawa III for land and accommodated themselves to the *thangata* system. They had four children, three boys, all of whom are now dead, and Ida. Unusually for those days, Thamanga and his wife both belonged to the Dzimbiri clan. Some ten years or so after they had settled, other Dzimbiri clansmen from Machedo came to join them at Mpawa. One of them, Elestina Petulo, still lives close by at Chimwalira and as we shall see regards Ida Thamanga as her 'sister'.

Both the ladies are long-established residents, respected for their age and accepted as spokeswomen for the women of the village. But when Ida Thamanga's parents first moved to Mpawa, they came as outsiders to a village first built almost a generation before. Mpawa III was obliged by the *thangata* system to accept them and to offer them land. Ida Thamanga remembers a song from her mother's days which makes a sharp distinction between the 'owners' of the village and new settlers like herself. Significantly, it is a song sung originally by Lomwe plantation workers in Mozambique and addressed to their employers ('I'm working in hunger / The owners are full / It's a bad sign.') At Mpawa, where one might have expected the song to be addressed to A. L. Bruce, the words were changed to express the newcomer's sense of having to struggle for acceptance:

> I'm dancing in hunger,
> The owners of the village are full:
> > ee *It's a bad sign*
> > ee *It's a bad sign*

Ida Thamanga's memories are memories of her mother. Life for the women had not changed greatly since before the rising. It was governed by the same cycle of cultivation, with the same crops – sorghum, millet, and maize, cassava and *nandolo* and a variety of pulses – following the same seasons. Ida's mother would, during the planting season, leave for her garden very early in the morning, refusing to eat anything until midday because 'it would make her lazy'. Her methods were exactly like Che Simani's at Mpotola ten years earlier. Most of the crops were planted on raised mounds, while cassava cuttings were pushed into holes in the cleared ground. After a midday meal of *nsima*, eaten at home if work permitted or cooked by Ida and taken to her mother in the garden, she would be joined by Thamanga who had completed his 'task' at nearby Chimwalira estate. In the late afternoon there were various other duties, flour to be

Fig. 19. Washing clothes in the Namadzi river, Mpawa

pounded and washed at the river, water to be fetched and firewood collected from Nanyungwi hill. In the dry season there was time to relax, though the months of August and September were also the time for building or repairing houses, with the work shared as before between husband and wife.

There were changes, though, from the days before the rising. Maize was becoming increasingly popular as the staple grain crop. It was less drought-resistant than sorghum and did very badly when the rains failed in 1922. But it had advantages. It produced more grain – more flour – to the acre and for villages suffering a shortage of male labour that was an important consideration. It also ripened earlier than millet or sorghum, being harvested in May or June. This had not been an advantage in the days of cotton growing but tobacco was different, its peak labour demands coming in October to March and then in June to August, when men were needed in the tobacco sheds for grading and packing. Maize then could be harvested by both husband and wife, and the household *nkokwe* packed to the roof before *thangata* imposed its second main levy of the year. Sorghum was still grown in case the maize crop faltered, and millet remained popular because it produced better *nsima* and better beer and because the ancestors knew nothing about maize. Ida Thamanga remembers her parents making annual sacrifice under an *mpoza* tree and using the traditional millet flour and millet beer.

There was also more money in the family. With wages now paid regularly, Thamanga and his wife were drawn into the local cash economy. Items once made in the villages began to be purchased from outside. Clay pots, for water or for cooking, came from the market at Thondwe, which was beginning to attract customers from as far as Zomba for the range and quality of its pots. Iron hoes were brought at Karim's near the Magomero ginnery and even reed mats and baskets and the carved wooden spoons and woven plates for *nsima* were purchased from itinerant traders. Mrs Thamanga senior kept chickens and bought goat meat occasionally from Njuli market or fish from traders who came, as in the nineteenth century, from the shores of Lake Chilwa. The fish 'of the old days used to be very good. They had fat of their own so no extra oil was needed' when they were boiled with tomatoes and onions. Bark cloth disappeared altogether. *Biriwita* cloth, which had once been a luxury, worn by the men as a loin cloth and by the women for complete cover with a belt at the waist to help support a baby on the back, took over from bark cloth as the poorest kind of wear. Patterned prints, still at 3d a yard, came within the range of more and more married women. The tailor with his sewing machine on the veranda at Karim's had more to do than simply provide hems, and began to produce skirts and blouses as luxury items. Husbands who had to pay for these items, sometimes under threat of separation, were not always pleased:

> Tailor,
> Measure me with your eyes
> ee Tailor,
> Measure me with your eyes
> > *My husband is jealous*
> > *He sleeps on the veranda.*

Compared with the opportunities available in Chiradzulu district it was a tiny economy. All the local markets – at Njuli, or Blantyre, or Thondwe, or later at Mwanje – lay off the Magomero estate, and the women who went with their husbands' wages or carrying baskets of flour or pots of millet beer for sale felt themselves to be poor when they got there. Money was preferred to the older barter system, since it could be stored and released people from having to make instant decisions about exchange. But no one accumulated anything which

159

could have been termed capital. The demands of the *thangata* system
made it impossible for any man to set up as a trader or storekeeper or
carpenter or builder, or for Che Namaponya of Njenjema to continue
working as a blacksmith, while the wages of *thangata* kept economic
opportunities to a minimum. In 1922, builders and bricklayers in
Chiradzulu district were earning 20/- per month, while even a road
capitao earned 15/-. That was the year in which a man called Johanne
opened a tea shop at Magomero on the model of similar enterprises
which were flourishing in Chiradzulu. The shop survived for three
months before it had to close for lack of custom.

Thamanga's wife was best known as a storyteller and her reputation helped her to gain acceptance among the women of the village to
which she had come as an outsider. She would tell her stories at beer
parties or at night at the fireside, especially when there was a full
moon and the children were allowed to stay up late. Ida Thamanga
retells these stories and remembers two in particular which were
among her mother's favourites. Both are stories about men who tried
to impose their view of things on women and were defeated.

The greedy man
> Mother,
> > *madedede*
> Mother,
> > *madedede*
> She is calling,
> > *madedede*
> > > Why is she calling me?
> I don't know, mother,
> > *madedede*
> > > How many dishes are there?
> Mother, what shall we do?
> > *madedede*
> > *madedede*
> > *madedede*

There was a certain married man who was very greedy. He used to go to dig in
the garden and his wife would stay behind to cook. He used to eat two large
baskets of *nsima* and three large baskets of relish and he would drink up a
whole big pot of water. The man would be digging in the garden waiting and
when the food was cooked the wife would send her boy to go and call his
father:

> Father,
> > *madedede*

Father,
>   *madedede*
She is calling,
>   *madedede*
>   Why is she calling me?
I don't know, father,
>   *madedede*
>   How many dishes are there?
Mother, what shall we do?
>   *madedede*
>   *madedede*
>   *madedede*

The man used to come from the garden, and as soon as he arrived he would order his wife 'Tell me my name! Tell me my name!' The wife didn't know his name and she said so. Then the man used to eat all the food she had cooked, two baskets of *nsima* and three baskets of relish and a whole pot of water, and he would have a rest and then go back to the garden. The woman became very tired of all this. One day when she was going out of the house, a little fieldmouse struck her on the leg. She was surprised and said, 'Why are you hitting me on my leg?' The fieldmouse said, 'Why don't you answer your husband when he asks what is his name?' The wife said she didn't know his name. Then the mouse said, 'Today, when you've cooked and you call him from the garden to come and eat, if he asks "Tell me my name! Tell me my name!", tell him that he is Chikangale [praying mantis].'

Then the woman sent the boy again to call the husband to come to eat. Again he said, 'Tell me my name! Tell me my name!' And she said, 'But aren't you Chikangale?'

> Chikangale gets up
>   *Chikangale ee*
> Poor Chikangale, poor man,
>   *Chikangale, Chikangale,*
> A man's son, where will I dance?
>   *Chikangale ee*
> She has spoken my name
>   *Chikangale ee*
> She thinks I'm Chikangale
>   *Chikangale, Chikangale, Chikangale*

After this the husband went out to the river bank and he drowned himself.

The hunter

There was a man who was a hunter and he got married. When he went out hunting and came back with the meat his wife used to be pleased and she used to cook it to eat. But his wife's mother always said, 'No, I don't want to eat your meat. No, I don't want to eat your meat.' This went on for a long time and always his wife's mother refused to eat the meat. So the hunter said, 'I don't like this. Why won't she eat my meat?' And he decided to do something about it.

Now his wife's mother had a big farm of groundnuts. When it was time to harvest the groundnuts, the hunter took some animal skins and he made some drums. He said to his wife, 'Where are you going?' and she said, 'We are going to the farm to harvest the groundnuts. You should come with us to the garden.' But he said, 'No, I am going to see my mother.' But the hunter was lying. Instead of going to see his mother, he went to his wife's mother's farm and he took his drums and he hid beneath a pile of grass which had already been cut. Then his wife and his wife's mother came to the farm and they began to work harvesting the groundnuts. When the hunter felt that they had harvested enough, he began beating drums and singing:

> I'm famous, ee
> I'm famous, ee
> I'm famous, ee
> I'm famous, ee

When his wife's mother heard this song she asked her daughter 'Where's that drumming coming from?' But the daughter didn't know. The hunter stopped drumming and singing and the two women went back to harvesting the groundnuts. As soon as they began to dig the hunter started up again with his singing and drumming and his wife's mother began dancing. She kept on dancing right up until sunset when it was time to go home. When they arrived back at their people said, 'But is that all the groundnuts you have harvested? What have you been doing all this time at the farm?' So the wife lied that her mother had been held up by a fit of vomiting. She said, 'When my mother was sick I didn't have the time to come home so I waited. Then I saw she was all right so I took her to the farm but she has been resting all day.'

The next day at the farm the same thing happened. When the two women went to harvest the groundnuts the hunter started beating his drums and singing, and his wife's mother danced until sunset.

Then a man who stayed close by began to get suspicious. He went to see the wife's father who was his friend and said, 'I want to ask you about your wife. She's always talking about her garden but when she comes home I don't see anything. What is happening in the garden? What she tells me is that whenever she goes to the garden her daughter gets sick, but I also heard your daughter say it was your wife who was held up by vomiting.' The husband did not know the answer to this, so his friend told him, 'Tomorrow, when you see your wife is going to the garden, as soon as she leaves the house you follow her. Then you can go and hide somewhere so you can see what is happening in the garden.

Next morning, the hunter's wife's mother got ready, and collected all her things to take to the farm. But her husband had gone on ahead and was hiding in a different place to where the hunter was also hiding. As soon as the mother-in-law arrived, she just had time to dig once with her hoe when the hunter started up with his drumming and singing. The boy was playing music and the father-in-law saw his wife dancing – jumping up and down, *kunumpa pamene paja*, jumping up and down. Then the man said, 'Oh, so this is what is going on in the garden?'

Then the man called his friend and said, 'Look over there for me. Have a good look under that pile of grass.' And the friend went there and he found the boy playing with his music and immediately the boy ran away taking his drums with him and the music stopped.

Of the men described in these stories, the Hunter is by far the more menacing. The Greedy Man has gained an unnatural ascendancy over his wife, supplanting her in the role of cultivator and consuming far more than his fair share of the household food. But his power rests on no more than the secret of his name. The power of names, through its association with witchcraft, is a real power. Mrs Thamanga, for instance, would not reveal the names of her children or her husband. The Greedy Man, however, is easily outwitted by a message delivered through the fieldmouse. When his name is revealed he is destroyed.

The threat posed by the Hunter is an altogether more serious matter. The Hunter is the freest of agents, dependent on nobody, living by his individual efforts and skills – the capitalist virtues in a world without money. The story begins with his marriage. By the custom of the time, the Hunter should at once have turned to cultivating the family farm. Instead, he goes out hunting, brings home the meat he has killed and offers it to his mother-in-law. The challenge is an open and direct one. Instead of being dependent on his wife's lineage he is trying to make them dependent upon him. The enormity of this is underlined by the methods he uses. Superficially, by interrupting the harvest, he is ensuring that his mother-in-law will have to turn to him for her supply of food. But the image of her dancing helplessly to his drums, with its undertones of sexual taboo, emphasises the degree of social disruption the Hunter is trying to bring about. It takes the combined efforts of the woman's husband helped by a family friend to restore order. The Hunter's threat is averted. But he remains a free agent, outside the system, and the story has nothing to say about his wife's future.

These are well-known stories and their age and origins are uncertain. It would be misleading to connect them specifically with the 1920s and with Mpawa where they were told. Neither so much as mentions *thangata*. Nevertheless, the fact that they were popular then indicates that they were found meaningful. They illustrate

163

tensions appropriate to the times. For, faced with the failure of the Chilembwe rising and the poverty to which they were condemned by the *thangata* system, people reacted by recreating a theory of society based on the role of women as the producers of food.

The idea was a familiar one, its starting point the extended family. The key figure was the head of the female line, the maternal grandmother from whom everyone was theoretically descended and in whose name the family land was held. The daughters of the lineage when they got married were given land to cultivate and their husbands came to live with them in their villages. The sons of the lineage would look for wives and land in other villages, returning home if the marriage ended through death or through divorce. Land or other property was inherited through the female line. A husband had no authority over his own children but he was responsible for the discipline and welfare of his sister's children. This being the case, the 'family' was much more than the individual household, and the bonds of kinship with all the obligations they imposed – of sharing work or distributing food or helping to reconcile disputes or joining together for religious or social rituals – spread far beyond the separate villages. In theory, a woman with three daughters and three sons would on their marriage – the daughters at home, the sons in other villages – have spread her family across four different villages. By the time these had also each raised to the age of marriage three daughters and three sons, the lineage could theoretically be spread over twenty-eight villages, the ramifications becoming enormously diverse from the third generation onwards.

On the other hand, there were circumstances in which both the household and the village were treated as entities. Each household had its own *nkokwe*, one or more bins in which maize, millet and sorghum were stored. The *nkokwe* belonged to the wife. Even though the husband had woven it, and even though the fields had been cultivated and the harvest gathered by communal labour, once the grain was stored it became the wife's property, the means by which she fed her household throughout the year, and no man and no other woman would touch it. Similarly, the village had coherence as a unit. The land belonged to the village, not to the lineage. It was the headman who was responsible for its distribution. Land which had once been allocated could not be taken back by the headman unless it had been left uncultivated, but the headman remained responsible for finding land for fresh settlers and for arbitrating boundary disputes. The fertility of the land was also vested in him in that his duties included the organisation of such rituals as initiation and rain-making, including the *chopa* dance. Most headmen had slightly better farms than their fellow-villagers. Mpawa, for instance, cultivated all eight acres of the original Magomero peninsula and he had another garden in the *dambo* 2 km to the east. But they received no tribute beyond a high degree of respect. When a headman died, it was the women of the village who had the loudest voice in choosing his successor from among the younger brothers and nephews of the deceased in the female line.

Nowadays, the old women regret the decay of customs which they describe as established from time immemorial. Only reluctantly and under detailed questioning about biographies will they acknowledge breaks in the pattern – the occasions when estate managers intervened directly in the choice of a village headman or when women on their marriage made 'a special arrangement' to live in their husbands' home villages. The gaps between custom and practice are easily demonstrated. As we have seen, the people who originally settled the villages came from a variety of different places. They were brought together with their common language, Mihavani, by their common experiences as refugees living briefly under Yao chiefs in Blantyre and Chiradzulu districts, and by their deliberate manipulation of their clan names. But they were not related except in the smallest of family groups. Even in the mid-1920s, when the villages were a generation old and when some of the earliest settlers had infant grandchildren, the kinship links within and between villagers were less important than the links of ordinary friendship and of shared experience. Obviously, those people who did have a small circle of relatives enjoyed advantages in the sharing of labour and the distribution of food within the extended family. But these advantages were lessened by the facility with which those without kin could invent families. People who claimed to be linked by clan, or who had attended Chilembwe's church together, or whose grandparents had been neighbours in Mozambique, or who simply liked each other, would employ the language of kinship to express their relationship. Elestina Petulo, for instance, calls Ida Thamanga 'sister'. Their real relationship is that they have been close friends since childhood and that their parents lived briefly in the same village in Zomba district before settling at Mpawa. Even the most disadvantaged people of all, the unmarried and never-to-be-married women, could adjust to the pattern. If kinship involved shared labour, then the sharing of labour could be made the basis of kinship. As a women's song from Njenjema's expressed it,

> *You, it's all right,*
> *You it's all right,*
> Though I'm not married
> *You it's all right,*
> Though you don't bathe
> You are my relative,
> Though you don't bathe
> You are my relative,
> *It's all right, you are my relative*
> *So long as you dig the garden.*

The terminology of kinship, then, became the means by which people who were not necessarily related described their society. Custom was not a set of conclusions derived from experience but a pattern imposed upon it.

Behind the custom was an even more basic contradiction. The villages were labour compounds. It was not, in practice, through his marriage that a man secured access to land. It was by performing *thangata*. Faced with any man who asserted this, 'custom' was helpless. If a man insisted on living in his home village, there was nothing his wife could do about it. Divorce would not simply deny her the benefit of his meagre wages, it would leave her liable to *thangata* herself. One of Elestina Petulo's most bitter childhood memories is of her father's decampment to Southern Rhodesia. He had sampled *thangata* and rejected it, and he never returned to his family at Mpawa. As soon as his absence was detected the rangers arrived, threatening to burn down the hut where Elestina was cooking her mother's *nsima* and she had to promise them that her mother, who was working in the garden, would turn out for field labour the following day. From the late 1920s onwards it became, in fact, increasingly difficult for women to find husbands who could accept the various requirements and restrictions.

In these circumstances, the themes of the stories told by Ida Thamanga's mother at Mpawa's in the 1920s take on a special urgency. Having accompanied her husband to Mpawa's during World War I to escape *tenga-tenga* and having obtained land through his *thangata* labour, she was faced with the difficult task of arguing that *she* was the resident and *he* the visitor. Her attack on men who tried to evade their ancestral responsibilities – the Greedy Man, the dangerously independent Hunter – has to be understood as an aspect of a struggle for resources between the sexes within a system which left women unusually vulnerable. In making their case, the women had certain advantages. One was that in the absence of the men on estate duty the village gardens were cultivated by their wives. It became difficult for a man to get a woman to grow his food while he performed *thangata* except within the context of the custom. The *thangata* system worked by coopting custom, the people adopting after 1915 a view of themselves which matched in important respects that of their landlord and their colonial rulers.

A second advantage was that the custom the women were trying to re-establish had historical validity, the pattern having been followed by their grandparents back in Mozambique. It could be presented, in the wake of the Chilembwe rising's failure, as a return to tradition in which men exchanged their authority as husbands and fathers for the status of brothers and uncles within their grandmothers' lineages. In a system in which a man's sisters raised heirs for him, he could become the focal point of a much larger network of relationships than simply through his marriage. The women, then, were offering something positive, the chance of becoming a kind of headman within the extended family. The difficulty from the man's point of view was that no woman grew food for her brother or her uncle. In the economics of the *thangata* system a man's marriage remained his most important relationship.

Most important of all, however, was the fact that by denying the *thangata* system in this manner, by insisting that their villages *were* villages following the custom of their ancestors and not the labour compounds they threatened to become, both men and women were able to preserve some sense of their dignity and value. From the summit of Nanyungwi hill in the middle of Mpawa, the houses of the Europeans at Magomero were just visible. But after the failure of armed resistance under John Chilembwe, people stopped looking in that direction. There is no further mention of the white men, nothing about *thangata* in the dance songs or pounding songs. The world shrank to the banks of the Namadzi river, and people who had once looked back to Mozambique and forward through John Chilembwe's teachings now found intellectual refuge within the confines of their village systems. In contradiction of the facts, custom was asserted as a defiance of their exploitation. They were there, they insisted, because they chose to be there and they were doing what they chose to do. Custom became an alternative form of resistance, a doctrine thrust in the face of reality. It was a narrow, inflexible, necessary, practical and honourable posture for them to adopt. But its long-term effect was to discredit custom itself. As soon as the men had the power and means to reject it they did so firmly.

This reaction lay in the future. First came a shift in the impact of *thangata*, a further twist of the landlord's knife. By the late 1920s as the world slump deepened, it was clear that Nyasaland's tobacco boom was over. For the third time in the Protectorate's history, a crop which had become the rationale of the planter community's existence came under threat. Prices collapsed and by the end of 1927 much of the crop remained unsold. The impact of this decline, however, was unlike the earlier collapse of coffee or of cotton. Over two decades, the Nyasaland economy had changed significantly.

The first of these changes lay in the rise of a new tea industry in Mulanje and Thyolo districts. Tea was yet another crop in which Scottish missionary mystique was invested. Jonathan Duncan, who imported the first coffee plants in 1878, had also raised two tea bushes in the grounds of the Blantyre Mission, and it was seedlings from these bushes which were planted at Mulanje in 1891 on Lauderdale and Thornwood estates. By 1905 there were 260 acres under tea in Mulanje district with a combined production of 2,500 lb of made tea, and in 1908 the first tea was planted in Thyolo district on Bandanga estate. In those days, however, the prospects for cotton focused everyone's attention, under the impact of W. J. Livingstone's experiments at Magomero. It was not until World War I, when it had become clear that cotton had no future as a plantation crop, that the tea industry began to expand significantly. Between 1915 and 1935, the acreage under tea in Mulanje and Thyolo quadrupled and tea became second only to tobacco in Nyasaland's table of exports.

Tea is a perennial crop, the bushes coming into full production after seven to eleven years and remaining productive for another sixty or more years. Unlike cotton or tobacco, for which each year's crop in the Shire Highlands was a speculative raid on freshly cleared land, tea required care in the selection and marking out of plantations, properly terraced gardens to make best use of surface water, the regular and scientific application of fertilisers, and an experienced labour force capable of observing precise plucking and pruning requirements. Tea, in short, required a commitment of capital and expertise over periods far in excess of earlier agricultural enterprises in the Protectorate. In fact, it was many years before tea was grown in

Nyasaland to its own exacting standards, but the contrast with other crops was clear from the start. When the world slump drove tea prices down in the late 1920s, tea was not a crop which permitted widespread retrenchment. Even the plucking of the bushes had to be continued to maintain the tea 'tables' until prices rallied following an International Tea Agreement in 1933.

The second change in Nyasaland's plantation economy lay in the rise of a new tobacco industry in the Central region. In May 1920 two planters from Zomba district, A. F. Barron and R. W. Wallace, leased 2,000 acres on the Mbabzi stream, 16 km from the tiny settlement of Lilongwe. Significantly, they both held land between Namadzi and Thondwe, bordering on the A. L. Bruce Estates, and they moved north in search of opportunities for expansion denied them by Harry Johnston's legacy in the Shire Highlands. The move was the start of a new industry, which rapidly developed three sectors. The first was flue-cured tobacco grown on private estates employing wage labour. The second was flue-cured tobacco grown by tenants on private estates who were offered land, seedlings and advice on cultivation in return for rights of purchase over the crop. The third and most important by volume was fire-cured tobacco grown as a cash crop by peasant producers for sale to European buyers.

The circumstances of this production were very different from those prevailing in the Shire Highlands. Comparatively little African land was alienated. Even in the mid-1930s, when the first rush was over, some 30,000 acres only had passed into European hands compared to the near one million acres owned by planters or plantation companies in the south. There was no *thangata* system and though labour could be tied to planters or buyers through a variety of devices (ranging from tenant production to advances to peasant growers of money and equipment), all labour was paid. Finally, there were no immigrants from Mozambique to be used by planters or by chiefs and headmen as tobacco growers. Planters paid their labour, and chiefs who wished to have their tobacco grown cheaply had to resort to using tax defaulters. The tobacco boom in the Central Province was thus a very different affair from the destructive scramble it became in the south. By 1932 Lilongwe and Dowa districts alone were producing more than half of the tobacco grown in Nyasaland.

This was despite restrictions on African production of dark-fired tobacco introduced by the planters as their response to the world slump. The main function of the Native Tobacco Board, which was instituted in 1926, was to protect planter interests from African competition. African growers had to be registered and the size of their farms was restricted. Marketing opportunities were curbed. Malpractices at the buying stations remained uncorrected and unpunished. Prices were fixed with the costs of the board's operations being charged indirectly to the African growers, who in some years received less than 50 per cent of the local value of their crop. Meanwhile, despite the fears of over-production which were used to justify restriction, tobacco cultivation on the private estates expanded.

These new industries – tea in Mulanje and Thyolo and tobacco in the Central Province – were able to withstand the impact of the depression, the tea companies relying on the long-term nature of their investment and the tobacco planters cushioning its impact by restricting African production. In the Shire Highlands, however, the three large plantation companies with their undeveloped estates reacted to the world slump by simply abandoning most of their activities. As early as 1914, the Blantyre and East Africa Company had been forced to write down its £1 shares to 16/-. The company decided to concentrate on tea production at the Lauderdale and Bandanga estates, and by 1935 owned three tea factories and had acquired three more estates at Glenorchy, Limbuli and Zoa. These investments, however, involved a mere 35,000 acres of the company's total land holdings of 175,000 acres in Zomba, Blantyre, Thyolo, Mulanje and Chikwawa districts. The rest stagnated, the company maintaining tenant production of cotton and tobacco as sidelines in lieu of *thangata*, but doing nothing by way of development and refusing to sell any of its land until after World War II.

Meanwhile, the British Central Africa Company was veering towards bankruptcy. In 1921, having never once declared a divided, not even during the tobacco boom, it was forced to raise £200,000 on first mortgate debentures simply to carry on trading and in 1924 the company went into liquidation and had to be reconstituted, its £1 shares being written down to 10/-. This was the company which owned 372,536 acres of the Shire Highlands. A settler scheme in 1919 attracted some fifty British ex-servicemen, with the prospect of purchasing land after an initial period of training. But at prices ranging from 30/- to £3 per acre and with the immigrants 'reliant on the African for what they could learn about planting', the scheme was a failure. By 1930, when the 10/- shares had to be written down to 5/-, the company still controlled 340,568 acres, of which a derisory 620 acres were actually under tobacco. Sisal and cotton had been abandoned altogether and tea production had yet to start.

On A. L. Bruce Estates Ltd., matters were only marginally better. By 1932 the accumulated losses were more than £60,000 and A. L. Bruce was financing a bank overdraft of £14,000 and a loan of £15,000 at 6 per cent interest as well as the earlier debentures of £18,000 at 6 per cent. Only the prospect of one day selling the estates for a price which would cover these losses kept the company in business. Meanwhile, between 1928 and 1932 all the thirty-one plantations on the Magomero estate were abandoned.

Six years later, Captain Kincaid-Smith, who became General Manager after Major Sanderson's death, described to a government Commission of Enquiry exactly what he thought had gone wrong. Noting that dark-fired tobacco had first been grown on European estates, he explained:

Unfortunately, however, it was discovered that this type of tobacco could be very successfully grown and cured by the individual native without a great deal of European supervision or expense or elaborate buildings ...With such an attractive and lucrative method of earning money, the native remaining his own master, and working only when he felt inclined to do so, with an army of eager buyers ready to buy his production on the spot, the rot was bound to set in ... Native production, no matter in what commodity and in what country, had invariably resulted in the eventual ruination of the European planter ... In our neighbouring territory of Southern Rhodesia, it is illegal for a native to plant tobacco and the prosperity of that country, as compared with Nyasaland, is obvious for all to see.

Developing this theme, writing at his desk in the house where William Jervis Livingstone had been killed, Kincaid-Smith enlarged on his view of the Protectorate's agricultural history:

One may say, 'Why should not a native grow what he likes in his own country, Nyasaland being a Protectorate?' This outlook may be ethical, but it does not bring prosperity to the country, neither is it fair to owners of freehold land. In the majority of cases these are private companies whose owners or directors were persuaded, about 1889, to take up large areas, send out settlers, and invest vast sums of money in the country in order to develop industries. At that time there was no government, neither was Nyasaland British property. It was to justify the erection of a government, and the Protectorate added to the British flag, instead of the Portuguese, that these people, sentimentally interested in the country, agreed.

Subsequent developments and Colonial Office policy have proved a poor reward for their spirit ...

171

It is a fascinating argument, a bizarre reversal of the original moral proposition of which Magomero was itself the symbol that colonial intervention was justified to destroy the slave trade and teach Africans the rudiments of commerce. In its place is raised a new doctrine, common to the planting community in the 1930s, of the duty owed to the landlord by both Africans and the administration, to compensate for the sacrifice made on their behalf in colonising Nyasaland.

In many ways, Captain Kincaid-Smith was an analogue of William Jervis Livingstone and, as we shall see, he very nearly suffered a similar fate. A large, bluff man, he liked to have his boots on the table when conducting an argument, and he expressed himself in short staccato bursts of loud assertion. He was incapable of listening to counter-arguments, resorting to bluster when contradicted and easily becoming confused. Like W. J. Livingstone, he had no head for figures or for the minutiae of estate administration or for the laws of the Protectorate. He was soon in debt to everyone, to his workers, to his European staff (witholding the wages of one 'in his own interest as he was addicted to liquor'), and to the administration over tax revenue. Barnes, the Chiradzulu district commissioner, called him 'a menace to the district' because of the 'intense hatred' of his African tenants. As with W. J. Livingstone, even his fellow-planters disliked him. Yet, again like W. J. Livingstone, he made one substantial contribution to the Protectorate's economy.

In 1933, Kincaid-Smith negotiated a contract with the United Africa Company to supply dark-fired tobacco to West Africa. The West African market had previously been monopolised by the United States, but a shift by American growers into bright Virginia tobacco for cigarette and pipe smokers had left a small but lucrative gap in West Africa, where smokers preferred a tobacco heavy with nicotine of a kind best grown in Zomba and Chiradzulu districts. The requirements were exacting. Five leaves, cured to precise standards and each measuring between 19 and 21 inches had to be tied into 'heads' in such a way that ten 'heads' weighed one lb exactly and a cask of 2,500 heads weighed 250 lb. After grading and packing, the tobacco was shipped via London to Sierra Leone, where Creole and Lebanese merchants operating along the West African coast used it as a currency for trading in palm oil, palm kernels, groundnuts and cocoa. By 1937, other tobacco growers were following Kincaid-Smith's example and Nyasaland's exports of dark-fired tobacco to West Africa had reached 330 tons. To this day Nyasaland has retained a *de facto* monopoly of the West African market.

Meanwhile, for the first time since 1924, A. L. Bruce Estates began to balance its books, registering a tiny profit on its local account of £704 in 1935. In achieving this, Kincaid-Smith had one enormous advantage. He was getting most of his tobacco free.

In 1928, another Natives on Private Estates Ordinance had been passed, altering yet again the rules governing *thangata*. Pressure for a change had come from both sides. The administration remained dissatisfied with the operation of the 1917 Ordinance which had allowed tenants to pay a cash rent in lieu of *thangata*. This had seemed a necessary reform following the Chilembwe rising. Faced, however, with the threat of mass evictions from the estates, the administration had collaborated in breaking its own laws, visiting estates like Magomero to sign up workers for factory or plantation labour without informing them they had any choice.

The landlords, too, were discovering inconveniences in the 1917 Ordinance. As the world recession began to bite they had less and less use for *thangata* labour. By the mid-1920s, some of the people settled on their land had been living and working there for a generation. There were children born on the estates approaching adulthood and marriage. What had looked in the years before World War I like a captive labour force, eminently exploitable because tied to the land, suddenly began to appear like a hoard of dependent relatives, exhausting the soil with their methods of cultivation, eroding the river banks with their dry-season gardens and deforesting the land with their hut building and cooking fires. For almost the first time the planters of the Shire Highlands looked ten years ahead and they began to have visions that when the recession was over and plantations were once again profitable their estates would be exhausted, eroded, deforested and over-populated.

Mass evictions seemed the solution. But the expulsion of thousands of people onto over-populated Crown Land areas was a political impossibility, and the landlords discovered that despite their threats in 1917 their rights in the matter were unclear. Few people knew or understood the law and those who did were confused about its application.

The root of the problem, as so often, lay with Harry Johnston. Many of the Certificates of Claim issued by Johnston to ratify land purchases in the Shire Highlands had included a non-disturbance clause intended to protect the rights of African residents. In 1903, the Blantyre and East Africa Company had sought to prove that no

Africans were protected by these clauses, their practice of shifting cultivation making it unlikely they were still occupying the sites they had occupied in 1894, and that therefore all residents were liable to *thangata*. It was this case which provoked the famous Nunan judgement, including the withering description of land alienation in the Shire Highlands quoted earlier. Judge Nunan interpreted Johnston's intentions as having been to protect African rights without qualification. He placed the burden of proof that Africans had forfeited their rights firmly on the landlords, the effect being that all tenants were treated as being protected up to the date of his judgement.

It was a famous judgement which scandalised the planter community, and it was followed necessarily in 1904 by legislation which defined the rights of Africans under the *thangata* system. As has already been noted, none of the protective clauses of this ordinance was ever actually enforced. Nor was the ordinance of 1917 ever put into effect. So broad was the gap between the law and the practice of *thangata* that both administrators and landlords lost all track of what the law said. Thus in 1923, when 2,000 tenants had been given notice to quit in Blantyre district alone, the Attorney-General claimed that landlords had the right to evict Africans who could not prove they were occupying the same land they had occupied in 1894, in defiance of the Nunan judgement which had declared precisely the opposite. The administration moved quickly, preparing to prohibit evictions without government consent. The planters protested, only to discover that 'the practice of *thangata* is by law illegal'. There was deadlock, followed by a realisation on both sides of the need for a new ordinance. The result was sheer farce.

The ordinance itself was relatively straightforward. African tenants were entitled to a hut and sufficient land to support themselves and their families, together with grass and poles for hut building and firewood for cooking. For these facilities they had to pay rent, in one of three ways. First they could pay a cash rent at a rate to be fixed by a District Rent Board, at between two and three months' wages at the average rate for the district. Secondly, they could do *thangata* labour, each month's work performed between October and February counting as one-third of their obligation to the landlord and each month between March and September counting as one-sixth. In practice this meant *thangata* extended from three to six months, depending on when it was performed. Thirdly, and most significant of all, tenants could by agreement pay their rent by cultivating a cash crop which the landlord was obliged to purchase at the market rate. The amounts required would also be fixed by the District Rent Boards. Tenants who failed to pay one of the three forms of rent could be given notice to quit. This could be done, however, only after five years and no more than 10 per cent of the population could be evicted at one time.

After the ordinance was passed the Attorney-General protested bitterly about the ensuing confusion. It had been a difficult bill to draft since 'no model from any other colony could be found' and 'from its inception the bill has been misunderstood and misinterpreted by those who are expected to know better ... 90% of queries could have been answered by assistant DCs I have examined in the past, including those who failed!' He gave examples. What happens if a man is absent when notice to quit is given? Answer: pin it on the hut door. What happens to the wives when men are evicted? Answer: they too must leave, since the ordinance does not recognise customary land tenure. The ordinance provided for men having up to three wives: what happens if a man has four wives? Answer: the ordinance 'does not provide for super men'.

These questions came from district commissioners alarmed to discover that for the first time they were expected to pay serious attention to what was happening on the private estates. The landlords took longer to comprehend what they had agreed to. At first they were delighted at what the ordinance seemed to have given them. Instead of employing *thangata* labour on loss-making plantations they could accept cash crops in lieu of rent. When shortly afterwards the equivalents were fixed by the District Rent Boards as 150 lb. of tobacco in Chiradzulu district and 144 lb of tobacco in Zomba district, the prospect of profit seemed secured. Whereas African-grown cotton and tobacco had undermined the plantation economy, the landlords had regained the initiative by, in effect, converting their estates into concessions within which they held monopoly rights of purchase over the produce.

But were the landlords obliged by the ordinance to *pay* for the tobacco grown by their tenants? Or was the tobacco to be offered 'in lieu of' rent? In all the discussion before the ordinance was passed, the landlords had assumed the latter. Now they were aghast to discover they were expected to buy the tobacco at market rates. For six years they protested vigorously. The new ordinance, it was argued, had disadvantaged them further, forcing them into competition with Crown Land growers who were being heavily subsidised with free seed and advice and transport by the government through the Native Tobacco Board. This was a specious argument – the costs of the NTB were being borne by the Crown Land growers – but there was a core of truth to the landlords' protests. The effect of the 1928 Ordinance was that tenants could fulfil their obligations under the *thangata* system simply by growing tobacco. If the landlord could not afford to buy it he had no further rights in the matter. In this respect, the ordinance simply maintained economic stalemate.

Against this background of confusion and mutual distrust it is not easy to establish what was happening on the private estates during the 1930s. No longer immune to the law, the landlords acquired a vested interest in misinformation which the government was slow to penetrate. On the Magomero estate, tenant production of dark-fired tobacco began in 1928 and over four years the company abandoned all thirty-one of its plantations. The estate was divided into sections, ten in Zomba district, four in Chiradzulu district and three in Mulanje district, each under the control of European section managers, whose duties were to supervise the production and the collection of the prescribed quantities of tobacco from the tenants in their sections. These quantities were initially fixed at 150 lb for Chiradzulu district and 144 lb for Zomba district. In 1936, when tobacco was grown for the first time in the three Mulanje sections, the quantities were equalised at 200 lb for each district.

In Bowadi, Mr Martin Wisikesi, son of Wisikesi Nthitiwa, who was imprisoned for two years after the Chilembwe rising, remembers clearly how the new *thangata* of the 1930s worked:

These were given weights – 200 pounds. If you just reached the target you were not given money, but if you exceeded this target you were given money for the remainder. However, if you did not reach the target you had to pay money on top of the tobacco.

Given the landlords' initial confusion and subsequent resistance to the 1928 Ordinance, the precision of this testimony carries great weight. There is little doubt that many and perhaps the majority of A. L. Bruce's tenants experienced the new *thangata* as a compulsory levy. But it is unlikely to be the whole truth. At Mpotola, for instance, the old men say they were paid for their *thangata* tobacco, perhaps because Mpotola's position as group village headman meant his people had to be better treated. Even elsewhere, some money changed hands. Throughout the 1930s, tenants continued to pay their hut tax to the *boma* and not even Kincaid-Smith was foolish enough to make those payments impossible. Nor was the system a static one. In 1933, when it had become obvious that tenants were supposed to be paid for their tobacco, Kincaid-Smith introduced a deferred credit system. Tenants were given a signed 'chit' when they handed over their tobacco on the understanding that they would be paid when the tobacco had been graded and sold and Kincaid-Smith had the cash in hand to pay his debts. By 1939, as we shall see, it had become obvious to the administration that these chits were not being honoured. It was the story of W. J. Livingstone's labour records over again.

Two conclusions suggest themselves. The first was argued long afterwards by K. Barnes, the district commissioner for Chiradzulu, who claimed that Kincaid-Smith had been embezzling company money. The second and perhaps more likely conclusion is that, as in the years prior to the Chilembwe rising, the new *thangata* system was too elaborate for a handful of Europeans to enforce. Much tobacco was extorted though the amounts were usually less than 200 lb per tenant, and some tobacco was paid for though at prices less than those prevailing on neighbouring Crown Land areas. But the system itself was as arbitrary and disorganised as it had been under W. J. Livingstone himself. There were also hints of a return to physical violence.

For the people in the eight villages on the banks of the Namadzi river, however, the effects of the new ordinance were straightforward. From 1932 onwards, for the first time since the first year of their settlement, the men were able to spend all of their time at home in their villages.

To grow their dark-fired tobacco the men needed gardens. Instead of selling their labour to gain access to land they were now cultivating land to gain access to land. But where was this new land to be found and under what terms of tenure? Before 1928, the men's daily absence from the villages for up to eight months each year had made possible a compromise between the *thangata* system and village custom. *Thangata* had worked by coopting custom, both in the sense that the women grew the labourers' food and more profoundly in that custom provided the defeated rebels with a framework which helped to preserve their sense of their own identity. But with the men now living at home this compromise was severely strained.

To produce 200 lb required half an acre of fertile land which had to be found either in a man's home village or, more often, in his wife's where he was living. In addition, a man needed a river-bank garden for his nursery, plenty of firewood for curing the tobacco, and a semi-permanent barn – a long open-sided thatched hut with bamboo racks from which the leaves would be hung over slow-burning fires.

177

It was difficult for the women who 'owned' the village to concede these things without also conceding that for the future certain property rights were vested in the men. The implications of this change came very slowly. It was some years before it came to be assumed that when a man died his tobacco land, his curing barn and his hoes would be inherited directly by his sons. But a turning point had been reached. There could be no question of the women resisting this development. Though attempts were made to describe the tobacco land as 'different' and 'outside the village', the fact remained that if the men were unable to produce tobacco whole households could be evicted.

Other changes further weakened the women's position. The administration's view of the new ordinance was that it placed private estate tenants in the same position as Crown Land cash-croppers, in that they were given the right to produce tobacco for sale at market rates. Alternatively, if they found work off the estates they could pay their *thangata* in cash at rates fixed by the new District Rent Boards. In practice, these provisions had little relevance and most men on the Magomero estate continued to experience *thangata* as a compulsory levy. But there were some growers who were paid for their tobacco, earning up to 30/- per year, and there were even a few men who discovered and exercised their right to seek employment elsewhere. In 1931, for instance, fifty of Kincaid-Smith's tobacco graders went to work for the season in Lilongwe. Most important of all, however, was the market for dark-fired tobacco in Chiradzulu district.

It was illegal for tenants to sell their *thangata* tobacco off the private estates. But the shift to village production had created new problems of security for Kincaid-Smith and his section managers. It was far easier to check whether a man had reported for work than it was to monitor his movements twenty-four hours a day. For those growers prepared to risk arrest by smuggling their tobacco across the estate border, the rewards were small but genuine. Officially, tobacco growers in Chiradzulu district had to be registered with the Native Tobacco Board, instituted in 1926. In practice, the registration cards were traded. Tenants could rent them from registered growers for one shilling per day in order to sell their tobacco at the official markets, a process aided by the fact that the entries on the cards were usually illegible. Commenting that 'this practice is common', and that 'only a few of the offenders are caught and convictions are few', the district commissioner noted too the resultant discrepancy in official production figures. The average Crown Land grower produced 317.26 lb of cured tobacco for sale to the Native Tobacco Board. The average grower on the Magomero estate produced 120 lb of cured tobacco for sale to Kincaid-Smith. Bruce Estates' tenants were not being lazy; they were being smart. They were selling their highest grades of tobacco off the estates and giving Kincaid-Smith their 'x' grades in lieu of *thangata*.

The effects of these stirrings of male entrepreneurship should not be exaggerated. Even in Chiradzulu district the economy remained a tiny one. The loopholes which gave tenants limited access to it were loopholes only. The best a man from Njenjema or Bowadi might hope for by 1933 might be to smuggle 150 lb of tobacco across the boundary and sell it for 2d per lb, earning him less than his *thangata* labour had done in 1925. Nevertheless, on however tiny a scale and however illegally, he had become a cash-crop farmer in his wife's village where he normally spent most of his time. This development coincided with changes in the way the villages were being administered.

In 1924, an amended version of the District Administration (Native) Ordinance (DANO) had been passed, extending the provisions of the 1912 Ordinance which had provided the means of imposing discipline on Chiradzulu district in the months following the Chilembwe rising. Under the amended DANO, 'village areas' were to be created and village headmen appointed with duties similar to those laid down in 1912. But village headmen were now empowered to hear civil and minor criminal cases, assisted by up to ten male village councillors. Principal headmen, appointed by the Governor, and section councillors, appointed by the provincial commissioner, were to administer 'sections' made up of 'village areas'.

Despite the air of bureaucratic unreality conveyed by the language of this ordinance, the powers delegated were real ones. Principal headmen could hear cases referred to them by the village headmen and could charge a fee. They could arrange marriages and administer divorce. They were responsible for tax collection which, in practice, conferred advantages in the control of labour. They controlled afforestation, a significant power in tobacco-growing areas but also involving poles for hut building and much local industry. They were to issue beer licences. They acquired for the first time clearly defined powers over the village headmen, with consequences for the allocation of land. The position of principal headman was obviously a post worth fighting for and in Chiradzulu district in the late 1920s competition was fierce as the applicants staked out their claims.

Tactics varied. Courtesy calls on the resident and cooperation with his demands remained a key method of courtship. Geographical accident played a part. With only five principal headships available, Malika stood little chance unless Mpama's claims could be discredited. But the biggest factor was 'Anguru' immigration. When the five lucky principal headmen were chosen in 1930, Mpama was selected because his version of history had prevailed, and a minor headman called Nyimbili was chosen by A. L. Bruce Estates to administer the area south-west of the Namadzi river. The other three were Nkalo, Likoswe and Kadewere, whom Nkanda at Mulanje still protested was merely his agent. All three had come to prominence because of the large number of 'Anguru' villages under their control. In Nkalo's case, 90 per cent of the population he administered were immigrants from Mozambique, while the number of villages in Kadewere's section had risen from twenty-two in 1918 to eighty-three in 1928, making him by then the biggest chief in the district.

In 1933, following further ordinances, Mpawa, Nkalo, Likoswe, Kadewere and Nchema (replacing Nyimbili, who died in 1930) became 'native authorities' for Chiradzulu district. Across the Namadzi river in Zomba district, five more native authorities were appointed. They included Mlumbe and Malemia, whose ancestors Bishop Mackenzie had attacked at Chirumba and Chikala, together with Chikowi, a close relative of Mlumbe's, who was put in charge of the southern section of Zomba district. Chikowi had succeeded to the chieftaincy in 1928 after many years with the Public Works Department as a road *capitao* and was regarded as 'a loyal supporter of the government'. He lived just north of Ntonya hill and among his subordinate village headmen were the descendants of Chisunzi and Kankhomba, who had once ruled the whole Shire Highlands. Chikowi's responsibilities included the northern section of the Magomero estate, extending to the north bank of the Namadzi river.

In effect, with the introduction of Indirect Rule, some of the chiefs of the Shire Highlands, carefully vetted and poorly paid, were incorporated into the lower ranks of the colonial bureaucracy. But there was an unconscious irony in the term 'native authority'. The 'native customs' they were responsible for administering represented a codification by colonial officials of the powers the chiefs claimed they had wielded in the years before their defeat in the 1890s. Nothing illustrated this more clearly than the effects of the new structures on the women whose interpretation of custom was very different.

Village headmen, for example, had always been chosen by the

women. Now the women's choice had to be ratified by the authorities and the headmen had to work with up to ten village councillors, all of them men. The right to cut wood for hut building and for fuel had been vested in the household. This pattern had changed as the men became tobacco growers, needing huge amounts of firewood for curing their tobacco, and it changed again as the control of trees came to be vested in Nchema and Chikowi. The effect was that the women had to forage further and further away from home to find their fuel. Beer making was a women's industry. For single women it was virtually their only means of raising money for hut tax, and most married women brewed beer occasionally, either as payment for communal labour in village gardens or for sale in the markets at Mwanje or Njuli. From 1930 onwards, they officially needed Nchema's or Chikowi's permission.

The most drastic effects, however, of the new arrangements were on marriage. For a woman a husband was essential if *thangata* was to be avoided. During the days of *tenga-tenga* there had been a steady flow of new settlers on the estates, many of them potential husbands, and the increasing land shortages in Crown Land areas had sustained this flow, providing the women with choices. From about 1925, this flow ceased. Major Sanderson had no uses for further settlers and the women were actually forbidden to marry men from off the estates. The contradictions between *thangata* and custom had become explicit.

For a brief period after 1928 the rules changed again. Tobacco was a man's crop and there was no work for the *ambeta*. Then Kincaid-Smith reintroduced chillies as a company crop, all single women being forced to cultivate one quarter acre of chillies as their *thangata*. Once again, a husband had become a necessity and women were increasingly forced into polygamous marriages.

It was at this juncture that the colonial administration ceded to native authorities the power to adjudicate divorce suits. In 1931, a meeting of the chiefs with Nchema present was warned that the pretexts on which men were being granted divorces were far too flimsy. 'Custom', explained the Englishman to the Africans, demanded that if a man insisted on divorce he should pay compensation. The DC noted he was spending the bulk of his time on divorce cases in which bad decisions by the chiefs averaged three per day.

To Akite Chiunda of Mpotola, reflecting on the *thangata* system, its worst evil was its assault on women. After all that has been said about forced labour this seems a surprising judgement. But Akite Chiunda is remembering the *thangata* she experienced from the 1930s onwards, when it was difficult to find a husband and the penalty for failure was *thangata* labour for the women.

In the old days before independence, husbands and wives worked together but the husband could use all the money for drinking without considering his wife. These days, there's a division. Women sell their crops and men sell their crops, so that a woman can also drink with her own money. I got this cloth after selling maize at Mwanje. If I had been working with my husband I wouldn't have got this.

During that time most men who lived on government land did not get married to women on the estates because they were afraid. People on the estates got married to each other. A man could have three wives.

These days, we women are free. In those days, men dominated because they were the ones who did *thangata*.

By being 'free', Akite Chiunda means a return to the custom she understands:

Q: Do men come from other villages to marry in this village?
A: Yes.
Q: Which land does he cultivate?
A: His wife's land.
Q: Doesn't the land belong to the family warden?
A: No, it belongs to the women.
Q: What happens to the land when the man dies?
A: It is the women's land.

It was the story of the Hunter and his defeat over again.

There is another clue on how the women felt about the erosion of their autonomy. It is the evidence of spirit possession or *nantongwe*.

The cult of spirit possession swept through central and southern Africa in the last quarter of the nineteenth century. To the north, the same cult was known as *vimbuza* and to the south as *madzoka*, and among other peoples further afield it had other names. But the phenomenon was the same and it was a comparatively recent one. There had been nothing quite like it in Chigunda's village in Magomero in 1861.

The belief that a person's ancestral spirits might speak to him or her was not a new one. Chibaba had appeared to Chigunda in a dream in December 1861 and warned him to beware of the English missionaries. Nor was there anything new in the idea that the spirits might employ a human medium to convey messages concerning the health of the people and the fertility of the land. What was new, as the century neared its end, was the sudden proliferation of the spirits who possessed people and a change in the language of possession from benevolent prophecy to social protest.

The word *nantongwe* refers to different stages of an illness which lasts for a month and sometimes longer. *Nantongwe* is the illness itself, usually a splitting headache which might be accompanied by 'heart palpitations', it is the medicine for that headache, and it is the night-long ceremony with drumming and dancing and singing at which the medicine is 'thrown away' once the patient has been cured.

There are different accounts of the cure, reflecting the methods of different doctors but linked by a consistency of symbolism. Florence Liponda of Mpotola remembers her grandmother preparing an infusion of herbs for the patient to drink over a month. In Bowadi, where Emily Makuwa is the 'nurse', she prepares an infusion of herbs but, before giving it to the patient, offers a sacrifice of flour to the ancestors. At this, if the medicine has been correctly chosen, the patient will fall down in a faint. Some of the medicine is then poured through a hole burned in the blade of a hoe and the rest is administered.

In Ntholowa, where Eliza Simoko suffered from *nantongwe* as a young girl and remembers seeing the spirits who possessed her, the medicine was prepared from the bark of a tree called *bwazi* and then tied to her wrists, ankles, back and her waist. On the same day a banana stump was planted in the bush, and sacrifices were offered there one month later when the medicine was 'thrown away'. Iness Ntungama of Njenjema gives a further account. Her memory is that the person suffering from *nantongwe* would herself direct people to go and kill a kind of mouse called *mapanya* and mix it with other medicines to be drunk.

On the day when people came to dance *nantongwe*, sweet beer called *thobwa* was brewed, *nsima* was cooked and chickens were killed. The doctor came in the late afternoon, with four assistants. They made a further sacrifice, scattering flour under the *mpoza* tree used for prayers, and the women sang and danced *nantongwe* songs. One of the assistants took a razor and cut a lock of the patient's hair, ran around the house, cut another piece, ran again around the house, and so on until her head was shaved. Lines were drawn on her face with red ochre and she fell into a trance and began talking. Florence Liponda remembers that 'they speak chiChewa [Nyanja] and they usually mention dead people. Everyone understands.' Other

183

accounts insist that although the *nantongwe* songs are in Chewa and Lomwe, the patients speak 'in Nguru ... only old people can understand the language because the patient might speak in the language with which we came from Mozambique'. Aggrey Tebulo from Njenjema goes further, claiming that there is a special *Nantongwe* language which is understood only by those who have suffered from *nantongwe* and by nobody else.

Florence Liponda explains what happened next:

The women dance and dance and dance. If the medicine is the right type for the patient, she jumps up from the mat and runs into the bush and falls there. The medicine people follow her singing and find her sleeping in the bush. Anything which they find there where she has fallen, whether it is a mouse or a grasshopper, they take it and get the flour lump and put the animal or insect inside this lump of flour. Whenever in the future the patient has a headache they would take some of the flour from this lump and make porridge and let her drink this. They would say the headache came from the bush. They'd tie the lump to a mat for safekeeping while the animal is still inside.

With this, the cure was complete. In the morning, one of the assistants was chosen as the patient's adviser. Flour was spread on the ground beside her. She was washed and then given part of the cooked food which everyone present proceeded to share. All that remained was to pay the doctor and the dancers their agreed fees. The *nantongwe* was over.

Ceremonies like this occur nowadays in many societies throughout central and southern Africa. As with the stories told by Ida Thamanga's mother in the 1920s, it would be wrong to explain *nantongwe* exclusively in terms of the early 1930s. Nevertheless, there are aspects of the ceremony which has just been described which suggest *nantongwe* had a special importance in the circumstances of the new tobacco *thangata* and of Indirect Rule.

One clue to this is that the spirits possessing the patients were invariably named as the spirits of recently dead relatives. Women in the north of Malawi practising *vimbuza* were much more ambitious in their range of possession, naming remote ancestral figures or famous hunters or the chiefs of hostile neighbours or even colonial officials as the spirits to be exorcised. Keeping *nantongwe* within the family was a further demonstration of how inward-looking the villages had become since the Chilembwe rising's failure. But it also suggests a context for the cult. Over the thirty years since the villages had been established they had ceased to be merely collections of refugees. Partly this was because there were children born in the villages with married children of their own so that families were beginning to be linked in complex networks. But it was partly, too, because of the facility with which those without families could invent relationships, the terminology of kinship being the means by which people expressed their friendship and mutual dependence. *Nantongwe* gave these relationships historical depth. It conscripted the recently dead to speak on behalf of custom just at the moment when custom was threatened by changes in the economy and in the patterns of authority.

A second clue is the prominence given to the language question with the possessed women speaking 'in tongues'. The first language spoken in all the villages (except Mpotola) had been Mihavani, and by the early 1930s this was still what most of the women spoke. But the men had been working since the days of Listonia alongside Mpotola-speaking, Shirima-speaking, Atakwani-speaking and Marenje-speaking men from other villages and under Yao and Nyanja-speaking overseers. A new language was emerging, soon to be christened 'Lomwe', though in fact very different from the Lomwe spoken across the border in Mozambique. It began as a creole spoken in the works gangs. By the 1930s the men were operating in two linguistic worlds – one in the villages where they spoke Mihavani to their wives, and one outside where they spoke the new 'Lomwe creole' necessary to wider communication. Meanwhile, for the women, Mihavani was becoming the language of their small, private and threatened world. *Nantongwe*, with its gift of tongues, part challenged and part accommodated this seepage of change from outside.

A third clue and certainly the most dramatic is provided by Florence Liponda, whose grandmother was one of the *nantongwe* doctors. Relating *nantongwe* specifically to the 'time of tobacco', Mrs Liponda describes how her grandmother's house was appropriated by her grandfather as a barn for curing his dark-fired tobacco. He 'had closed all windows and door so that the smoke should meet the tobacco'. A family row erupted. By custom the house belonged to the wife; by *thangata* it belonged to the husband. The wife's father-in-law, who had no rights in the matter, lost his temper. He threw fire on the veranda 'so that the fire outside met with the fire inside the house. Now my grandmother stood on the veranda clutching the wall of the burning house because she wanted to die in her house. People came and dragged her by the arm ...' The old lady survived the fire but never recovered from her distress and died shortly afterwards. In

185

describing her grandmother's treatment of *nantongwe*, Florence Liponda lays stress on the messages delivered by the ancestors, which 'everyone understands'. Nothing could illustrate more vividly the problems of ownership and succession brought to the villages by the new *thangata* system.

Nantongwe is an expensive ceremony. No husband whose wife became possessed could have been pleased about the costs of curing her. The arrogant and aggressive behaviour of the women when possessed and the words of some of the songs used during the ceremony seem to suggest that *nantongwe* was, in part, a means of redressing the balance in villages the men seemed poised to take over:

> I should buy
> > *A pair of big shorts*
> I went there, and the Governor was crying
> > for me to buy a pair of big shorts
> > *A pair of big shorts*

These shorts are the long baggy khaki shorts sported by *askari* and court messengers, whose status the possessed woman is temporarily claiming. It would be misleading, though, to place the main emphasis of *nantongwe* on sexual politics. Husbands under the *thangata* system had to be courted or mollified, not abused. All accounts of *nantongwe* in the villages are agreed on two things. First, that men were also afflicted, though in nothing like the same numbers as women. Secondly, that the most frequent causes of the 'headache' were quarrels between women.

These quarrels could and can be extraordinarily bitter. Listening to the allegations which women make against each other, using the *manong'onong'o* or licensed gossip of pounding or drinking songs, one wonders how they are able to go on living together in the same village. The women accuse each other, often by name, or laziness, of pride, of filthy habits ('She shits in the cassava garden'), of lacking a husband to work for them or an uncle to protect them. They call each other prostitutes or the mothers of illegitimate children. They join together in mocking women who are childless or who have given birth to boys only, so that they will 'eat ashes' and 'drink urine' in their old age with no daughter to cook or fetch water for them. They call each other ugly or 'black'. The songs go far beyond humour in the bitterness of their complaints and they cannot be explained away as public criticism intended to maintain standards. Most terrible of all are the songs making allegations of witchcraft:

Fig. 20. The graveyard at Mpawa

> You bewitch
> *You bewitch*
> You bewitch
> *You bewitched my child and it died innocently*
> I have never forgotten
> *I have never forgotten ee*
> I have never forgotten
> *I have never forgotten ee*

There are many such songs, opening for the outsider a window on the sufferings of a society where children had and have only a 50 per cent chance of surviving infancy:

> Maize has a market
> Sorghum has a market
> Maize has a market
> What about my children?
> *My children's market is the graveyard*
> What about my children?
> *My children's market is the graveyard*
> You are a backbiter
> You are a witch
> You are a gossip,
> My children,

> You will kill them because of jealousy.
> My children,
>   *You will kill them because of jealousy.*

It is striking how very different such songs are from earlier pounding or drinking songs such as 'When I tell my husband, let's marry ... This place is wonderful' which was quoted earlier. In that song, sung in Mihavani and dating from the earliest days of Mpawa's settlement on the Namadzi river, political comment was combined with family affection and a sweetness of expression which can still be heard in songs across the border in northern Mozambique. By contrast, women's songs from the 1930s onwards are abrasive and accusatory. Significantly, this shift in their tone and content corresponds with the beginnings of a shift in their language. The more 'Lomwe' the songs are (or in recent times, the more 'Chewa'), the more bitter they become.

The link between such 'gossiping' and *nantongwe* is direct, for *manong'onong'o* is given as one of the main causes of the 'headache'. If 'you gossip about someone who has the disease she can fall down wherever she is and become sick'. This is the theme of one of the best known of the old songs used in the *nantongwe* ceremonies:

> As I was going over to Ntholowa
> As I was going over to Ntholowa
>   *ee i ee a – ee*
> I found some girls pounding
> I found some girls pounding
> The mortars were saying things
> The mortars were saying things
> I shouldn't have heard
> I shouldn't have heard
>   *ee i ee a – ee*

Part of the ceremony's purpose was to indicate that such talk was causing great distress and should be stopped.

The link between *nantongwe* and witchcraft is equally explicit. It is difficult to be certain that the link was established as early as the 1930s, but there is some evidence of an increase in witchcraft accusations related to the fall in living standards throughout Nyasaland during the world slump. The most famous of the witchcraft eradication movements, called *nchape*, swept through the colony in 1932. *Nchape* was believed to have originated in Mozambique, though it was introduced to Nyasaland by an African doctor called

Maluma from Mulanje. *Nchape* means 'wash' or 'clean out'. It was in fact a mild purgative made from an infusion of mahogany bark but the *nchape* doctors claimed that it had the power both to detect witches, forcing them to confess and hand over their implements, and to offer immunity against witchcraft. Answering the needs of the early 1930s, *nchape* raced through Nyasaland like a bush fire. Late in 1932, it came to the villages on the Namadzi. All people were ordered by Mpawa III to attend a meeting in the *bwalo* at Nazombe where his sister was married to the headman. *Nsima* was cooked and dozens of chickens were killed as relish. *Nchape* was added to the food and everyone present had to throw into the cooking pots a hair from his or her head. When the food was eaten, the guilty confessed their witchcraft and the innocent had been 'inoculated' against witches. No one on this occasion was punished but everyone felt safer.

At some stage, perhaps also in the 1930s, perhaps more recently, *nantongwe* took on the added character of an antidote to witchcraft. Instead of becoming possessed by the spirits of deceased relatives, the sufferers could be possessed by evil spirits manipulated by witches in the community. 'Sometimes,' says Effie Musa, 'she is possessed by the spirits of relatives. But sometimes people just bewitch her so that she suffers.' 'Some people are bewitched to get *nantongwe*,' says Emily Makuwa. One of the best known *nantongwe* songs is an answer to the witches:

> I was dead and now I am alive
> Those are ashamed now who wanted me to die
> I've come back
>   *I've come back*
> I've come back.

The cure was the same, the evil spirit being exorcised.

There was not much the women could do to resist the developments of the 1930s. Indirect Rule and the new *thangata* had left them unusually dependent on men and tensions between women were unusually destructive. *Nantongwe* was at hand in the culture as a means of formalising their distress. As another of the *nantongwe* songs put it:

> Words in my heart
> Words in my heart
>   *e – e – e – e – e – e*
>   *I will bring them out*

The effect of the ceremony was to restore the sense of community:

> My ashen friend, let's get together and visit each other
> *Ashen friend*

Equally significant was what *nantongwe* declared about the basis of community. The symbols used in the ceremony referred to a confrontation more profound than that between women and men, the village and the town, or the traditional and the colonial. *Nantongwe* came from the bush. It was, says Eliza Simoko, 'when a person dreamed about wild animals.' *Nantongwe*, says Aggrey Tebulo, 'is a headache coming from an animal.' By contrast, the cure involved the use of hoes, of millet beer and millet flour, and of freshly planted banana stumps, all symbols of cultivation. It involved a wild dash through the bush at night until the patient collapsed and the offending animal was imprisoned in a lump of flour.

The greatest danger the women could envisage was the collapse of the community into the bush which had been cleared when the villages were first built.

The balance of power in the villages was shifting perceptibly to the men. Despite the women's attempts to assert the claims of custom, the new tobacco *thangata* had its own irresistible logic. But *thangata* was affecting the villages in another way. Denied education or the opportunity to develop skills and denied economic incentives, the men, too, were increasingly isolated from the main currents of political and economic life in Nyasaland.

In 1926, John Chilembwe's Providence Industrial Mission at Mbombwe had been permitted to reopen. The new leader was Dr Daniel Malekebu, who in 1907 as a young man had been taken to the United States by Miss Emma DeLany, one of Chilembwe's original American Negro missionaries. He returned to Nyasaland with medical degrees and in 1926 was allowed to reconstitute the mission with support from the National Baptist Convention Inc. The New PIM expanded rapidly. By 1929, Dr Malekebu was rebuilding Chilembwe's shattered church on the original scale. By 1935, he was able to celebrate in the rebuilt church 'Ten years of Effort in Nyasaland'. A day of prayer was attended by leaders and delegates from Blantyre, Thyolo, Mulanje, Chikwawa, Zomba, Ncheu, Dedza, Lilongwe, Chinteche and Kasungu districts. Each leader in turn came forward with a hymn and a prayer and an account of the progress of the mission in his district. John Chilembwe's reputation had proved a firm foundation and support was also coming from Southern Rhodesia and South Africa.

Meanwhile, Dr Malekebu had maintained the social and political aspects of Chilembwe's teaching. In 1929, he founded the Chiradzulu District Native Association with Chief Mpama as president and Fred Njilima, son of Duncan Njilima, as secretary. This association, one of many springing up throughout colonial Nyasaland, began at once a campaign of protest. Land alienation and the *thangata* system, cheating at the tobacco markets, and restrictions on African businesses formed the agenda at monthly meetings. Just sixteen years after his death the authentic accents of John Chilembwe were once again being heard in Nyasaland.

The Chilembwe tradition, however, was in sharp conflict with the politics of Indirect Rule. Indirect Rule was essentially conservative. It employed its own concept of tradition, suitably modified, and it drew its personnel from chiefs and headmen, creating them where necessary. Intellectually, it was based on theories of the 'tribe'. These had been much refined in recent years by anthropological study, but in essence they remained similar to those which had been held by the missionaries at Magomero in 1861. A 'tribe' was still a collection of people with a common ancestor, a discrete language, a centralised and hierarchical system of government and in normal circumstances fixed territorial boundaries. Some tribes, such as the Yao, were assumed to have advanced towards nationhood. They were, as *A Handbook of Nyasaland* put it, 'intelligent and quick'. They spoke 'perhaps the finest of all Central African languages'. They lived in 'square houses' and cultivated 'personal cleanliness'. They were also a people with a history, in marked contrast to others who had only customs and folklore.

In his 1936 report for Chiradzulu district, District Commissioner Barnes elaborated further on these ideas. The Yao, he declared, had their origins in Mozambique as family units or *mbumba*, small female-headed communities often living many miles apart. Under pressure from the Portuguese and Arabs of the east coast, they had coalesced into larger communities living under minor chiefs who became responsible for security. A later stage, as the wars intensified, was the formation of still larger communities, the family groups thus evolving into the 'tribe' or into sub-sections of the tribe under paramount chiefs. At this point of development, which coincided with the migrations into Nyasaland c.1860, there were three levels of power: the paramount chiefs, the subordinate chiefs, and the village

191

mbumba usually headed by the nephew of the village 'mother'. Although the paramount was essentially a military figure, his position 'rested largely on his reputation for fairness'. No Yao paramount ever had the power of a Zulu or Ngoni chief: if a Zulu chief was like Caesar, the Yao paramounts were more like British prime ministers!

The Yao, then, were a tribe with a history; they had evolved through the proper stages into something like a nation. The problem in dealing with them was that this fact had not been understood by the colonial authorities:

The policy pursued by us till quite recently has been to break the power of the big Chiefs and has led naturally to a regression – a detribalising – back to the old loose system of the 'Mbumba'. and now we have altered our policy and are trying to undo what we have done and return to the system we originally found.

After writing this section of the report Barnes went on leave and it was left to his replacement, A. C. Kirby, to investigate the history of the 'Anguru'. The 'Anguru', it transpired, had evolved in the opposite direction. Originally united, they had disintegrated into family groups and were no longer a 'tribal unit'. What Kirby's investigations had revealed to him was that the term 'Anguru' was a fiction, this discovery by a twist of colonial thinking being adduced as fresh proof of their inferiority.

The 'Anguru' were unpopular. They had been unpopular in February 1915, but as the world slump cut commodity prices to such a point that even crops levied in lieu of *thangata* were no longer profitable, the arguments that had been used in the run up to the 1928 Ordinance took on redoubled force. Planters saw themselves afflicted with a resident 'Anguru' population which was rapidly consuming their one remaining asset, that is, the land itself. As A. J. Tennett of the Mangunda estate in Thyolo put it, with all the aggrieved innocence of a man entirely responsible for his position:

The whole of my land has been deforested by these Anguru and there is not a single indigenous tree left apart from those growing on the banks of streams, the cutting of which I have forbidden. In a very short period the fertility of this land will either have been exhausted or washed away and will become desert. These Anguru will then move of their own accord, just like locusts and will possibly go back to Portuguese territory whence they came.

Early in World War II, rumours circulated in Nyasaland that the Colonial Office intended to buy out landlords and abolish *thangata*. Spokesmen for the planters, who began to fear they might be displaced by 'Anguru' they had themselves settled on their land, lashed out in letters to the *Nyasaland Times*. Why should Britons die, raged one, 'to make Nyasaland a safe boozing den for alien Nguru?' There was insufficient space in the paper, clamoured another, to show 'from the history of this people the steps by which they became in turn slave trading gangsters, irregular soldiers, cringing starving unclothed refugees, and finally under a safe benign government: slothful, drunken and vicious'. The older colonial historiography was turned on its head. All along it had been the 'Anguru' who were the slave traders. They were 'Candid bandits, their prey human flesh and blood, and having gorged like the hyenas they were they returned *ku Mangulu* for the most part replete'.

The wheel of opinion had come full circle: the former 'raw Anguru' were now the cannibals. But if such malicious imbecilities were to be countered with any effect, two things were clear: it had to be done through the same medium and it had to be done in the same terms. The 'Anguru' needed spokesmen who were literate in English and, despite their disparate origins, they had to become a 'tribe'.

No one from the villages on the Magomero estate was equipped to present the 'Anguru' case in such terms. The men who could do so came from Crown Land areas throughout Nyasaland, where limited opportunities to gain an education had been available for two generations. Among the most prominent of these in Nyasaland during the 1930s and 1940s was one whose career is especially illuminating. His name was Lewis Mataka Bandawe and, like the people in the villages on the Namadzi river, he was a Mihavani-speaking immigrant from Mozambique.

Bandawe was born at Mulumbo, Mpawa's original home, in 1887. He had attended the school founded at Mulumbo by John Gray Kufa in 1896 and in 1899 had been sent by Kufa to Blantyre for further training. He became a teacher and in 1913 he returned to Mozambique to a post in a new station at Mihecani, south-east of the Namuli hills near the town of Alto Moloque. He remained there until 1928, working as a teacher, acting for long periods as head of the mission, and translating the New Testament into 'Lomwe' – actually, into the Shirima language spoken in the district of Alto Moloque. On his return to Blantyre, he broke with the Blantyre Mission and became a clerk and interpreter in the judicial department, eventually reaching the rank of deputy registrar.

With his long experience of both Nyasaland and Mozambique, Lewis Bandawe was ideally placed to become the spokesman of the despised 'Anguru' people. He understood the imperial accents of Indirect Rule and the room for manouvre they offered. He began to speak of 'a vast country' east of Lake Chilwa, extending from Yao territory in the north to Sena territory in the south and from the Nyasaland border to the east coast. It was a country populated by 'the mighty Lomwe tribe' and its 'sub-tribes', which he identified sweepingly as 'Amihavani, Ashirima, Ameto, Amakua, Amunyamwel Amunyamwelo, Atakhwani, Akokhola, Amerenje, Amaroro, Achuwapo and others'. All these sub-tribes, he claimed, spoke languages derived from Lomwe which, equally sweepingly, he identified with the new Lomwe creole emerging in Nyasaland. All of them looked to the Namuli hills, the heartland of the Lomwe people, as their ancestral home. These were arguments the administration understood.

In 1943, Bandawe founded the Alomwe Tribal Representative Association. One of its first acts was to petition the government to have the word 'Anguru' banned as a term of offence from all official documents and replaced by the term 'Lomwe'. Disturbed by the tone of the letters in the *Nyasaland Times*, the government acquiesced. Thus, under Bandawe's auspices, the various groups which had entered Nyasaland from Mozambique became a tribe.

Arguments like these in alliance with the new politics of African nationalism were of little relevance to the people living in the villages on the Namadzi river. None of them spoke any English and only a few of their children were learning to be literate in the Nyanja used at Chimwalira and Mpotola schools. In 1915 they had been in the forefront of the anti-colonial struggle. But their main target had been the estate manager and it was the symbolism of their action, as planned by Chilembwe, which gave it a nationalist dimension. There is nothing in what the men and women say of their circumstances in the 1930s and 1940s which connects directly with Lewis Bandawe's concerns or with the formation, also in 1943, of the Nyasaland African Congress. *Thangata* remained what it had always been, levelling and impoverishing, a block to all development.

Yet suddenly, almost inadvertently, in January 1940, the villagers won their case, striking a blow against the *thangata* system from which it never recovered. Twenty-five years to the month after William Jervis Livingstone had been killed, there was talk of a second rising. Intervening personally, Governor Mackenzie-Kennedy dismissed Kincaid-Smith and hustled him from the territory. For

Alexander Livingstone Bruce in Edinburgh, the episode marked the end of a long road. Abandoning at last the duty enjoined in his father's will to bring Christianity and Commerce to Africa he made plans to sell the Magomero estate.

Captain Kincaid-Smith had become general manager in 1931. It took him nine years to bring the estate to the point of crisis, almost exactly the time taken by W. J. Livingstone from the introduction of cotton growing. Kincaid-Smith's first act was to send out his rangers to uproot all cassava gardens. Cassava, he argued, drained the soil of nutrients and rendered it unsuitable for tobacco growing. The opposite was, in fact, closer to the truth, but Kincaid-Smith was responding to widespread gossip in the planter community about soil exhaustion. What made cassava the symbol of this concern was precisely what made it a focus of resentment: it was a crop particularly identified with the Lomwe. The matter became bogged down in legal niceties. Was cassava, under the terms of the 1928 Ordinance, an annual crop? Could the fact that some varieties took more than a year to mature be justification for banning it? The administration dodged the issue, forbidding Kincaid-Smith to ban cassava but allowing him to discourage it.

Kincaid-Smith's second initiative came in 1933. By then, landlords throughout the Shire Highlands had discovered, through the very volume of their spokesmen's protests on the matter, that they were indeed expected to pay for the tobacco under the ordinance in lieu of *thangata*. For A. L. Bruce Estates this was a serious matter. The company was hopelessly in debt, and in no position to pay out cash against anticipated sales. Kincaid-Smith's solution was a system of deferred payments. The men were issued with signed chits, cashable late in the year when he had begun to dispose of the tobacco and had money in hand.

Again the administration dithered. The delay in payments caused 'discontent'. One of its consequences was that tenants had to pay their hut tax at the higher rate of 9/- applicable to those who failed to pay their tax by 1 October. But there was nothing strictly illegal in what Kincaid-Smith was doing. Meanwhile they continued to file their reports.

By 1938, matters were beginning to get out of control. Kincaid-Smith's chits were clearly not being honoured, the tobacco graders in the Magomero sheds had not been paid for several months, and even the salaries of European section managers were in arrears. Still the administration did nothing. They had begun to nourish the hope that

195

Kincaid-Smith might overreach himself, removing at a stroke the long-festering problem of *thangata* on the A. L. Bruce Estates. 'The possibility', wrote Barnes, 'of a sudden unexpected bankruptcy is always to be kept in mind.' 1938 would be a key date. It marked the end of the second quinquennium under the 1928 Ordinance when Kincaid-Smith would have the right to evict defaulting tenants and the administration would be called in as arbiter.

In the event, 1938 was a turning point for quite different reasons. Kincaid-Smith's proposed evictions totalled only 127, far short of his 10 per cent entitlement. The fact was that he had lost interest in his tenants. Suddenly and unexpectedly he was buying most of his tobacco from Crown Land growers.

In 1938, the Native Tobacco Board opened new tobacco auction floors in Limbe and Lilongwe. It had been forced to this measure by complaints about falling prices through the 1930s and by allegations of malpractices at the tobacco markets, where the habit of taking 'overages' – writing down 60 lb of tobacco as 40 lb – had become the buyers' most secure means of profit. As so often with colonial decisions, the reforms were as resented as the abuse. Crown Land growers were outraged in March 1938 to find that the rules had changed. Without any prior warning, growers were required to grade their own tobacco in seven categories from Extra Special Wrapper to Filler no. 4, each grade being sold separately in a market lasting all day. Prices, too, were down as the buyers hedged against possible losses on the auction floor and as the NTB covered its own costs. The growers protested by throwing their tobacco away or by burning it outside the markets.

Some of them, though, had the idea of selling it to the private landlords, who were delighted to find their sheds overflowing with Crown Land tobacco. True, Kincaid-Smith's cash-flow problems worsened dramatically, for the Crown Land growers were in no mood to accept his chits. He eased them by borrowing and by cutting back sharply on estate purchases.

In February 1939, testifying to a Commission of Enquiry into the Tobacco Industry, Kincaid-Smith concluded his interview with a question which took the commission by surprise: 'May I ask you a question? Is there anything in the laws of Nyasaland regarding the amount of maize a native is allowed to grow on a private estate?' It was an intriguing question which went to the heart of the system. Unlike cassava, maize was indubitably an annual crop permitted under the ordinance. But what happened if the tenants grew a surplus for sale in the markets at Chiradzulu, Blantyre and Zomba? 'This year,' Kincaid-Smith explained, 'there has been a tremendous increase. If they are going to grow maize on our land and sell it, it is going to defeat our object as tenant growers of economic crops'. His problem was that by rejecting low-grade tobacco the previous year he had inadvertently released his tenants from their *thangata* obligations. According to the ordinance, if he did not choose to buy their tobacco and had not specified an alternative crop, he had no further rights over them.

In March and April when the new season's tobacco markets opened, Kincaid-Smith became the biggest purchaser of Crown Land tobacco, despatching the best grades to the West African market. When he sent the residue back to the Limbe auction floor, the buyers walked out in mass boycott. Once again, he was unable to pay the wages of tobacco graders at the Magomero sheds and by the end of the season some £800 was owed to 600 of his tenants. To recoup these losses Kincaid-Smith had to persuade his tenants to grow tobacco once more.

On 13 December 1939, he called a meeting of all tenants at the Magomero factory. He dressed for the occasion in his captain's uniform and presented as his spokesman Captain Parker, the DC for Zomba district, who 'informed the natives of their obligation to the landlord' and complained that they were planting too much maize at the expense of *thangata* tobacco. The meeting became a shouting match, Kincaid-Smith losing his temper and the men protesting they were not being paid.

At once the rumour swept through the Shire Highlands that with the outbreak of war Africans were to be compelled by the military and the *boma* to grow tobacco without payment. Exactly what followed is unclear, though to the administration it had a horrifying starkness of import. A priest of the Nguludi Mission intercepted a letter 'written by one native to another'. Leaders of the Watch Tower churches in Mulanje and Chikwawa districts were holding meetings across the Portuguese border at a village called Matamera. There was to be a rising in January 1940, beginning with the killing of 'several selected Europeans'. To these sinister coincidences – discontent on the A. L. Bruce Estates, the African Christians of the Shire Highlands, the first January of the war, an intercepted letter at Nguludi – was added a further detail. The Catholic Apostolic Church of Christ at Ncheu, scene of the subsidiary rising in 1915, also appeared to be involved.

Was there any substance in the rumours? Governor Mackenzie-

Kennedy was in no mood to await events. Captains Kincaid-Smith and Parker were summoned to Zomba and asked to explain themselves. One by one the damaging facts emerged, not only about the shouting match at Magomero but about the unpaid wages, the unhonoured chits, the confusion over estate records. Kincaid-Smith's nervous bluster alienated his audience, and one outright lie sealed his fate. It was agreed he should be removed. The Governor cabled his commanding officer, outlining the position and requesting his transfer to Nairobi 'or some other distant station at the earliest possible moment'.

Had there ever been substance in the rumours? Nothing happened, no leader was ever named or arrested, and no one in the villages today remembers anything of the matter. Perhaps all the colonial government heard was the rattling of the skeletons in its own cupboard. Whatever the truth, it was undeniably a belated victory for John Chilembwe. His was the name invoked in all the anxious discussions, and the consequences were much more than simply the demise of Kincaid-Smith. With his departure, *thangata* itself began to disappear from the Magomero estate. J. Sibbald who took over as general manager was not the man to walk in Kincaid-Smith's or W. J. Livingstone's shoes. He had worked for the company for twenty-one years and he knew his limitations. *Thangata* was not abolished but, with one exception, it ceased to be enforced. All eviction notices were withdrawn and all wages paid up to date. The exception concerned unmarried women who were still required to harvest Sibbald's chillies for another eight years.

Meanwhile, Sibbald concentrated on the West African market and obtained his tobacco from two sources. The first was tobacco grown on the estate. As tobacco prices rose in the 1940s men in the villages began at long last to experience the benefits of cash-cropping. There was no need for compulsion when the prices were right and the only remaining complaint about *thangata* was the 20-shilling rental charged to those who sought work off the estate. So much had the atmosphere changed with Kincaid-Smith's departure that Crown Land growers began for a brief period to rent plots from Sibbald to grow their tobacco on the vast uncultivated acreages of the Magomero estate. Sibbald's second source of tobacco was the Limbe auction floor. From 1941 onwards he began purchasing dark-fired tobacco at Limbe, regrading it for the West African market, and reselling the remnants at Limbe along with the surplus from the estate itself. By incurring such costs in wages and purchases, Sibbald drove up his local expenses from £17,106 in 1939 to £58,463 in 1942. But his gross revenue jumped from £15,724 to £70,906 over the same years, giving the company a local profit of £12,443 in 1942. Under Sibbald's management A. L. Bruce Estates was ceasing to be a fiefdom and was becoming a business.

For A. L. Bruce himself, ageing in Edinburgh, these developments came too late. His accumulated losses had already compelled him in 1938 to sell off the Likulezi and Kada estates in Mulanje district. But it was the scandal over Kincaid-Smith with its bitter reminder of the events of 1915 that persuaded him to abandon his commitment of forty-six years. As he explained afterwards, the company had 'had a most unfortunate financial record' and he could not expect his daughter 'to shoulder the responsibilities which I have done'. Even the profits being made by Sibbald in the early years of the war were largely swallowed up by wartime taxation. He resolved as soon as the war was over to sell the Magomero estate and cut his losses.

So at long last the Livingstone family was retreating from Magomero. On 4 January 1945 there appeared in the journal *East Africa and Rhodesia* the following advertisement:

Old established tobacco estate in Nyasaland with modernised factory at present handling over 1 million lbs leaf annually. Large acreage available for development other products. Estates 'mark' has very valuable goodwill with regular buyers in UK and other markets ... Very good reasons for wanting to sell.

The Nyasaland authorities had not been informed. This seemed, commented Governor Sir Edmund Richards, an extraordinary omission, 'in view of the purpose for which this estate was apparently purchased originally'.

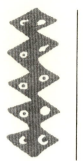

4 | 1945–1985
'John Chilembwe will
make everything shine'

Nowadays for drivers on the Blantyre–Zomba road, the Magomero turnoff, which is roughly half way, is marked by a cluster of painted signs. The biggest and oldest reads:

MALAWI YOUNG PIONEER ENTERPRISES
NASAWA POULTRY UNIT / NASAWA FARM
ZOMBA
YOUTH SPEARHEAD FOR PROGRESS

Next to this are advertised the NASAWA TECHNICAL TRAINING CENTRE, the MAGOMERO COMMUNITY DEVELOPMENT TRAINING COLLEGE, and KAMUZU VOCATIONAL REHABILITATION AND TRAINING CENTRE FOR DISABLED PERSONS. Less conspicuous is a small wooden sign reading MIN OF FORESTRY & NATURAL RESOURCES, MAGOMERO TREE NURSERY, WORLD ENERGY PROJECT. Just beyond these notices is a roadside market, the vegetables piled on rough tables or on pieces of sacking spread along the verge. They are cheaper than in Blantyre or Zomba and it is worth stopping.

Branching east is a dirt road. It is a kilometre to the Magomero Community Development Training College, which occupies the former offices of A. L. Bruce Estates Ltd. The tobacco grading shed has been dismantled leaving a concrete yard, but the ginnery where many of Chilembwe's supporters worked can still be picked out among the classrooms and dormitories. Up the hill is A. L. Bruce's house, now the residence of the college principal. In the garden of a neighbouring bungalow are the graves of W. J. Livingstone and Duncan MacCormick. The inscriptions, incorrectly dated but admirably neutral, read 'Killed: 25 January 1915'.

Byond the Magomero College is the Vocational, Rehabilitation and Training Centre for Disabled Persons, and beyond that is the old estate road to Nasawa. This dirt track, crazy with boulders and

200

tyre-slashing stones, winds between bald hills and lush river-bank gardens, crossing the Namadzi by a perilous bridge just north of Njenjema. The drive gives a perspective to economic development in the area.

Just before Nasawa, the road divides the sloping plain where W. J. Livingstone opened one of his first two cotton plantations with labour from the villages on the Namadzi river. Today it is used for tobacco and three brick tobacco barns dominate the left side of the road together with workers' houses. They are owned by the Malawi Young Pioneers, whose company Spearhead Enterprises recently went bankrupt. People from the villages have no access to this land though they sometimes supply labour at unofficial *ganyao* rates.

Nasawa itself is dominated by two institutions. The first is the Nasawa base of the Malawi Young Pioneers, a national youth-training scheme with bases throughout the country. School leavers come to Nasawa for a ten-month course in agriculture. The base contains a farm and poultry unit and a plantation of mixed trees, all maintained as part of the students' training. There are barracks with a parade ground and an assault course, for the students spend much of their time on political and para-military activities. They wear uniforms and have a brass band audible at Mpawa when the wind is from the north-east. Opposite the base is the Nasawa Technical Training Centre. Students at the centre spend up to four years learning such trades as building, plumbing, electrical engineering and car mechanics. They qualify with the Malawian equivalent of the London City and Guilds diplomas and they are guaranteed jobs if they are successful.

Beyond the wire fences the track divides. The right fork cuts south past an abandoned maize mill and across a patch of waste land to Nasawa's old village, before turning parallel to the Namadzi river and continuing downstream through Ntholowa, Mpawa, Nazombe and Komiha. The main track continues straight to Chimwalira, a large village with a market, a rectangle of shops, a number of churches and a government primary school. The *dambo* land surrounding it, the best land in the area north of the Namadzi river, is known to envious villagers as 'the Scheme'. It belongs to an agricultural settlement scheme organised by the ruling Malawi Congress Party.

All these activities – community development, youth training in trade and agriculture, a school for the handicapped, a settlement scheme – appear at first glance as the consummation of a long tradition, a secular expression of something not unlike Bishop Macken-

201

zie's original vision. Nowhere else in Malawi is there such a collection of welfare and educational facilities. The name Magomero still retains its connotations of moral investment.

Yet, in practice, none of these institutions impinges directly on the lives of the people in the villages on the Namadzi river. The villagers use the twice-weekly market and the shops at Chimwalira, and a few of them send their children to Chimwalira school. At Nasawa there is a government dispensary used by most of the women, and a station for the government's Agricultural Development and Marketing Corporation (ADMARC), where villagers sell their cash crops. But there are no local young people at the Magomero Community Development College or at the Technical Training Centre or the Young Pioneer base. When the Chimwalira Settlement Scheme was inaugurated in 1964, all but a tiny fraction of the farms were awarded to outsiders. This has been for two decades a matter of policy. A former principal of the Community Development College proposed that community development should be practised on neighbouring villages. He was told the college was a national institution and should not be used to confer local benefits.

This policy is easily defended. Malawi has potential divisions along regional and ethnic lines and the government is obliged by commonsense and its terms of credit to appear impartial. The consequences, though, are unfortunate. The effect is to deny villagers access to land and buildings they have laboured in since 1901. Occasionally, people from Nasawa are admitted to the Young Pioneer base to perform 'traditional dances' for distinguished visitors. Otherwise, the high-security fence excludes them from its luxuriant vegetable gardens and poultry farm. The villages lie in the shadow of developmental institutions which do not in any way acknowledge their existence. This experience heightens their sense of exclusion from the main currents of contemporary Malawian life.

A. L. Bruce's advertisement in January 1945 that the Magomero estate was for sale caused consternation. Opening a new file called 'Disposal of land owned by A. L. Bruce Estates Ltd', the chief secretary inserted as the first item a copy of the report of the Commission of Enquiry into the Chilembwe rising.

Bruce's advertisement had concluded: 'Very good reasons for wanting to sell'. By 1944, the company's accumulated losses totalled £64,244 and, as Bruce later explained to the Nyasaland government:

You have seen the Company's accounts for a considerable number of years and therefore you will be aware that until recently the Company has had a most unfortunate financial record. In order to carry on at all not only had considerable sums to be borrowed on debenture, but I personally have had to advance substantial sums and in addition I have been compelled to guarantee the bank overdraft ... I am reluctant to breach such a long association regarding which I have most pleasant recollections in addition to worries.

It hardly seemed a strong bargaining position. In fact, Bruce's single concern in the discreditable wrangle that ensued was to secure a price for the Magomero estate which would cover these losses.

The government, meanwhile, was awaiting the report of the Abrahams Commission, which had been set up to examine yet again the question of land in Nyasaland. In a spirit of optimism about long-overdue reforms, Governor Richards cabled Oliver Stanley, the new secretary of state for the colonies, recommending the purchase of Magomero, the 'largest homogeneous block of privately owned land now remaining in Nyasaland'. Asked whether the purchase would be an 'economic proposition', Richards invoked the names of Bishop Mackenzie and Livingstone.

[The] original grant of this large tract of land ... was made as a memorial to David Livingstone to be used in perpetuity for the welfare of Africans ... In fact, the land has always been run as a private business, the position of native residents has been unfavourable in comparison with Africans on Native Trust Land and welfare organisation has been negligible.

Pressed for an actual policy, the governor outlined four options. The estate could become Trust Land; it could be run on present lines with the government as manager; it could be turned into reserved land with new rules of cultivation under a land settlement scheme; or it could be run as a cooperative for the benefit of the tenants. 'I must confess', he concluded, 'my chief thought was the opportunity to redeem some 33,000 people from what is in the strictest sense a state of serfdom.'

Stanley was receptive to the idea of a cooperative, but there remained the problem of the price. The government was prepared to offer no more than 5/- per acre for the whole estate. Even this figure was exhorbitant. Despite the years of talk about European expertise, the Magomero estate 'has been very badly treated and soil has been abused, the natural woodland destroyed, the grassland overgrazed and the stream banks neglected all for the sake of producing as many cash crops as possible'. Mildly contesting this point, Bruce shifted the argument from past failures to present successes. Sales in West Africa for the estate's dark-fired tobacco were running at 637,000 lb. An official minuted sourly that most of this tobacco was being purchased on the Limbe auction floors.

Bruce's price was determined by his overdraft. But the government, too, had anxieties it was concealing. Aware that the company had become little more than a processing plant for the West African market, it was aware of the consequences. In the years since Kincaid-Smith's departure, the *thangata* system had virtually ceased to operate. Few tenants paid rent in money or tobacco and A. L. Bruce's Register of Tenants was, yet again, hopelessly inaccurate. Any new landlord, however, purchasing the estate with an eye to plantation production, could be expected to enforce his rights under the 1928 Ordinance, demanding rents, evicting defaulters and causing endless political trouble. A comment that the Magomero estate was 'saturated with Africans' was circulated in the hope of putting off private buyers.

Meanwhile, the result was deadlock. Though Governor Richards would for 'political and administrative reasons' have been willing to pay 10/- per acre for the whole estate, he was permitted to offer no more than 5/-. When Bruce turned this down, the governor was left hoping the Abrahams Commission would clarify policy and strengthen his hand.

The commission reported in 1946 and attempted a compromise which was doomed to failure from the start. The justice of African grievances that 'Europeans are holding large tracts of undeveloped land while natives are suffering the acute pangs of land hunger' was acknowledged. But there were to be no powers of compulsory purchase. Instead, a Land Planning Committee was established to do the job everyone had assumed was the commission's responsibility. The committee was to recommend which estates should be bought by government and in what order. It collected information from district commissioners and from the more pliable of the native authorities, including Nchema and Chikowi. But it also co-opted as members Sir William Tait Bowie of the Blantyre and East Africa Company, Kaye Nichol of the British Central Africa Company and Sibbald of A. L. Bruce Estates Ltd, together with representatives of the African Lakes Company and the Livingstonia and Blantyre Missions. The committee proposed that 497,365 acres in the Southern Province should be made available to government together with 65,129 acres of the Central and Northern Provinces. In return for this generosity, *thangata* would continue to be enforced on the estates remaining in private hands. In a confidential appendix, the core of the committee recognised the inadequacy of these measures and warned of serious African discontent unless more land changed hands. Compulsory purchase, however, might 'prevent the further investment of European capital'.

Such pusillanimity gave the Nyasaland government little help in its dealings with A. L. Bruce Estates Ltd. In July 1947, Sibbald told the land-planning committee that the whole Magomero estate was to be sold to Campbell, Carter and Acrin. The price was £80,000 and the sale was to be completed within ten days. Acrin planned to use the estate for ranching, for growing flue-cured tobacco and for the production of fruit juices. The African residents would all be placed 'on contract' and would be concentrated in large villages throughout the estate. This operation would be carried through by Sibbald himself, who would also stay on to handle the West African tobacco sales.

The government acted swiftly. Acrin's London representatives were summoned to a meeting at the Colonial Office, were warned of the intention to purchase private land and were presented with yet another copy of the report into the Chilembwe rising. When Acrin backed down, Bruce was outraged. The government then approached Acrin, offering to repurchase the estate for 6/- per acre if Acrin bought it for less. When Bruce got wind of this proposal, negotiations broke down completely.

Had the authorities but known it, Bruce's position was becoming desperate. Purchasing tobacco on the auction floors meant high prices and a high proportion of wastage after the West African leaves had been graded. Losses in 1948 were £19,376, and further losses of £27,346 in 1949 brought the accumulated deficit to £109,777. While negotiations remained officially suspended in a show of strength, the company was taking its first steps towards complete liquidation. What saved A. L. Bruce, providing him out of nowhere with a long queue of prospective purchasers, was the Shire Highlands' famine of 1949.

The famine of 1949 was probably the worst the Shire Highlands had suffered since 1863, when Rowley guessed helplessly that nine out of ten Mang'anja people died. Certainly it was the worst famine since 1922. Colonial officials claimed at the time that no one died of hunger

205

in 1949. This claim was, to say the least, disingenuous and there is ample evidence that despite distributions of free maize many hundreds died of hunger or of famine-related illnesses.

The heart of the problem was that, despite the slow expansion of the Nyasaland economy, the bulk of the country's food was still being produced on family farms in the villages. Villagers were well able to feed themselves and understood the problems of production on the soils available to them. But Trust Land areas were becoming increasingly overcrowded, with some families trying to survive on less than two acres of land. At the same time and partly as a consequence, there was an increasing number who expected to secure their food by purchase. These included workers in Blantyre, Limbe and Zomba, and the families of labour migrants using money remitted from Southern Rhodesia and South Africa. They also included the tea estates of Mulanje and Thyolo districts, whose agents toured the villages of the Phalombe plain buying up maize, cassava, pigeon peas and beans to feed their labourers. Demands on the village farmers were increasing by the year. Meanwhile, the Native Tobacco Board which, despite its name, was responsible for all African cash crops kept prices artificially depressed. Food was already short in the early 1940s. When the rains failed in December 1948, the system collapsed.

In the villages on the Namadzi river, the season opened promisingly with good rains in November. At Mpawa, Julitta Chimatule, who was then in her mid-thirties, remembers her garden was planted with maize, millet and cassava and that the crops were doing well by early December. Her neighbour Alfred Chimene's tobacco plants were even more advanced, having been moved the month before from their river-bank nursery. But from 3 December to 3 February, virtually no rain at all fell in the Shire Highlands. Maize ripened prematurely and meagrely and the cassava plants lay dormant. A few showers fell in February, when people planted pigeon peas and sweet potatoes together with a fast-maturing variety of cassava called *chilingano*. But there were no more rains until mid-November. It was a year in which the villagers' staple foods simply could not grow.

At Mpawa and its neighbours, people were luckier than most. They had plenty of land and the Namadzi river kept flowing throughout the year. It was even possible for people to carry a little water to their gardens. Mrs Chimatule could not live on her harvest of millet and maize. But she reaped enough to brew beer and buy flour with the profits. Mr Chimene's tobacco was poor but it produced just enough cash to ward off the famine's worst effects. In any case, village farmers knew how to cope with famine. While the government imported maize for sale in the towns, villagers fell back on older techniques of survival. Sorghum, for instance, was drought resistant and most households had a patch of sorghum as insurance against a bad year. There were sorghum harvests even in 1949. There was a variety of emergency foods which could be gathered in the bush. Mr Chimene remembers digging up banana roots and drying them in the sun for his wife to pound into flour. A kind of wild yam called *miwole* and a type of grass called *mauzu* could be found as close as Nanyungwi hill. Some of these edible grasses, fungi, fruits, tubers and roots required long and careful preparation to make them safely edible. But the knowledge survived from the 1922 famine of how to exploit them.

Many men, including Mr Chimatule, preferred to walk to Mabuka's in Mulanje district where some rain had fallen and there was cassava for sale. For those who had relatives there the return journey took three days. But most men simply offered their labour on *ganyao* terms, spending three weeks working on people's farms, walking back to Mpawa with their wages of dried cassava and then returning next morning for a further 'contract'. To this day, in women's pounding songs, the famine is remembered:

> Boy's mother, be quiet!
> Boy's mother, be quiet!
> Be quiet!
> O – ye – ye
> Your husband is gone to Mulanje
> Your husband is gone to Mulanje
> To work for dried cassava
> So you will have food.
> You – e – e – e
> You – e – e – e
> You – e – e – e
> You are arrogant!

The point here is that there were husbands who did not take this trouble. There were also some who never bothered to come back.

One of the reasons for this was that cruelly in 1949 *thangata* gave a dying spasm. Tormented by his cash-flow problems and perhaps hoping to demonstrate to potential buyers that the system still worked, A. L. Bruce made a final attempt to exact rents in cash and in kind. In September, DC Watson found a number of broken-down huts on the Magomero estate. They belonged to men who had sought work off the estate in an effort to buy food for their families. Destroying huts

207

was illegal as well as unpardonably harsh in a year of famine. Watson returned in October to visit Nasawa, Mpawa, Komiha and Mpotola, where he camped overnight. He was relieved to find people coping with the drought, with food in all the villages and ample seed for the coming season. As a precaution, though, famine-relief centres were established at Jenela and Matiti. Watson reported one complaint. Chief Chikowi asked him to place *capitaos* in Chimwalira market to maintain price controls and stop profiteering.

As this indicates, some villagers were much better placed to cope than others. The famine served to highlight divisions, some as old as the villages themselves, others just emerging as the *thangata* system was relaxing its hold. The advantages of a garden in the village *dambo* or on the banks of the Namadzi were much greater than in normal years. Mpawa III, for instance, who farmed the eight acres of the original Magomero peninsula, was able to grow and to distribute a variety of emergency foods. The very old and the very young were the most vulnerable of all. The old were less able to travel or to forage. Few children were conceived in 1949 and those born were sickly, while babies not yet weaned suffered from their mothers' insufficient milk. It was a difficult year for unmarried women. Those without husbands to forage or to travel to Mulanje depended for the most part on what they could produce in their gardens and in 1949 some of them starved. A few supplemented their income through *ganyao* labour for neighbours with dry-season gardens. Some, like Mrs Chimatule, brewed beer for sale, and some took up prostitution. At the famine-relief centres, food was almost invariably distributed to men on the assumption that they were heads of families.

Reflecting on the famine a year afterwards, Provincial Commissioner Barnes was most affected by the collapse of village customs:

There were people in the villages very nearly dead and the village communities doing nothing to assist . . . this came as a great shock to me. I have been 26 years in this country and I never imagined for a moment that the African village community had ceased to look after its own people, and that points to the fact that your old customs of community life are breaking down very fast.

Barnes was commenting on the Southern Province as a whole and his conclusion was not quite justified by his evidence that women, children and old people had often been abandoned. What he had witnessed was not a general collapse of community life so much as proof of the famine's severity. Those who in normal years ate from the *nkokwe* or household grain bin were the only group that mattered. Women fed their children and their husbands, eating inside with the door shut so that neighbours could not see they had food. Mrs Chimatule was supported by other women when she told me she had no food that year for her brother or for her uncle. 'Perhaps,' she said quietly when I pressed her hard, 'perhaps for my mother.' The corollary is that survivors remembered 1949 as the year of divorces, when many 'broke their marriages' and only the strongest relationships endured.

In November, the rains returned. It was in October and November, when emaciated villagers tried to clear fresh gardens that most of the deaths occurred. The rains were good. By January, people were eating pumpkins and perennial sorghum and by March there was maize in abundance. No one bothered growing tobacco. Maize prices had been doubled to 1d per pound, making it the most profitable of the cash crops, and Sibbald was forced to buy all his tobacco for the 1950 season on the auction floor. The 1949 famine, then, was the last year of *thangata* and it marked the system's effective end.

For A. L. Bruce in Edinburgh, however, the famine was a godsend. At its height, Governor Colby issued instructions that the tea planters of Mulanje and Thyolo should no longer expect to buy food from village farmers. Instead, they should use estate land to grow their own supplies of maize, beans and cassava. Rumours began to circulate of the consequences of this instruction. In April 1949, Provincial Commissioner Barnes heard that 3,000 acres of the Magomero estate in the Sanje area were being sold to Lujeri Tea Estates and that a further 23,000 acres near Chikomwe were being sold to a new agglomerate of tea and tobacco companies. The fact that this information was not entirely correct (Chikomwe Farms bought two plots of 9,000 and 3,000 acres) was part of the problem. A. L. Bruce had no intention of letting the government catch wind of his plans.

As over the next twenty months no less than fourteen new landlords moved on to the Magomero estate, the government found it impossible to keep abreast of events. By the end of 1950, 92,794 acres had been sold at prices of up to £2 per acre. They comprised seventeen new private estates, the lion's share being a block of 40,000 acres south of the Namadzi river which was bought by I. Conforzi, the largest of the Thyolo planters. Some of these transactions involved members of the government's own Land Planning Committee. They included the purchase of 2,250 acres at Chimwalira by Malcolm Barrow on behalf of Nyasa Tea Estates.

The government's land policy was in ruins. The famine, coupled with the refusal of tea companies to use tea land for maize pro-

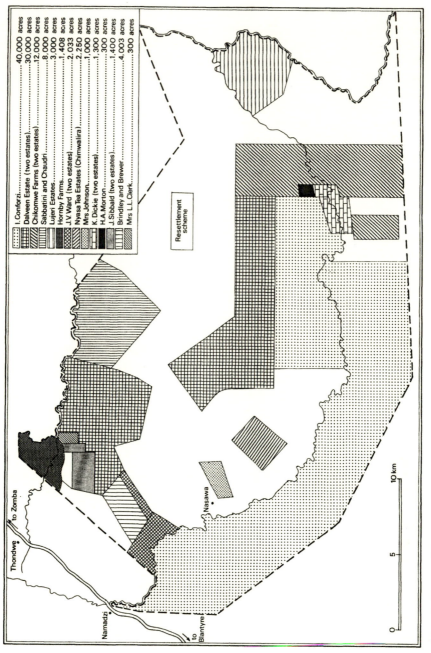

Map 4. Former Magomero estate in 1953

I. Conforzi.....................................40,000 acres
Dalveen Estate (two estates)......30,000 acres
Chikomwe Farms (two estates)....12,000 acres
Sabbatini and Chaudri.................8,000 acres
Lujeri Estates...............................3,000 acres
Hornby Farms...............................1,408 acres
J.V Ward (two estates)..................2,033 acres
Nyasa Tea Estates (Chimwalira)...2,250 acres
Mrs Johnson................................1,000 acres
K. Dickie (two estates)..................1,300 acres
H.A. Morton.....................................300 acres
J. Sibbald (two estates)................1,400 acres
Brindley and Brewer......................4,003 acres
Mrs L.L. Clerk...................................300 acres

Resettlement
scheme

to Zomba
Thondwe
Namadzi
to
Blantyre
Nasawa

0   5   10 km

duction, had created a land boom from which A. L. Bruce in the nick of time was able to benefit. The Magomero estate was reduced to a patchwork of separate enterprises, some of them individual farms, from which African residents were already being evicted, and others 'resident tenant' estates on which the new owners were already applying the full rigours of the 1928 Ordinance. Capitulating, the government reopened negotiations on Bruce's terms, purchasing the remainder of the estate for £40,571. The price was 12/6 per acre, a figure which set a precedent for all future land purchases.

In its last two years of trading, A. L. Bruce Estates Ltd made a profit of £50. But the sale of land netted £183,302, more than enough to cover the loans, overdrafts, debentures and accumulated losses since 1913. It was not quite enough, however, to pay off the shareholders. A squabble broke out among Livingstone's descendants over the division of these spoils. Plans to liquidate the company were opposed by Diana Livingstone Bruce with the support of Maria Nyasa Livingstone, W. J. Livingstone's daughter, who had witnessed her father's beheading in 1915 and who had inherited her mother's shares. It took over five years of legal wrangling to resolve the dispute but under a new firm of liquidators the company was wound up in March 1959. Shareholders received 52/9 per £1 share on the remaining capital of £142,425.

Even then, A. L. Bruce Estates Ltd was not quite dead. There was a flurry of interest in 1964 when it appeared bauxite was to be mined at Mulanje and enquiries were made about mineral deposits at Likulezi. To this day the heirs of Alexander Low Bruce retain mineral rights at Magomero, subject to a 5 per cent royalty.

The government's plans for the 75,000 acres of the Magomero estate it purchased in 1952 were based on a distinction. The bulk of the land, 46,700 acres in the east, was badly drained and sparsely inhabited. This was designated Public Land and was to be used for an ambitious resettlement scheme. The remaining portion in the west was to be treated as Trust Land. No settlement would be permitted, but measures would be taken to curb soil erosion. The distinction reflected how far the government had been outmanoeuvred: the land it had bought was either waterlogged or overpopulated.

In January 1953, the agricultural experts moved in. Like the missionaries in 1861 they came to help Africans make better use of their resources and their errors were similar to Bishop Mackenzie's. This comparison is not merely fanciful. J. E. R. Emtage, the resettle-

Fig. 21. Burrup's grave, photographed by J. E. R. Emtage

ment officer, was a cultured man who was to publish sensitive accounts of the missionary settlement. He was aware of the parallels with his own efforts.

The eastern portion was surveyed, providing detailed information about areas A. L. Bruce had always treated as remote bush. Emtage remembers mile upon mile of white-thorn and knob-thorn trees so closely packed they looked like a plantation. However, there were over 21,000 acres of sandy loam overlying brown clay and a further 8,000 acres which were potentially fertile if properly drained. For the rest, 14,700 acres of *makande* dark clay, the costs of drainage would outweigh any possible advantage.

Once allowance had been made for afforestation and for roads and housing, some 24,000 acres remained available for husbandry. It was proposed that 3,000 families from Trust Lands in Chiradzulu and Thyolo districts should be resettled on eight-acre plots, each measuring 100 by 400 yards. Significantly, the ultimate source of this estimate of African requirements was the 1904 Ordinance governing the *thangata* system. The plots were to be cultivated as follows: one acre of grain (maize and millet), one acre of cash crops (cotton or tobacco), one acre of legumes and one of grain in rotation, the remaining four acres lying fallow for four years. These crops by 1953 prices would produce an income of £45 per year, £32 of this in cash and the rest in the value of subsistence. Tenure was to be vested in men and inheritance was to be by the nearest male heir. No plots could be sub-divided and tenants who failed to follow the general plan of cropping would be evicted. There was to be an access road eight miles long, a system of boreholes, and provision for draught-oxen to be available for hire at 7/6 per day.

The good intentions of the resettlement scheme are manifest. Nothing could have been more in keeping with the Magomero tradition than this combination of effort and investment in defiance of what the Africans involved actually required. The plan was that whole villages should be shifted from Chiradzulu and Thyolo districts. But in order to move they had to cease being villages. Each man was to live on his separate eight-acre farm, his house next to his private borehole, unencumbered by the real or notional obligations of kinship. The same unconscious assumption had lain behind Bishop Mackenzie's week of Christian marriages. There was nothing for widows or daughters or second sons in the arrangements so simply devised, and wives were to lose all economic independence. As Emtage says, engagingly, 'We didn't get as far as thinking that one out.'

As the scheme moved from theory to practice other difficulties arose. There was flooding in 1955 and many of the newly built houses had to be evacuated. The land itself proved 'most intractable' and 'heroic effort' was needed to cultivate it outside of the rainy season. The cropping rules had to be abandoned in the effort to find something that would actually grow and cassava and sweet potatoes came back into favour as 'land opening crops'. This idea came not from the experts. It came from a flood of 'trespassers' from Chiradzulu and Thyolo. In order to preserve the scheme's original intentions these squatters had to be evicted. By 1958, only 1,041 of the proposed 3,000 smallholdings had been marked out and of these a mere 351 had been taken up.

Meanwhile, western Magomero, north of the Namadzi river, was being turned into 'a miniature district'. Over the next five years, Nasawa acquired a number of facilities. The most popular were a dispensary and an official market for cash crops. This was run by the African Produce Marketing Board which had replaced the Native

Tobacco Board, and its opening confirmed the new opportunities which had come with the ending of *thangata*. In addition, Emtage established a tree nursery and a small plantation. The nursery prepared young citrus, guava, pawpaw, mulberry and banana plants for distribution in the villages, together with jacaranda and Pride of India trees. Of these, only the mulberries and pawpaws were distributed with any success though across the river, on I. Conforzi's new estate, Mpotola planted an impressive orchard of orange and lemon trees. The Nasawa plantation consisted of ten acres of Pride of India and *cassaya siamia*, trees chosen for their resistance to white ants and intended for use in bridge and hut building. In the event, *malimo* trees with spindly pole-like branches and broad drooping leaves have proved more popular in the villages.

It was during the years 1953 to 1955 that Nasawa, Njenjema, Ntholowa, Mpawa, Nazombe and Komiha took on their present appearance. The Namadzi river was protected with a ridge extending for ten miles from Njenjema to beyond Machereni and 250 miles of bunds were constructed to channel the surface water. Contour ridging was introduced and, as we shall see in a moment, imposed with surprisingly little opposition. But the biggest change in the villages' appearance came with hut concentration. In Emtage's words, the aim was 'to stop them building huts all over the place and in the middle of gardens'. At Mpawa houses were moved away from the river-bank and the gardens and rebuilt alongside the road or on the bare rock immediately beneath Nanyungwi hill. Efforts to persuade people to exchange plots and consolidate their holdings were less successful. Villagers valued the access to different kinds of soils the existing system gave them.

In the monthly reports of agricultural officers we are offered the fullest picture of the agricultural year since the missionaries kept their journals in 1861. In 1953, the rains began on 30 November with heavy showers. Within two days, tobacco plants five inches tall had been transferred from river-bank nurseries to gardens and by 6 December all the season's maize had been planted. Then the rains stopped. By mid-January, both tobacco and maize had flowered prematurely and there were many gaps. Meanwhile, people had planted sorghum and pigeon peas, both of which had been slow to sprout, together with groundnuts which had flowered quickly and looked healthy. Even the cassava, though, which had been planted before the rains, looked patchy and pests like stemborer (which

Fig. 22. Mpawa from Nanyungwi hill

attacked grain crops) and *ukupe* beetle (which attacked pulses) were active.

In early February, three inches of rain fell. The maize 'recovered marvellously' and the first cobs were harvested. So, too, was *sumbwe*, the grain sprouting from last year's perennial sorghum. Villagers were rushing to plant fresh cassava gardens and 2,300 pounds of short-term sorghum seed were distributed from Nasawa as an anti-famine measure. In March, there was further heavy rain and people continued to plant cassava and sweet potatoes. Tobacco curing had begun with the first leaves being plucked and at Nasawa tobacco prices reached 8d per pound. Beans were also being harvested and the pigeon peas had recovered well after a poor start. The biggest surprise was the long-term sorghum which was flowering with every prospect of a good crop. The short-term variety had failed completely.

Quite suddenly, from May onwards, the whole tone of these reports changes. The measured optimism is gone and the year turns out to have been a bad one with only twenty-eight inches of rain. Tobacco was a disappointment. Only seventy-six tons were sold and few people were bothering to re-register as tobacco growers for 1954–5.

There was sufficient maize, especially from *dambo* gardens, for people to have a small surplus for sale to European buyers. But it was the traditional crops such as sorghum and pigeon peas, together with the emergency crops such as cassava and sweet potatoes, which had saved the year.

Two aspects of these reports are especially interesting. The first is that the strategies of survival on the banks of the Namadzi river in 1953–4 were very similar to those in Chigunda's village in 1861–2. More maize was being grown than ninety years earlier and there was a greater dependence on cassava and pigeon peas. But, except for the contour ridges, there was little the missionaries would not have recognised. The second aspect is the re-education of the experts. There were certain things to be done with this land and the villagers knew best what they were. When the rains faltered, sorghum, cassava and pigeon peas, those disregarded crops, proved reliable. The following February, when the rains were unusually heavy, the same agricultural officer noted with fresh surprise, 'sorghum is apparently unaffected by conditions and makes good growth'.

This is not to say the experts were invariably wrong. Hut concentration has stood the test of time and few people today use for their compounds land which could be used for crops. Similarly, as the population has increased and gardens have become smaller, older methods of maintaining soil fertility by leaving land fallow have become impractical. Everyone today practises contour ridging, using last year's trash as this year's green manuring, and the richest farmers buy fertilisers. In adopting new crops, farmers have followed the incentive of prices, abandoning tobacco and growing sunflowers and cowpeas because they saw their neighbours growing them with profit.

Village farmers, in short, have proved willing to adapt to changing conditions. But they have been able to select for themselves what was beneficial and to reject bad advice. Their most stubborn loyalties have been justified in the long term. Sorghum and cassava are still widely grown as insurance against a bad year. Emtage in his retirement argues that it has been the Lomwe devotion to their pigeon peas that has 'saved the life of that land'. The land 'looked as if it was too much walked upon and sat upon and everything else, and if it weren't for the *nandolo* . . . *nandolo* is nitrogenous, you see, and I'm sure it has kept the land alive'.

These comments are made with the advantages of hindsight. At the time, in the dry season of 1953, Emtage's programme of bunding and contour ridging met with hostility in the villages. There was heckling and the threat of violence and on one occasion police had to be summoned to restore order. The other major controversy of those weeks was the launching of the Central African Federation. A women's song from Mpawa linked the two issues by mocking Emtage's African *capitaos*:

> Federation capitoes
>   *e − e − e*
> Sooner or later you will die
>   *e − e − e*
> Contour ridging capitoes
>   *e − e − e*
> Sooner or later you will die
>   *e − e − e*
> e − e
>   *You will die but you don't know it*
> a − i − a
>   *You will die but you don't know it!*

In 1951, Britain had decided to link Nyasaland with Northern and Southern Rhodesia in the Central African Federation. The decision disregarded the strong opposition of Africans in Nyasaland and Northern Rhodesia to any transfer of sovereignty from London to Salisbury. Dr H. Kamuzu Banda from his surgery in north London and Harry Nkumbula, leader of the African National Congress of Northern Rhodesia, had already published a hostile memorandum. As British plans went ahead to launch the federation on 1 August 1953, African opposition intensified.

On 17 July in Chiradzulu, a meeting was arranged to call for the sacking of Chief Mpama. The organiser was Malika, whose predecessor had been a friend of Chilembwe. Malika had lost out in 1929 in the competition to become a native authority. Now the DC ordered his arrest. The following morning a large crowd marched to the prison at Chiradzulu *boma* singing hymns and demanding Malika's release. Two days later there was an attempt to depose Chief Nkalo. On 28 August, a further meeting was arranged to call for the dismissal of Chief Kadewere. This meeting was banned but when police tried to enforce the order they found a large and angry crowd surrounding Kadewere's house. They rescued him after a series of baton charges and removed him to Blantyre. Africans responded by setting up road blocks, destroying bridges and burning down Mpama's house. The political arrangements made in the aftermath of the Chilembwe rising were, after thirty-eight years, beginning to fall apart.

Chiradzulu was not the only focus of protest in 1953. In Ncheu, Paramount Chief Gomani had launched a campaign of civil disobedience involving the non-payment of taxes and the deliberate breach of the agricultural rules and of controls on hunting. When the DC arrested Gomani the chief was released by a crowd of his supporters and took temporary refuge in Mozambique. The worst riots occurred in Thyolo district. They began in August on J. Tennett's Mangunda estate with the arrest of a youth on a charge of stealing oranges. Rumours spread that he had been killed and a crowd stormed the house demanding the 'body' be handed over. When the DC for Thyolo read the Riot Act the crowd refused to budge. There was shooting and one demonstrator was killed.

By the time order had been restored throughout the Protectorate late in 1953, eleven Africans had been killed and seventy-two injured. The Commission of Enquiry attempted to prove that federation was not the main cause of the disturbances. This was not entirely disingenuous. Africans in Nyasaland had a confusing variety of anti-colonial grievances and, as the events in Chiradzulu and Thyolo had shown, anger could be expressed in very local terms.

What the commissioners failed to understand was the degree to which the federation issue had become for Malawians the basis of a new coalition of protest. There were dangers for the country in this. Concealed within the apparent unity of the coalition were profound differences of vision of the form a future independent Malawi might take. After Malawi's independence in 1964, these differences erupted in the upheaval of the Cabinet crisis, when the country's best-trained young men were driven into exile. For the time being, however, African clerks and schoolteachers, villagers and some chiefs, tenants and residents on Trust Land, Christians and Muslims, men and women, the Northern, Central and Southern Provinces could all find common ground in opposing federation as the entrenchment of settler rule. Opposition to federation became, in effect, a substitute for nationalism as all the country's political energies became concentrated on negating a single decision.

Yet, by January 1954, Congress had been forced to acknowledge defeat. The party passed into the hands of younger radicals like Henry Chipembere and Kanyama Chiume. In 1956, these two were elected with other Congress figures to the Legislative Council and, as the Devlin Report later noted ruefully, began using their position 'to harass and criticise the government ... Hansard has become a best seller among educated Africans'. It was Chipembere who in November 1956 wrote to Dr Banda inviting him to return to Nyasaland and lead the anti-federation struggle. Dr Banda had been out of the country for forty-three years, studying and practising medicine in the United States, Britain and Ghana. On 6 July 1958, he flew home to an ecstatic welcome by thousands of cheering supporters. The date and the occasion have since been enshrined in the state rituals of independent Malawi.

Dr Banda brought a new urgency to the campaign, spurred on by the threat that the three territories were to be completely amalgamated. When the scale of popular enthusiasm proved of itself insufficient to sway the government, Congress resurrected its 1953 programme of civil disobedience. The government reacted by declaring a state of emergency. On 3 March 1959, Dr Banda and Congress officials were arrested. In the disturbances which ensued, fifty-one Africans were killed and seventy-nine wounded. When the Commission of Enquiry under Lord Devlin spoke of Nyasaland as a police state, the fate of federation was effectively sealed. In September 1959, the Malawi Congress Party was formed with members drawn from the old Congress and the following April Dr Banda was released to prepare for new elections to the Legislative Council. These were held in August 1961. The MCP won all twenty seats elected by African voters.

From this moment, independence, which followed in July 1964, was inevitable. So, too, was the collapse of the coalition in the Cabinet crisis, when Chipembere and Chiume were driven into opposition abroad and Dr Banda assumed supreme power.

What part did the people in the villages on the Namadzi river play in these events? The answer is, very little.

Ever since the Chilembwe rising, the Nyasaland authorities had assumed Magomero was the flashpoint of the Protectorate. They had been genuinely alarmed by the Kincaid-Smith affair in December 1939, and were equally worried by the fiasco of the sale of the estate. Bad relations aggravated by boundary disputes between African residents and several of the new landlords were carefully monitored by the police and intelligence services. The worst incident occurred in August 1952 when R. W. Cleasby, the manager of Malcolm Barrow's Chimwalira estate, was beaten up in Chimwalira market.

Headman Nazombe, Mpawa III's brother-in-law, had brought a

219

basket of fish to sell at the market. During the morning a fire broke out near the home of the estate manager. Cleasby sent two of his *capitaos* to the market to summon help in putting out the fire and then, when the traders were reluctant to leave their goods unprotected, arrived himself in a dangerous mood. He kicked over Nazombe's basket of fish and punched him twice, knocking him unconscious. The other fish traders set upon Cleasby, banging his head against a tree until he too lost consciousness and had to be carried home by his *capitaos* with a fractured rib.

The government was keen to prove it had been right to anticipate trouble and investigators poured into the villages. They had little difficulty in establishing that Cleasby was 'very much disliked by all the Africans in that neighbourhood, who have given him the nickname *Mahafu* ("halves") because of his habit of dismissing his employees and giving them half pay'. Behind this hatred were genuine grievances, particularly over land. But there the matter ended. After all the official warnings, and all those re-readings of the report on the Chilembwe rising, it was hard not to feel that the Cleasby incident had somewhat failed to come up to expectations.

One year later, in the dry season of 1953, Emtage was heckled and his *capitaos* satirised, and he remembers his dependence on the authority of Mpawa III, the oldest of the ruling headmen, to keep protests over contour ridging within reasonable bounds. But the work was completed and there were no riots comparable to those in Chiradzulu or Thyolo. The fact was that government officials were once again out of touch. They were wrong to assume that these villages remained in the forefront of political protest.

There were three reasons why this was so. The first, as we have already seen, lay in the long legacy of the *thangata* system. Chilembwe's inheritance had long passed into other hands, hands of men whose mission education and business and agricultural skills equipped them to combat colonialism on its own terms. The second was that conditions had changed slowly but profoundly since the departure of Kincaid-Smith in January 1940. By 1950, after a last turn of the screw during the 1949 famine, *thangata* had ceased operating. The causes of the riots at Tennett's Mangunda estate no longer existed at Magomero, and most people were better off in 1953 than within living memory.

But there was a third reason, unremarked by staff at the resettlement scheme. In the villages a different kind of political and economic transformation was taking place. With their labour no longer tied to the land, men from the villages were seizing the opportunity, available for three generations elsewhere in Nyasaland, to earn better wages by migrating to Southern Rhodesia and South Africa. Meanwhile, as one group was moving out, other men were moving in. Men from overcrowded Chiradzulu, Blantyre and Thyolo districts were marrying the widows, *ambeta* and abandoned wives who, with *thangata*'s demise, had suddenly become extremely eligible. It was an unofficial settlement scheme, by-passing Emtage's ban on settlement in the western part of the estate. Their arrival coincided with, and was largely concealed by, his programme of hut concentration. The new men were interested in land, especially the red soils of the villages on the Namadzi, and in growing cash crops for sale at Nasawa. When branches of the Congress party were formed in the villages, it was these new settlers who became the local secretaries, treasurers and chairmen.

Frank James was born in Mpotola in 1907. He was seventy-five years old when I spoke with him there and had already lived half as long again as most of his contemporaries. Because of his age he was respected as a historian. He was short and wiry, but gentle and thoroughly alert. If the story he told was not altogether consistent, this was because there were certain themes he wanted to emphasise.

The original Mpotola was a Yao chief who had migrated from Mozambique. Four of them had travelled together – Kumpama, Nkanda, Chikoja and Mpotola. They had driven away the Mang'anja and Mpotola was the owner of the land. Then, having insisted in the presence of the chief's nephew on Mpotola's pre-eminence, Mr James told a different story. The emphasis this time was on the flight from Mozambique at a time of war and famine of a mixed group of Yao and Lomwe peoples. They had settled first at Thamanda in Mulanje and then heard there was land available on the Namadzi river. Mpotola, their leader, agreed with W. J. Livingstone the terms of their *thangata*. Then they cleared the bush and built their present village. The village was Muslim in those days. Later, because of Baison Chiunda, who supported John Chilembwe and became Mpotola II, it became Christian. Frank James is a Christian and has been since childhood a member of the PIM.

As a child before the Chilembwe rising, he can remember working on Mwanje plantation, picking boll worms from the cotton. 'Listonia', he says, 'was a harsh person': 'People were not allowed to have lunch and they were beaten up while working. If a person suffered from toothache he used to beat his cheeks. He also used to beat up dead bodies.' He spent half his life under the *thangata* system, first at Mwanje and later growing flue-cured tobacco at Chikomwe and Chiradzulu. After 1932, he grew his dark-fired *thangata* tobacco at Mpotola, abandoning his wife, whose name and home village he refuses to mention. Unlike the majority, tobacco growers at Mpotola were paid for their *thangata* tobacco.

He was forty-three years old when Conforzi purchased the Chiradzulu section of the Magomero estate. Mpotola and Bowadi remained subject to the *thangata* system until Malawi's independence in 1964. But it was a modified *thangata*, governed by a new ordinance passed in 1952, which clarified the rights of tenants. This gave them the option of paying an annual rent if they worked off the estate or if they sold their cash crops to someone other than the landlord. Frank James decided to celebrate his freedom. In 1953, he left for Southern Rhodesia, following in the footsteps of so many of his fellow worshippers at the PIM. He took a job in Salisbury as a garden boy earning £5 per month. By the standards of *thangata*, this was wealth. He stayed in Salisbury for four years, returning home in 1957. Life back home in Mpotola was unexciting in comparison and he missed his travels. He produced this comment with a grin which transformed his face, making the men around laugh out loud with pleasure.

In 1958 he returned to Southern Rhodesia. This time, he found a job as a houseboy earning £7 per month. 'I spent it all there,' he said with the smile of a man who had squandered a fortune. It didn't matter that he paid no rent, for his wife had long since found another husband. He stayed on in Salisbury until 1970. 'I liked the place,' he explained with a simplicity which reduced issues like federation and UDI to a proper perspective.

For Frank James, freedom from *thangata* has made the second half of his life a prolonged celebration. He looks an old and satisfied man. He now farms two acres in the village of his birth and finds them sufficient for his needs.

Wadmeck Chikopa was born in 1935 and now lives at Ntholowa. He was seventeen years old when the government purchased the remaining portion of the Magomero estate and he belongs to the first generation of men who missed *thangata*. He is a tall, long-limbed man with a bald head and a smooth, young-looking face. Though he speaks some English he preferred to talk in Lomwe for the sake of accuracy. He is a highly articulate, well-informed man, especially on matters of local history. It was he, for instance, who took me to see the Mang'anja forge – Zachurakamo's forge – and who explained how it had operated.

In 1954, he got a job in Salisbury as a film projectionist, moving on to Gwanda after three months to do the same job for better pay. His next move was to Johannesburg, where he worked on the Witwatersrand as a feeder-technician, repairing mine compressors and pumps. He returned to Ntholowa briefly in 1959 and then went back to South Africa for a further five years, coming home finally in 1964, 'because I had heard of the self-government in my country'. Meanwhile, he had been paying school fees for his sister's son, a pupil at Zomba Secondary School, and he had saved the considerable sum of £292. When the nephew left school he entered Lilongwe Training College, again with Mr Chikopa's support, to qualify as a teacher. Before completing this course, he passed away.

It was the collapse of many years of hard work and investment. Mr Chikopa had two more nephews, however, and he still had his savings. When they, too, entered secondary school he took on the task of supporting them. He put his money into a grocery in Chiradzulu, but the business went bankrupt largely through the strain of paying the school fees before it was properly established. Finally, he turned to cash-cropping on his wife's land at Ntholowa. He grows maize for subsistence and tobacco, sunflowers and cowpeas for sale, the cash crops occupying the land after the maize has been harvested. Even so, there are family arguments about the use of the land and Mr Chikopa has interesting things to say about the pressures of 'custom':

Q: According to Lomwe custom, men were supposed to stay in their wives' homes and cultivate the women's gardens?

A: This custom was brought from Mozambique. The first chiefs who came into this area were called by the *boma* and they were asked which custom they wanted to follow and so they chose the custom which requires the man to live in his wife's village and this agreement was written down. But today it is difficult because people get educated and when they get a job and get a lot of money they find problems in being ruled by their in-laws. Those who pay *lobola* [bridewealth] are better off because these problems don't occur...

Q: With this shortage of land does the custom present any problems?

A: Yes, there are problems because if a man works hard on a woman's land the owners say he is profiting on their land. If they decide to divorce the woman and go back home you find the land is already divided up.

There are contradictions in these comments. Mr Chikopa, who is putting his sister's sons through school, is plainly working within the custom. Yet his activities as a labour-migrant, shopowner and commercial farmer pose a challenge to custom and his investment in education looks to a future outside the village.

Moffat Manonga, named after David Livingstone's father-in-law, is the secretary of the local branch of the Malawi Congress Party. Like his friend James Ngoleka, who is the branch chairman, he is not originally from Magomero. He was born at Kapichi in Thyolo district in 1930 and he grew up there under the *thangata* system. When he was fifteen years old he was given an accordion and he began to compose songs. Soon he had established a reputation as a musician in the Lomwe-speaking villages of Thyolo and Chiradzulu. He would be invited to perform at weddings and beer parties, earning a fee both from the organisers and from the guests who would request particular 'records', using the English word for his best-known songs. In 1952, he played at a beer party at Nasawa. He found that *thangata* had ended and that there were many unmarried women and plenty of land. Mr Manonga joined what became in 1953 a minor stampede of husbands from Blantyre, Chiradzulu and especially Thyolo districts.

For the women it was plainly a buyers' market. But it is easy to see why Moffat Manonga was extremely eligible. He is a quiet and very gentle man, very 'Lomwe' in appearance with his jet black skin and thick hair and eyebrows. He speaks thoughtfully and almost without emphasis, pausing between words. This is especially true when he is talking of his musicianship. Through his marriage, he gained a sizeable farm. Even after it has been sub-divided twice, he retains the use of five acres, twice the average for Nasawa. Custom and his talent have served him well. Yet again there are contradictions. His most popular songs were about the problems of husbands living under Lomwe custom:

> They like them because when I sing it seems they have already told me their problems.

Q: Do you sing songs about complaints made by men who go to stay in their wives' villages?

A: Yes. Men complain they are being ill-treated by their in-laws.

Q: What other topics do you sing about?

A: These are the only ones.

When the farm was sub-divided, the first part went to his wife's niece but the second part went to his own son.

Fig. 23. Moffat Manonga's blacksmith's shop

From the start he treated the farm as a commercial venture, using his earnings as a musician to employ labour on *ganyao* terms. He talks regretfully about never having had enough capital to hire machinery as well as labour. By the early 1960s, opportunities for professional musicians in the villages were decreasing. People organising parties preferred to use radios and record players for entertainment, and performers who were not adopted by the Malawi Broadcasting Corporation were soon doomed to unemployment or amateur status. Mr Manonga secured his position in two ways. He became secretary of the local branch of the Congress party, giving him a powerful voice in the village he had joined by his marriage, and he became a blacksmith, the first to make a living in the area since Zachurakamo.

His business has two branches, one at Chimwalira market and the other in Nasawa just outside the Young Pioneer base. Like Zachura-kamo he can re-handle hoes and repair knives and axes. But the bulk of his trade is in repairing bicycles. Like the radios and record players which destroyed his career as a musician, these bicycles have been bought with the profits of labour migration. This business brings in enough money for him to buy fertiliser and hire local labour to cultivate his five acres. Back home in Kapichi, his two brothers are farming land they inherited directly from their father.

Facing inwards along three sides of the open rectangle of Chimwalira market are eight tiny shops, all owned by Africans and replacing the single Indian shop of the 1950s. One of them is run by Mr Mangomba. He was born at Nasawa and is now in his early forties. He was a young man at independence in 1964 and he had a primary school leaving certificate but no secondary education. He worked first on his parents' land at Nasawa, but in the early 1970s he went to Johannesburg and spent four years in the gold mines. When he returned home he had saved £187, which he planned to use to start a business.

The shop which he rents from the owner Mr Singano is entered by a flight of steps leading up to a wide veranda. It consists of a hot, tiny zinc-roofed room with a wide counter running across the middle. On one side the customers, all women, wait patiently and suckle their babies. On the other, Mr Mangomba presides. On display are tiny packets of Rinso, long bars of Lifebuoy soap, razor blades, Encor aluminium saucepans and enamel cups and plates, and also matches, radio batteries, salt, sugar, coca cola, cooking oil, and pieces of coloured 'Java' cloth with bright printed patterns. In the corner is a drum of kerosene with a metal jug and a funnel. 'It varies,' he explains, using a fluent mixture of Lomwe and English words. 'Today I am just selling safety-pins only. Sometimes, just a bit of coca colas. Once in a while somebody buys cloth. Soap they buy, but not all the time.'

The radio plays incessantly and attracts women who have come only to listen. Customers have to shout above the noise. When I spoke with Mr Mangomba it was playing a song with the repeated lines 'When you're in love with a beautiful woman, You watch your friends', and he tapped the rhythm on the counter as he explained about his business. He is proud of his wife. There is a framed picture of Akazi Wa Mangomba (Mrs Mongomba) hanging above the doorway to the storeroom at the rear. She looks a very large lady with an Afro-style wig. Mrs Mangomba is a South African who returned with him from Johannesburg. He paid bridewealth for her and the marriage has not encumbered him with local in-laws. He employs *ganyao* labour to cultivate the small patch of land at Nasawa he inherited from his father, and he is a staunch member of the *Chiyembekezo* (Adventist) church at Mpawa:

I started a long time ago. Now I get enough from here to feed my children and do other things. When you come to think of it, the three hundred kwacha I started with is still here. I haven't spent it. It's what you can see. I eat from it, I cultivate my garden from it, there's enough to do all this. I pay income tax and in good time.

Standing in shirt and trousers behind the counter of his shop, a small eager man with large eyes, Mr Mangomba looks the very epitome of a Samuel Smiles hero, a man who has broken with the past and is prospering.

Thirty-odd years after it is difficult to assess how many men, in the months following the ending of *thangata*, married into the villages on the Namadzi river or emigrated to work in Southern Rhodesia or South Africa. The fact that such movements occurred at all emerges only from biographies, and in villages where less than 16 per cent of the men reach fifty years of age the majority of those who were twenty in 1953 are already dead. Official census figures (for 1945 based on Bruce's register of tenants and wildly inaccurate: for 1966 too late to be helpful) provide no scale. The phenomenon is best explored not statistically but through its consequences. For the first time there was money in the villages.

The men moving in by marriage, outwitting the rules of resettlement, were attracted by the large gardens and the opportunities for cash-cropping. Official help was forthcoming. As if responding by a conditioned reflex to the word 'Magomero', the agricultural department distributed free seed in an attempt to re-establish cotton growing. In 1953, there were 204 cotton growers registered with the resettlement scheme. They cultivated an average of just under half an acre and earned on average 5/8. Tobacco growers in the same year cultivated quarter-acre plots and earned on average £2/15/-. It was the end of cotton at Magomero.

Other crops were more promising and for the first time producers had a choice of markets. Nasawa was only one outlet. Across the Namadzi river, Conforzi was paying good prices for *thangata* tobacco, and men from Njenjema, Ntholowa and Mpawa hired the registration cards of friends and relatives from Mpotola and Bowadi to sell their tobacco to him. Others of the new landlords – Dickie, Sabbatini, Morton, Du Toit, Du Preez – were keen to buy foodstuffs. Traders with such well-known names as Gunson, Chaudri and Abegg sent their agents to tour the villages. There was a sellers' market for maize

227

and pigeon peas at 1d per pound, for dried cassava at ¾d per pound and for cowpeas at 5d per pound.

Meanwhile, the men who had emigrated to Southern Rhodesia and South Africa were beginning to remit money home to their wives in the form of postal orders cashable in Chiradzulu or Zomba. Within three years, the first of them were returning home with their savings. Money was beginning to transform the villages, and the women who had been joyously released from the subservience forced on them by *thangata* soon began singing a different kind of pounding song:

> You, bearded man, you are holding me back
> > i – yee
> You, bearded man, you are holding me back
> > i – e, i – e, i – e, i – yee
> I would be in Limbe cooking for someone
> > i – e, i – e, i – e, i – yee, o – o
> Kazinga would be at my side for cooking
> > i – e, i – e, i – e, i – yee, o – o
> Fish would be there for frying
> > i – e, i – e, i – e, i – yee,
> You, bearded man, you are holding me back,
> > Your friends are at Lilongwe working.

This delightful song dates from the 1970s, but pressure from women for better clothing, housing and food had been expressed constantly in pounding songs since the ending of *thangata*.

As this suggests, the most fundamental change has been a shift in the balance of relationships. In villages where *thangata* had reduced all men to the level of field labourers there began to appear professional brickmakers and builders, carpenters and blacksmiths, breeders of livestock as well as commercial farmers and a variety of different kinds of traders. Money enlarged the scope of the villagers' economic contacts with Chimwalira market, drawing in traders from an area a hundred kilometres across. Money in the 1960s filled Chimwalira Primary School with boys and girls looking to a future beyond the village. The 'bearded man' song plays with images of the wife living in town surrounded by food – if only her husband first raids the economy as a labour migrant. It is a vision which stands in sharp antithesis to the old story of the Hunter, the dangerously individual entrepreneur described by Ida Thamanga's mother.

Moffat Manonga's reputation as a singer had been based on his songs about husbands being ill-treated by their in-laws. For the first time, such songs began to appear at Magomero:

My bicycle
My bicycle e – e
My bicycle
My bicycle e – e
My bicycle
My bicycle e – e
My bicycle is taken by my brother-in-law.
When I ask for it he says I am a billy-goat.
Though I am a billy-goat
My bicycle
I want it back!

In this song the 'billy-goat' is the 'visiting husband', who is nevertheless not prepared to see what he has bought with money earned by wage labour become his in-law's property. There are many such songs and it is by no means only the men who complain. In the following song, a woman is attacking her brother Waya who lives at his wife's village but still expects to have a claim on his sister's resources. There is a play on words between the 'cock' who 'marries' indiscriminately, even with his own sister, and '*tambala*', which is both the Chewa word for cockerel and the name of Malawi's coinage:

The cock is the one who is lucky
a – e
The cock is the one who is lucky to marry his sister
a – e
Waya has called me
a – e
He has eaten my tambala
He has eaten my tambala

These two songs were sung consecutively at Bowadi, the first by a group of young men and the second by the women in swift reply. They define the two sides of a general argument.

At the heart of this argument has been the question of investment, of how best to profit from the earnings from cash-cropping or migrant labour. The following song is one of a number by Edwin Sankhulani of Njenjema which are marvellously explicit in their treatment of family problems. Mr Sankhulani has been to South Africa and he used his earnings to build a house with a zinc roof. Later, he was divorced and lost everything:

At Njenjema, do not dare
At Njenjema, do not dare
To build an iron-roofed house

When you live in a women's village.
At Njenjema, do not dare
At Njenjema, do not dare
To build an iron-roofed house
When you live in a womens' village.
When you complain after the divorce,
After the divorce, you go to Mbiza's:
Mbiza just says, Leave the iron sheets
              because you have children!
When you complain after the divorce,
After the divorce, you go to Mbiza's:
Mbiza just says, Leave the iron sheets
              because you have children!
When I come I stand a distance away
Weeping,
Father,
I am crying for my iron sheets
   My iron sheets hurt me
Father,
   My iron sheets hurt me
Father,
   My iron sheets hurt me
Father,
   My iron sheets hurt me

Since the 1950s, the men have been looking for ways of avoiding this fate. Few have gone so far as Mr Mangomba, who brought his wife from South Africa. But even Wadmeck Chikopa is attracted to the idea of bridewealth as a means of satisfying in-laws. His own attempts at investment – in education, in trade, and in commercial farming – neatly illustrate the options available.

Education has for decades been a popular means in Malawi of investing the profits of labour migration. The rewards were jobs outside the village as schoolteachers, clerks and pastors, or further afield with the plantation companies of Mozambique or the mines of Southern Rhodesia and South Africa. By the late 1950s, however, when the first labour migrants from the former Magomero estate returned home with cash in hand, the benefits of education were already receding. This may seem paradoxical with independence approaching, but the days when primary education alone guaranteed a job had gone and the competition for secondary-school places was, and remains, intense. The risk of losing one's whole investment through non-selection (or as happened to Mr Chikopa's nephew, through death) are very high. Official census returns for 1977 revealed that while half those in the appropriate age groups in the eight villages had been to primary school, less than 0.5 per cent had continued their education. In 1982, out of 800 pupils at Chimwalira Primary School, which serves an area of some 400 square kilometres, only four were selected for secondary school. Since the 1960s, then, only a handful of people have used education as a route from poverty and, unlike Mr Chikopa, most now regard that route as effectively closed.

Trade was Wadmeck Chikopa's second option. It is instructive to talk with his friends and neighbours at Ntholowa about the profits to be made as a tradesman. James Chambo, for example, pays a royalty of K1.45 (approximately 60p) for six feet of timber. After seasoning the wood he makes chairs, tables, beds, cupboards, doors and door frames. He charges K5 for a chair if he has to supply the timber or K2.50 if the timber is his customer's. Edwin Benes is a brickmaker and builder. He makes his bricks using clay from the undersoil on his wife's land and shaping them with a wooden mould. After they have dried in the sun, he charges 78 *tambala* (approximately 32p) for 1,500 bricks. This is seasonal work both because the bricks need hot dry weather (the cost of firewood is prohibitive) and because the dry season remains the time for house building even when people are employing a professional builder.

Jombo Mseula has a bicycle which he uses to buy dried fish at Nchisi on Lake Chilwa. He leaves for Lake Chilwa on Monday mornings and tours the markets of Zaone, Jenela, Khonjeni and Mwanje selling his fish before returning home on Friday evenings. The profit varies, but in December when food is scarce he can make as much as K6 per trip. He bought his bicycle after working in South Africa. Other trading possibilities mentioned by this group of men at Ntholowa were to make mats, though the reeds have to be bought at Phalombe, to breed chickens and pigs for sale at Chimwalira market, to buy a sewing machine and become a tailor, since there is none at Ntholowa and, if you were very rich, to own a maize mill.

There are two problems about all such ventures. The first is that there is a limit to the number of specialised traders the local economy can sustain. As James Chambo remarks, 'Money from carpentry depends on the orders people make', and the high price of fish when I spoke with Jombo Mseula had kept him at home for several weeks. All these men worked to supplement their income from farming and the rhythm of their trade continues to be dictated by the agricultural year. The second difficulty is that over the last ten years the opportunities for securing the initial capital – to buy a bicycle, a sewing machine, a set of carpenter's tools, a trowel and mould – have drastically declined.

In 1974, following a plane crash in which a number of Malawian miners returning from South Africa were killed, recruitment for the Witwatersrand ceased. The accident coincided with complaints from the tea companies of Mulanje and Thyolo about shortages of labour. Recruitment was renewed in 1977 but on terms which have meant that only experienced men may apply. Meanwhile, the labour market in Zimbabwe has also closed. Nowadays, the migrant has to sell his labour within Malawi and the opportunities are severely limited. Few men are willing to work on the tea estates, where Malawian labour is in competition with even more desperate workers coming from Mozambique and where a full day's pay will not buy one loaf of bread. There remains the option of working for tobacco planters in the Central Province or for the Agricultural Development and Marketing Board (ADMARC) in Lilongwe.

ADMARC is the heir of the APMB, which itself replaced the NTB. Workers are signed on at Chiradzulu *boma*. They are given transport to Lilongwe and accommodation in barracks with breakfast and a midday meal. The contract is for two or two and a half months and they are paid 81t per day, out of which they have to find an evening meal. Labour for the tobacco estates is recruited informally. Lorries tour the villages inviting people to sign on for work on farms in Kasungu and Mchinji, many of them owned by President Banda or his entourage. Housing and food are provided plus wages of up to K15 per month, but return transport is paid by the worker. There is little opportunity for any man born since independence to accumulate the kind of savings mentioned by Mr Mangomba or Wadmeck Chikopa.

There is a further dimension to this poverty trap. Each of the established traders talked of hiring labour on *ganyao* terms to work on the land while he turned his attention to business. Too much should not be made of this gap in wealth. In villages where even the prosperous earn less than K300 per year and where no one's wealth is entrenched, talk about 'classes' is pretentious. Nevertheless, there are people who are forced by hunger or taxes to work on *ganyao* terms for Mr Mangomba the shopkeeper or Mr Manonga the blacksmith. It is hard to establish who they are since no one admits to doing such work. Some are widows able to feed themselves but not to buy salt or soap powder or a new cloth. Some are people who miscalculated

Fig. 24. Interviewing at Mpotola

when selling their surplus maize and are left without food during the planting season. Some are people who suffered unexpectedly poor harvests because they gambled on the wrong crops or because the rains were patchy or because illness in the household affected their labour supply. Many come from outside the villages altogether, working anonymously, since it is a disgrace not to be able to feed oneself. This sets up a vicious circle, since to work on other people's land they have to neglect their own. Some, finally, are simply people unable at the last minute to find money for taxes or for their party membership card. 'We do not find where to get employment,' I was told at Bowadi, 'and so there are a lot of tax defaulters who are hunted in the bush like wild animals.'

Whatever the cause, the pay for *ganyao* labour is pitifully small. Payment in cash is between K6 and K8 per month. Payment may also be at 'piece' rates in cash or food. Eight paces of ridging earns 1t or one small Encor plateful of maize flour. Weeding five maize or tobacco plants (if the weeds are thin) or three plants (if the weeds are thick) earns the same rates. It is possible to subsist on such wages but no more.

Wadmeck Chikopa's third outlet for investment was commercial agriculture. During a recording session at Mpotola, Mr Matiki

233

Rabiano interrupted a song about Dr Banda's return to Nyasaland in 1958 to make a speech about the agricultural option:

Excuse me, my friends, I want to talk about the modern times, what I see. From 1951 I was putting on *biriwita* cloth and my mother put on *siti*. But today because of the coming of the Ngwazi [Dr Banda] things have changed for the better. I never knew a pair of trousers, but today I buy one, even one which is worth K30. I never knew how to cultivate. The colonial Europeans, Welensky, hid the technique of cultivating. But today we know how to cultivate and eat well. I am very happy about this because in the old days I knew nothing. I never knew a bicycle, worse still a motor car. There was nobody who could buy a car in this country, but because of the coming of the Ngwazi people buy cars and build iron-roofed houses. I will never go to employment even to Wenela, no, my employment is farming, that is where wealth is. A person from Wenela might come and borrow money from me after one month. We just trouble ourselves going to Salisbury or South Africa. The wealth is in the soil as the Ngwazi tells us. I will never go to work and be shouted at by a European, no! But I will shout at myself in my garden, that is where wealth lies. I can buy cattle from farming. We just trouble ourselves going to Wenela, leaving wives behind very insecure and maybe when coming back you find her married. Please let us work hard on the soil.

This speech provoked some barracking, partly because Mr Rabiano's K30 trousers were in a spectacularly dilapidated state and partly because such self-denigration for political purposes ('I never knew how to cultivate') always provokes derision in Malawi. It is a fascinating and rich statement, reducing the area's history to before and after Dr Banda, willing to be satisfied with the wealth of the very few, and summarising accurately the tone and content of Dr Banda's own speeches. But Mr Rabiano's main point that farming is better than labour migration drew general support. The speech moved on to stronger ground in its last sentences and there was no detectable irony in the applause at the end.

The agricultural option brings full circle the problems over custom. Is the land to be used primarily for subsistence? Or should it be used mainly for commercial farming on the assumption that a good deal of food will be purchased? The former implies self-sufficiency, the reduction of risks to the minimum. But people's expectations have gone up since *thangata* ended and many things are regarded as necessities which can only be obtained by purchase. Clothing, for instance, is a constant preoccupation in the women's songs and no wife, no matter how jealously she controls her garden, would tolerate a return to bark cloth. Two metres of cotton cloth in Mr Mangomba's shop costs between K3.50 and K5.50 and the tailor will charge a further K1.20 to make a dress. Clothing generates its own need for soap powder, for which there is no local substitute. Cooking oil has also ceased to be a luxury item. For women with so little firewood that cooking fires are fuelled by dry maize stalks, cooking oil is a necessity because it permits faster cooking and few people can afford kerosene. People also need cash for the oldest reason of all, to pay taxes. If they want to sell goods at the market they will need party cards. For anyone with yet larger ambitions – to pay school fees or to accumulate the kinds of capital possible in the 1960s – the balance of the argument shifts yet further towards growing crops for sale.

Commercial agriculture at village level, however, is a heartbreaking business. It is an extremely efficient type of farming, since the attention given to each acre of a family holding far exceeds that on the large estates. This does not mean simply that every piece of land is used, with even the anthills being cultivated with regard to their special fertility. It means that it is used throughout the year from November to early September and inter-cropped constantly, with pigeon peas or cowpeas (but never both) spreading through the dry stalks of the ripe maize, while tomatoes, cucumbers and green peas use the tall masts of sorghum for support. Village farmers have held constantly before them the vision of wealth in the soil. But the pricing policies of ADMARC have discriminated sharply against small producers. A surplus has been generated which has benefited the large estates, both through investment in infra-structure and through keeping labour costs down. In many ways ADMARC is an effective organisation, and its network of markets nationwide is the envy of neighbouring Zambia and Mozambique. But its profit margins have been excessive and there has been no reciprocal investment in village agriculture.

The obvious compromise and the one adopted by the majority of house-holds is to grow food and sell only the surplus, or to grow wet-season crops for subsistence and dry-season crops for sale. One of the reasons why tobacco has become less popular than cowpea is that it occupies land throughout the wet season. But even this compromise is somewhat artificial. Crops like cassava or sweet potatoes or even sorghum and pigeon peas do not fit this neat division of the seasons, and every crop makes a different demand on soil, time and labour. Government pressure on farmers to grow new varieties of hybrid maize further illustrates the point. Hybrid maize can only be grown with fertiliser, which means a cash investment, and can only be grown for sale since it will not store for more than a few months in village granaries. Credit is available only if it is grown single-stand and is not intercropped with cowpeas or pigeon peas. For these reasons it is not a crop which tempts the small farmer. One old woman in Bowadi responded to my questions by producing a handful of hybrid maize dust from her nkokwe and spitting on it contemptuously. Her crop had been harvested six months before.

Aggravating every other problem is the question of land shortages. Wadmeck Chikopa's six acres is a large farm by today's standards. Most households have access to between two and three acres. Compared to Chiradzulu district, where there are families struggling to survive on less than an acre, their plight is not yet desperate. But it is far too little for families to be able to avoid constant disputes about how the land should be used. Another of Edwin Sankhulani's songs describes the situation in many households:

> A noisy family
> *A noisy family*
> A noisy family
> Leaves the garden unfinished.
> In the morning we quarrel,
> In the afternoon we quarrel,
> The garden is too small.
> Tell, ee,
> *Tell the warden to come*

The effect is not simply to restrict the agricultural option. Land shortage in the 1980s is becoming as important a factor as the flow of investment in the 1960s in further undermining custom. In 1977, there were 202 children in Mpotola and Bowadi, including 102 girls. According to custom, the girls should all be allocated land on their marriages but simple arithmetic is forcing changes in the pattern. More and more women are marrying outside their home villages, cultivating their husband's land while he is absent for part of the year in Blantyre or Lilongwe supplementing the family's income. More and more men are insisting on the direct inheritance of property from father to son. As the size of the farms has declined, so too has the bargaining power of women. The villages have largely ceased to be 'women's villages'.

Ironically, the only place where this is not so is on the Congress Party's 'scheme' at Chimwalira. In 1964, the 2,500 acres of Malcolm Barrow's Chimwalira estate were finally taken over by the government of Malawi. The land was not returned to the villages which had originally owned it. Instead, another settlement scheme was devised and it was announced on the radio that land was available for allocation. Over the next two years the Chimwalira estate, with its prized *dambo* land, was carved up into smallholdings. One of the first to take up land was the scheme's first chairman, Mr Isaac Mahonya of Mahonya village in the north of the former Magomero estate.

In 1942, Mr Mahonya had enlisted with the King's African Rifles. He served for four years as a driver, in Kenya, Ceylon, India, and finally in Burma which he describes as 'six months of suffering'. During these years, his *thangata* obligations were cancelled and he was able to remit 15/- monthly to his wife. On demobilisation in 1946 he was given a further £46. With this cash he bought a set of carpenter's tools and set up in business in his home village. After his wartime experiences, politics came naturally to him and in 1959 he became chairman of his local branch of the Malawi Congress Party. When the Chimwalira scheme was organised in 1964, he became the scheme's first chairman, awarding thirty-five acres of *dambo* land to himself and summoning his friend John Sambani to join him. Mr Sambani had also served in the KAR. It was in India where they shared a house together that he met Mr Mahonya. Demobilised in 1946 with a broken leg, he used his gratuity to hire people to work on his wife's land. When the scheme was announced, his friendship with Mr Mahonya secured him a small farm.

Lewis Bonongwe, who is now seventy-four years old, was born in Thyolo. In 1952 he joined the stampede of husbands to the emancipated villages of the Magomero estate, marrying a woman at Mpawa. With David Alipawo, who arrived at the same time from Thyolo and married a woman at Nasawa, he founded the Nanyungwi branch of the Malawi Congress Party, serving the villages from Nasawa to Mpawa. Lewis Bonongwe became chairman and David Alipawo secretary. It was these party positions which secured them small estates with the Chimwalira scheme in 1964. Mr Bonongwe has fifteen acres and Mr Alipawo seventeen acres. Other farms vary in size from fifty to five acres.

Their earlier careers demonstrate that these are men of initiative and enterprise. But the Chimwalira scheme is in no sense a 'scheme'. The farms they hold are no more than their reward for political loyalty and since 1964 they have worked quite independently of each other. No equipment is held in common and there are no shared plans for cropping and harvesting, not even a sales cooperative. They grow maize, groundnuts and cassava, cowpeas and sunflowers and flue-

237

cured tobacco. Mr Mahonya remains sufficiently influential in party circles to have secured permission to grow burley tobacco, despite regulations restricting its cultivation to the largest estates. Labour comes from the surrounding villages and over a hundred people are employed on *ganyao* terms. Mr Mahonya, for example, employs between fifteen and twenty people and pays them 35t per day, less than half the Malawian minimum wage. He has just bought a tractor which the other farmers may hire from him. With labour so cheap the tractor will actually be more expensive, but Mr Mahonya finds the local workers rather slow and unreliable.

There are no regulations about land tenure. Twenty years on, the farms are being broken up as daughters grow up and are married. Many of the smallholdings are already being run by women, such as Effie Musa from Makoka and Alucia Chandamale from Ntholowa, both of whom were brought to Chimwalira by their former husbands. As a group these women speak very differently from the women of the surrounding villages. They all stress the importance of cash-cropping 'because money helps people: if you have no money you are very poor'. They all send their children, boys and girls, to Chimwalira Primary School and can afford the school fees of K3.50 per term for standards 1 to 5 and K5.50 for senior classes. School is 'very important ... Europeans didn't want us to go to school. His Excellency has taught us to like school and he has brought us adult schools so that anybody can know which buses to board.'

This strong party message, almost completely absent in the villages, is typical of the women of the scheme. They are full of praise for 'His Excellency Kamuzu Banda who gave us the freedom so that anybody can come to the scheme':

Q: Can people of Blantyre, Mulanje, Thyolo etc. come and grow crops here at the scheme?
A: No. Only people from around this area. Only about three people came from places far away from here.

Yet, according to Mr Mahonya, first chairman of the scheme and Mr Alipawo, current chairman, land allocation without regional preference was completed in 1966 and there have been no further smallholdings available since then. It is a fascinating contrast of emphasis. To the women, the scheme is already becoming a 'women's village', the only one in the area where there is sufficient land for custom to continue to operate, and new husbands are settling all the time.

Elestina Petulo, Ida Thamanga's 'sister', now lives at the scheme. She was born at Machado in Zomba district in 1925, the third of eight children. Her four brothers and three sisters are alive and in touch with her regularly except for Damiano, who followed his father to Southern Rhodesia and never returned. She has memories of Machado and of her grandmother Akunyaika:

> In the morning she used to take a broom and sweep, and then she set out for the garden. When she went there, sometimes she would leave *nandolo* on the fire and then tell us that when it is cooked, take some and bring it to the garden. Then we took some of it and also water and brought it to where she was. She used to eat there, then we took the plates home, that is what I saw.

Q: Was there any difference in what you did during the dry season and the rains?

A: The rainy season is a difficult time. Sometimes we used to run, I don't know where, it could be at the river while we were pounding. When our parents came back they would find we had made a fire and were warming ourselves. And the dry season was a time when we would walk around, pick fire-wood, come back with it, go to the river and pound, cook *madeya* [*nsima* made from the flour of maize husks] and give it to our elders. Sometimes we would play *masanje* at a place like that, cook things and come back here to give the elders.

This was a Christian family. Elestina's mother, Elizabeth, had been married in the Catholic Mission at Machado and her own initiation ceremony was a Christianised version of Akunyaika's:

> During my time we are Christians. So it differs from those who were not Christians, that is, during my grandmother's time they were not Christians. Those who are not Christians say insulting things to the girls. What is required is that the young girls be taught good manners. Christian girls are initiated separately from pagan girls.

Q: After the ceremony what happened?

A: After they come out the young girl pounds some maize and takes this to the one who looked after her during the ceremony called m'zina. Each girl had her own *azina*. There the girl's hair is cut, since at the real ceremony the hair was also cut. At the real ceremony the hair is cut and the girl is bathed by her *azina*. The whole body is then smeared with *nsatsi* [castor oil]. Now dresses are brought for the girls. After they are dressed up the girls are ready to come out. When they come out they assemble in one line.

Two features of this are especially interesting. The first is the ambiguity of Mrs Petulo's position as she moves between talking of

239

the benefits of the Christian version of initiation and 'the real ceremony' for the pagan girls. The second reflects this, being equally respectful of custom. It is that whenever she speaks of her adult experience Mrs Petulo submerges her own identity in generalisations and passive verbs.

When her grandparents died, the family followed their friends, Ida Thamanga's parents, to Mpawa. Almost immediately, Mr Petulo disappeared to Southern Rhodesia and never returned. It was then that the rangers arrived, threatening to burn down the house and Elestina, who was cooking *nandolo* while her mother was in the garden, had to promise they would both turn out for *thangata* the next day.

At the age of fifteen, Elestina married a man whose name she keeps a secret, whispering it inaudibly to the tape-recorder. Once again, she describes what happened entirely in terms of the custom:

During my time if a young man had a girl in mind he went off to tell his uncle about the girl. The uncle then went off to the girl's uncle and told him of his nephew's interest in the girl. After this, the girl's uncle called her and her parents and told them of the other person's visit. The parents asked the girl whether she really wanted the man. If she accepted, the girl's uncle told the boy's uncle about it. The two could then become man and wife.

The following year, her husband enlisted with the KAR and served for five years, ending up in Burma. She was pregnant when he left but the infant died. For five years she received a monthly remittance. As a KAR wife she was not subject to *thangata* and by the standards of the time she was privileged. In 1946, her husband returned with a small gratuity. They grew maize and tobacco for sale first to Sibbald and afterwards at Nasawa. She also brewed beer, using a blend of millet and cassava flour which has earned her a reputation.

Over the next twenty years she gave birth to ten more children and watched eight of them die in infancy. Only Catherine and Lazaro have survived. A century earlier Zachurakamo and his family lived out the same extended grief on this same site. Zachurakamo was denounced as *mfiti*. Mrs Petulo is a Christian and will not talk about witchcraft nor blame her husband. Nor did she join in the songs about witchcraft sung in her presence at Mpawa. It is, in fact, only through her passivity, her deliberate sinking of her own experience in the general life of the community, that we can gain any hint of what she has suffered. Every question that has a personal bearing is answered, simply and courteously, with a statement of what is customary.

Materially, she has done well. In 1964, her husband was given one of the new farms on the Chimwalira scheme. It was the KAR connection with Isaac Mahonya which secured his entry. Since his death, she has taken the land, brewing her special beer for sale at Chimwalira market to hire labour. Her two children are prospering. Catherine completed three years of primary education and is married and living in Blantyre. She sends money to buy clothes for Lazaro, who is a pupil at the Catholic Secondary School in Zomba. Mrs Petulo is the only mother from Mpawa whose child is in secondary school. The school fees are paid by the army.

Alice William's brother, Anderson William, is the current village headman of Bowadi. He has married away from the village, however, and by agreement she acts as 'headman'.

Unlike the villages across the river which were concentrated in 1953, Bowadi straggles for 2 km along a system of footpaths which fork and redivide between gardens in a bewildering manner. There is no road and many of the houses look dilapidated. There are also less trees than across the river or at Mpotola, just the odd mango or pawpaw or clump of bananas looking as if they have grown by accident.

There is no *bwalo*, but Alice William's house is the natural focus for gatherings and here everything changes. She is a small, neat and courteous lady who looks much younger than her fifty years. Her house is tiny but immaculate. The thatch is trimmed and overhangs a broad baked-mud veranda on all four sides. Inside, where she brought us a plate of bananas and peeled oranges, the floor and mud walls have the smoothness of plaster. Her clay pots and gourds are arranged in a corner and there are ledges and crannies in the walls for holding Lifebuoy soap or a box of matches or her comb.

She is a niece of the Bowadi who took part in the Chilembwe rising and the Chilembwe tradition remains strong. The village has its own PIM church. One of the niches in her house held a Lomwe Bible and among her duties as acting-headman are those of leadership in the church. Other responsibilities include keeping the tax lists and maintaining law and order. She does not hear cases – these are heard by her brother or referred to Mpotola. Nor does she interfere in land matters. 'There is no giving out of land these days,' she explains, 'because there is no land.' There is no doubt, though, about her ability to create harmony. As people arrived in response to her arrangements, everyone without exception greeted her by shaking hands, the women making a low curtsey, and then sitting on the ground until the session began with her introduction.

Alice William did not really want to talk about her life. Her answers were polite but brief and often negative. This was not because she was suspicious or felt we were being intrusive. She simply felt I was asking the wrong questions. She described the pots her grandmother made for sale. She was informative about clan names and about *nantongwe*. She explained what crops she grew and what she sold and where. School was important because 'we want our children to be able to board the right bus when they travel and also to read our letters since most of us are uneducated'. School fees, however, and the cost of uniforms meant that very few children could afford to attend. Those who do will work in town 'if they are lucky'. Only twice was she assertive. Once was when we asked about her problems and she replied with spirit, 'Poverty! We just work hard in the garden but we don't get money out of it.' The other was when describing the end of her marriage in 1977. 'My husband', she said indignantly, 'wanted to chase away our child so that we stay together.'

Then, at a second prearranged interview, came a surprise:

Q: Is there someone here who is good at story-telling?
A: Yes.
Q: Who is it?
A: Me, and I want to tell you a story.

The Woman who was Barren

There was a woman once who was barren. Then she picked up a cucumber and shaped it into a baby. She wrapped it in a cloth and laid it on the bed. She went out to work in her garden. Some other children came. When she came back she found the other children had eaten her cucumber, and she said 'Eeee! My child is gone! What should I do?' So she went and stood on an anthill and she started singing:

> Climb root, climb root,
> *Climb, it will climb me*
> My father and my mother
> *Climb, it will climb me*
> My baby has been eaten, climb
> *Climb, it will climb me*
> The cucumber is the baby, climb
> *Climb, it will climb me*

She stood on the anthill and went on singing. Then strange powers lifted her up into heaven. She found a man sitting there. He asked her, 'Were you crying for the child?' and she said 'Yes'. The man told her to go a little way and she

242

would find two big buckets. 'You'll find this bucket which is gleaming and beautiful and you'll find another one which is old and ugly. You must open that one.' Then she said, 'Is that so?' After hearing all these words she takes a few steps and she finds the ugly bucket. Inside there is a beautiful Baby. She picks up the child and goes to the water and she starts again singing that song:

Climb root, climb root,
  Climb, it will climb me
My father and my mother
  Climb, it will climb me
My baby has been eaten, climb
  Climb, it will climb me
The cucumber is the baby, climb
  Climb, it will climb me

Then she goes, she goes back to her home. Then everyone asks, 'Oh! Where did you find such a child? I want one too! What do I have to do? I want to go and find mine.' So the woman stood on the same anthill and began singing the same song:

Climb root, climb root,
  Climb, it will climb me
My father and my mother
  Climb, it will climb me
My baby has been eaten, climb
  Climb, it will climb me
The cucumber is the baby, climb
  Climb, it will climb me

She also is lifted up into heaven and she finds the man sitting there. 'But you, you will also find a shining bucket. Don't open that one. Go and look for the ugly one and if you open it you'll find a child in there.' But she says to herself, 'Oh, no, I'll open the beautiful one and I'll find a more beautiful baby in there with hair like a white man!' She opens the beautiful one and fire came out of the tin and she died there. That's the end of the story.

This story, with its combination of sexuality and supernatural order, its contrast between appearances and reality and its emphasis on children as the supreme gift, was premeditated. It was what Alice William wanted to tell me after hearing the kind of matters I was interested in.

Nachanza missed out on the husband boom of the 1950s. She was in her late teens when *thangata* ended and had already been conducting her own rebellion, partly against *thangata* but mainly against her father, who was an elder in the Presbyterian church at Chiradzulu. By

1953 she was an unmarried mother with a reputation for wildness. Since then she has had four more children, each by a different man, and has earned part of her living through prostitution. I asked for an interview, and she immediately demanded money, standing legs apart, right hand held out, her chin raised in defiance. In keeping with the joke I gave her 2t and so started a gleeful village rumour that she was now a two-*tambala* woman.

She is proud of her reputation ('I never got married. I just get pregnant, that's all'), and it was plain that in some ways the women are proud of her. She was the only person whose testimony they kept interrupting with, 'She is lying!', demanding ever-increasing frankness, and they squealed with laughter at her indiscretions:

Thangata was a real problem. We worked in the pepper fields and we picked pepper and when you scratched anywhere, especially your anus, it could get swollen and was very painful. I had my own house but no husband and one day I found the *thangata* people had cut down my house and it had fallen because I didn't go to work. They caught many of us girls to go and pick pepper. I tell you it was very painful when you scratched your anus!

She has earned the right to be humorous about marriage. Husbands, she says, 'just come to give us kids. They are like servants who produce kids for us.' She is splendidly contemptuous about village life and though none of her children has been to school believes in education as the only way of escaping and getting a decent job. Her anger about the memory of *thangata* is genuine. But her protest does not rest in complacencies about freedom and independence. She is just as angry with the Congress Party for forcing her to sell maize to buy a party card annually. On the subject of land, protected by her reputation, she says what no one else would say about the Young Pioneer base and the Chimwalira scheme: 'Land is becoming scarce because so much has been taken by the government and when you try to grow your crops on the government land they arrest you.' Not all her earnings have come from prostitution. She has land and grows food and cash crops. These include fire-cured tobacco which she sells at Nasawa ADMARC, earning further admiration by encroaching on what most of the village women regard as a male preserve.

At the end of her interview she again demanded money, rejecting my customary gift of soap or salt or sugar. Perhaps the two-*tambala* joke required correction. But she has never left home, except to sell maize in Blantyre, and she has never made the jump to becoming a professional bar girl in the townships. She has never, in fact, quite

Fig. 25. Women dancing *likwata* at Ntholowa

outgrown her adolescent rebellion. Yet no other interview was so entertaining or came so close to political frankness. No other interview produced such a sequel as hers.

Political discussion is taboo in Dr Banda's Malawi. To talk politics with Malawian friends is to be admitted to a special intimacy of trust. This was not something I could achieve in the villages. I arrived by car and by village standards was well-dressed with shirt, trousers, shoes, a camera and a tape-recorder. I had three girl students as assistants, all English-speaking and immaculately groomed. Our first conversations were necessarily of the party's approval of my work. In the months which followed, anything bearing on current politics was immediately suspect. When a question caused silence and a chill, followed by protestations of loyalty to Dr Banda and faith in ADMARC, I knew I had trespassed on a topic to be avoided.

After interviewing Nachanza, however, when I had thanked her and paid her, I asked as normal if I could record songs. Some of the women were still excited by Nachanza's performance. Laughing and ululating, they broke into the following:

> Let's go,
> Let's go,
> There's no need to wait,

Kamuzu returned from England
Yelele ee – e – e
  We found him asleep burned
  We found him asleep burned

The opening lines of this song are in Chewa and they parody the songs usually sung about Dr Banda's return to Malawi. The chorus line, however, is in Lomwe and it deliberately echoes a well-known Lomwe song:

We found him asleep,
We found him asleep
Naked,
    Uncle, uncle, look
    Your hairs are burned!

'Uncle' in this song is the mother's brother, normally the most respected person in the family but in this song mocked for disgracing himself by rolling drunkenly into the fire and burning his pubic hair. The new song combines parody and allusion to ridicule Dr Banda at several levels. In Chewa, the President's language, it provides a sarcastic twist to the normal praise songs by saying Kamuzu's return is a piece of ancient history it is no longer worth waiting around for. In Lomwe, the villagers' own language, he is exposed comprehensively as a foolish old man, not entitled to respect because he can't even protect his private parts.

Margaret Matemba's circumstances are the opposite of Alice William's. She is a visiting wife married to Mpawa IV.

It is impossible not to feel a little sorry for her. She was born in Namitambo in Chiradzulu district in 1949. Her parents and grandparents were members of the Zambesi Industrial Mission, the mission originally founded by Joseph Booth and one of the models for Chilembwe's PIM. Though land was short in Chiradzulu, her family worked hard and avoided alcohol, and lived close enough to Blantyre to be able to sell their surplus maize and sugar-cane. Margaret Matemba grew up taking for granted the printed cotton cloth her grandmother always wore, or aluminium plates and cooking utensils, a gramophone for entertainment, and such facilities as a dispensary and clinic, a maize mill and water piped from a communal bore-hole. After her marriage, it was a hardship to have to fetch water from the Namadzi river.

Her husband is several years older and they met when he was

Fig. 26. Margaret Matemba with Mpawa IV

visiting relatives in Namitambo. 'He just proposed to me,' she says, 'and I agreed and told my parents who told my maternal uncle so that he was informed.' They were married at the ZIM church in Namitambo. It was sensible to move to Mpawa. Her husband was already working as an assistant to the long-serving Mpawa III and was likely to be chosen by the women as his successor. In any case, there was more land available. From 1970 when he became Mpawa IV until 1985, her husband cultivated the eight acres of the original Magomero peninsula. Unlike the other women of Mpawa, Margaret Matemba regards land as plentiful and by the standards of Namitambo she is right.

But Mpawa is not her village and she talks as an outsider. She describes one specific duty. If a child in the village is stillborn it is regarded as never having known its father and is buried by the

247

women alone. A procession led by the headman's wife carries the body to a special part of the graveyard. Otherwise, she feels separate from village ceremonies. Behind her house is a small shrine for prayers. She takes no part, 'since this is not my house and I don't know their ancestors'. To be the headman's wife is an ambiguous privilege.

She has two sons and three daughters. The elder boy, who is nineteen, attended Chimwalira school briefly. None of the others has received any education. This, too, is less than she was brought up to expect. But her greatest grief has been the death of her sixth child. About the same time, despite his ZIM marriage, Mpawa IV took a second wife at the opposite end of the village. She did not volunteer this information. I found out afterwards when I met her to be accompanied to the church she joined as a result of these experiences and I asked about Che Mpawa's absence. The church is Anglican, a tiny grass hut constructed around the grave of Henry de Wint Burrup on the horseshoe-shaped peninsula of the original Magomero. The pastor is Edwin Gabriel, who was born in 1951 and has married into Bowadi. He has been trained as a lay superintendent – this was Horace Waller's title – and he founded the new church following a dispute in the Roman Catholic mission near Utwe. Sitting on the slope at Bowadi and looking down across the Namadzi river at the mission site, Mr Gabriel told me about the events of 1861 – about David Livingstone and Bishop Mackenzie, about the disastrous chase down the Shire river and about Burrup's return and death. But he had learned the story at school. It was new to the people of Bowadi sitting listening. It was new to Margaret Matemba when her grief led her to attend services in the new grass building erected in the middle of her husband's farm. In that faintest of echoes of the most distant of traditions, or perhaps only in the romance of the story itself, she seems to have found something to bind her to the village. In the best traditions of Anglicanism, she is a little patronised by Edwin Gabriel's wife.

As early as 6.30 the square was vibrant with men, children, babies and women in bright *chitenges*, shouting greetings, swaying with baskets on their heads, gossiping, laughing, drinking sweet beer, fingering cloth, prodding catfish, turning over sweet potatoes or cassava, holding eggs up to the sunlight, whispering to the 'native doctor', holding hands, waving away flies, flirting with the tailors at their sewing machines, feeling the breasts of chickens, untying cloth purses, calculating, bawling at a mangy dog, squatting under the fig tree to suckle babies, smoking, playing *bau* or shaking hips to the music blaring from radios in the bottle stores. It was Saturday market at Chimwalira in September.

I counted 102 sellers, though several came and went during the morning. Some have permanent stalls, rough wooden tables with a thatched cover. Most squat on the ground surrounded by baskets, with a reed mat or a piece of sacking on which their goods are arranged in small pyramids. The men are professionals. Behind each is an upturned bicycle with well-worn tyres, bought with the savings from a contract in South Africa. They have travelled for their supplies and their goods are stored in 50-kilo sacks which they ferry from market to market throughout the week.

Charlie Banda lives at the scheme. Every Monday and Friday he cycles to Chipiko store in Zomba to buy salt. Two kinds come in sacks, one coarse and white from South Africa, one coarse and grey from Mozambique. Table salt comes in packets which he carries in a knapsack. He cycles round the markets selling his salt in brown paper twists at 3t, 4t and 5t, making K3 profit on each sack. Mackford Kachere from Zaone specialises in beans. He buys in Thyolo, dealing directly with the villagers. By taking a smaller profit than ADMARC he offers a higher price and so secures his supplies. Occupying the next sales pitch is Kambalame, whose business is in groundnuts. His weekly journey by bicycle is to Ntaja, north of Zomba, where the local groundnuts have a reputation. He too is operating within ADMARC's profit margin.

The fishmongers have stalls at the back of the market. Four are from Lake Chilwa. They have brought their own catch – dried *chambo* slit along the belly and laid flat, smoked catfish with their tails in their mouths looking like coils of tobacco, and tiny dried *usipa* like strips of silver foil in 5t and 10t piles. Some, like Jombo Mseula, have made the opposite journey, cycling for suppliers to Kachula harbour and touring the local markets for a week's profit of K6. Some are middlemen to the middlemen, intercepting the bicycles and buying stock wholesale before walking round the markets to make K2. One man from Namadzi has a small van. He brings fresh *chambo* from Mangoche to sell at 20t, 25t and 30t according to size. These are high prices for Chimwalira and his business is precarious. He also has trouble getting petrol.

There are other men who carry goods from market to market. One cycles to the swampland, where the Phalombe river joins Lake

Chilwa, and buys reed mats. They sell at K1.15 and K1.35. One deals in sugar, table salt, curry powder and sweets, all packaged and obtained from Indian merchants in Limbe who are no longer permitted to trade in the villages. One with an enormous battered trunk is selling bars of Lifebuoy soap, tiny packets of Rinso, combs, mirrors, razor blades, pairs of scissors, matches and pieces of Java print. He also has a drum of cooking oil which he siphons into his customer's bottles. This man is undercutting the permanent Chimwalira traders like Mr Mangomba, but he cycles in – drum on his crossbar, trunk on his saddlerack – only on Saturdays. A fourth man deals in scrap metal which he hammers expertly into buckets, saucepans and mugs. On his bicycle, with them hanging about him, he looks like Don Quixote.

Just after 7.30 a lorry roars up, braking with dangerous panache under the fig tree. Several men jump down, passing between them ripe hands of bananas, and one remains behind as the lorry races off to other markets beyond Zomba. The Banana Cooperative Society of Thyolo has 727 members. Every Saturday they hire a lorry to get their bananas to as many markets as the rickety truck and their supply of petrol will allow. The bananas sell at 1t each. The lorry returns in the late afternoon to pick up the salesmen and unsold goods.

The 'native doctor' is Jagaja. 'Native doctor' is his own title for himself and he has a second sign in English reading 'Friends, Relatives, Don't Ask for Credit!' Few of his customers can read English but when he translates the sign it carries authority. Though Jagaja lives at Machereni he claims to be the son of a chief in Mozambique and the words 'Portuguese' and 'Mozambique' are used interchangeably to signify mysterious knowledge.

He lives by imagination and wit and what he sells are metaphors. They are spread out odorously on a table of planks, and I pick them up one at a time. This tortoiseshell is for children with rickets. Flakes of it wrapped in paper and tied round a child's knees will strengthen the joints. Sections of this lion's tooth, tiny slices costing K2, will strengthen the arms of miners on the Rand. This piece of bark with 'stars' in it when held up to the light brings good luck. A triangle of porcupine skin with the quills intact will prevent thieves ambushing me in my car. In this tiny corked bottle are stored 'sparks' made by water falling from a high place in Mozambique. Jagaja has collected and dried them and they too bring good luck. A bundle of wild grasses tied round the middle will keep families united. A kind of root called chimanga mudzi ('building a home') achieves the same result. Parts of a crab, pounded with other roots, are the treatment for someone 'running mad'. Parts of a monkey's paw, again pounded, will help children who are late in walking.

There are wrinkled pods and seeds and dried herbs for headaches, diarrhoea, constipation or barrenness. A root called *sakaziga* should be given to poultry if they are wasting away. A powder called *tibula* was offered as good for me 'if I was doing nothing with my wife'. Instead, I bought the whole lion's tooth, beating Jagaja down from K24 to K15. It is on my desk giving me strength as I write. But it is not a lion's tooth. It is the left tusk of a wart hog.

Of the women traders there is only one who rivals these men in the scale of her business and she surpasses them all. She is an ebullient woman, more like a West African market mammie than a Malawian. Her home is in Blantyre and she runs a small Ford van. She trades in clothes which she obtains wholesale in Limbe, buying them by the bale – K156 for a bale of fifty women's dresses, K110 for fifty men's shirts, K120 for fifty men's trousers. These items are spread out on reed mats and madam sits beside them, drinking sweet beer and eating sugar-cane, very much a woman of the people. She jokes with passers-by, telling a man his wife needs a dress or that his trousers are a disgrace. Trousers sell at between K4.95 and K5.95, giving her a profit of between 100 and 140 per cent. Again, these are high prices for Chimwalira. But clothes are a necessity and hers are the cheapest available. The reason is they are all second-hand, having been donated by charities in the United States.

The other women are like the remaining men. They live close by and Chimwalira is the only market to which they bring goods for sale. Some are providing a service, like the woman selling sweet warm milky beer at 2t per half cup, or her neighbour selling roasted groundnuts, or the man who has brought bamboo poles from his farm at Machereni at K1 for a bundle of ten. James Chambo, the carpenter from Ntholowa, has brought hoe handles to market. An old woman from Njenjema has a small bag of unhusked rice, just harvested from her *dambo* garden. She is selling it as seed for the coming season. Several women are selling fermented millet, tiny purple seeds sprouting after a week's soaking and ready for brewing beer. Off to the left, macabrely isolated between two goats' heads on poles, is the butcher. The heads indicate how many goats he has brought to market. His butchering is crude. The carcases hang upside down and he slashes at them with a cutlass. All meat is the same price and what you get depends on your place in the queue.

Alice William from Bowadi has harvested more finger-millet than she needs for flour and she has brought half a basket to market. Jaisoni Siliya from Mpawa has brought his 'X'-grade tobacco which he refused to let ADMARC have at the price offered. There are women selling cassava, pumpkin and cassava leaves, spinach, nandolo, sweet potatoes, sorghum, tomatoes, okra, piri-piri – anything, in fact, ready and in surplus. At least two dozen women are selling maize, not as in Blantyre or Zomba markets already pounded but in the grain at 1t per plateful. Some of these transactions are pathetically small. There are women who have brought three platefuls of maize to market in order to buy a single twist of salt.

During the 1960s, when many African states regained their independence, it was fashionable to describe them as having two economies, a small developed sector generating exports and a large subsistence sector involving the rural masses. Eventually, it was assumed, the 'modern' economy would triumph, abolishing 'backwardness' as Africans joined the developed world. A decade later, when the entrenched poverty of most of the new nations was all too evident, the two-economy model was replaced by analyses which stressed the vertical nature of exploitation in a single system, the wealth of the few during deriving from the poverty of the masses. Walking around Chimwalira market, there seems merit in both descriptions. Perhaps the right metaphor would allow for two economic spheres, one poised above the other but connected by a narrow passage as in an old-fashioned coffee perculator or a chemist's double-retort. There is no doubt Malawi's small elite subsists by drawing wealth out of the villages. No one at this market can get full value for their labour or their produce. Yet within each sphere, a good deal goes on without direct reference to the other. In its strictly circumscribed way, the market is its own world, hollowing out space for itself with a multitude of transactions. There is no escape here from poverty, but within the room permitted for manoeuvre there is enormous inventiveness and effort. The other sphere which sucks wealth from this can seem at times absurdly remote and insubstantial.

Take for instance, this man selling sheets of paper at 1t each. He squats strategically between the butcher and the woman selling roasted groundnuts. He has a pile of magazines with their staples opened so he can lift out the double pages. Hilariously, they are stamped *Not to be Removed from the Senior Common Room* and they turn out to be back numbers of the *New Statesman* and *New Society* from the University of Malawi. Among them is a copy of the Malawi government *Hansard*, recording debates from the fifteenth session of parliament held in 1979. The covers have already been sold but I buy the remaining pages for 11t. They contain a speech by the Honourable Gwanda Chakuamba, Minister for the Southern Region, Minister of Youth and Culture and Leader of the House:

It was a unanimous view of the House and undoubtedly the unanimous view of the people we in this House represent, that His Excellency's efforts and endeavour to uplift the standard of living for his people have borne fruits unsurpassed in the history of any developing nation in the world ... The rumours that were spread some time ago were merely day dreams. All Honourable Members of Parliament have sworn and pledged on their own behalf and on behalf of the people they represent, in assuring His Excellency that no dissident from any country outside this country will ever put his or her foot on any inch of the soils of their motherland, Malawi. And furthermore, the House wishes to assure His Excellency the Life President that in health or sickness, in life or death, in richness or in poverty, solidly they and their children shall ever remain behind His Excellency the Life President, Ngwazi Dr H. Kamuzu Banda.

Mr Speaker, Sir, I am equally delighted to report to you this that the standard of debate since the General Elections last year has been remarkably high ...

Only a handful of people at this market can speak English and fewer still can read. Their only use for this speech is to hold roasted groundnuts or wrap goat meat. Gwanda Chakuamba is currently in jail, serving an illegally long sentence.

I had one more visit to make. On my last Sunday in Malawi I attended morning service in the grass-walled Anglican church at Mpawa. Margaret Matemba was my escort and we walked the sloping path between her husband's ripening wheat and cowpeas to the peninsula where the Namadzi river makes its huge loop. Down by the five blue gums we were too early. It was not yet 7 o'clock and our first glimpse of an alerted Edwin Gabriel, the lay superintendent, was of him running along the track from Bowadi the other side of the river. We watched him vanish into a clump of *nandolo* and emerge zipping up his trousers. A small boy with legs muddy from the river arrived carrying a bundle wrapped in red cloth, and then Edwin himself was with us, breathlessly anxious, shaking hands and shooing us into the church. At the front was a low altar smoothed with clay. The red bundle was unwrapped to reveal a blue altar cloth, trimmed with white lace, and two aerosol tins which became vases, each with three

253

Fig. 27. Houses at Mpawa

marigolds. There was also a Chewa Bible and several prayer-books. By now others had arrived, seven boys in torn khaki shorts and five women and two girls, all barefooted. We arranged ourselves, men to the left and women to the right of Burrup's white marble cross and began catechism class.

Since this church was built under the blue gums in 1978, there have been no more *chopa* dances at Mpawa. 'Things have changed,' explained Mpawa IV to me. 'People still offer sacrifices but the response of the ancestors is not as it used to be in the old days.'

In the eight villages and at Chimwalira, there are no less than twelve different denominations with fifteen places of worship. The majority are the older churches – Anglican, Roman Catholic, Church of Central Africa Presbyterian (ex-Church of Scotland), ZIM and, most popular of all, PIM, with branches in Njenjema, Ntholowa and Bowadi. But newer denominations are represented by the fundamentalist Church of Christ, Assembly of God and the Adventist *Chiyembekezo*, a breakaway from the ZIM. Finally, there are the Ethiopian churches, Abraham, Masiye and Galilee.

Ethiopianism has its origins in the kind of stories once told at Magomero by Charles and William, two of the African members the UMCA missionaries had recruited at the Cape. The stories described 'blackness' as the mark of Cain, the sign that blacks were intended to serve whites forever as hewers of wood and drawers of water. It is hardly surprising that in southern Africa the first generation of educated black Christians should have rejected such ideas. From the 1870s onwards, different groups among the Wesleyans and Episcopalians began to mark out an alternative biblical tradition, linking such texts as 'Ethiopia shall soon stretch out her hands to God' (Psalm 68, v.31) with the baptism of the Ethiopian by Philip the Evangelist (Acts 8, 28–40). Southern Africa today has a great variety of these churches, many of them attempting to incorporate African religious practices into their rituals and theology.

There are difficulties, though, about describing the Ethiopian churches as 'traditional' or 'African'. Akite Chiunda admits that the Abraham church is by far the best attended in Mpotola, but she explains this is because 'It allows people to drink and practise polygamy, though many people don't have more than one wife because they don't have enough money to dress their wives.' This is not just the scorn of high Presbyterianism. Akite Chiunda, it will be remembered, described *thangata* as the time of polygamy, and she regards Ethiopianism as an affront to the real customs of her village.

255

Her comment goes to the heart of the advances Christianity has made in recent years.

There is a huge variety of beliefs and practices on offer and the pleasure village men take in theological disputation should not be underestimated. 'The Bible is a forest,' I was told after an argument about polygamy. 'When you're walking in it you can't see what is happening behind.' All the same, the denominations are on very good terms. At this morning's Anglican service at Mpawa, Edwin Gabriel has invited pastors from the PIM, Abraham and Masiye churches to meet me and all three are given parts in the service. On essentials, the churches are in agreement. All of them are under the control of men. The priests or pastors and the lay workers are all men and all of them preach that the man is head of the household. All agree, too, that a man who marries outside his congregation will be 'dismissed' unless 'he orders his wife to follow him to his church'. Asauka Alinapo of Ntholowa, who is over eighty years old, gave me a woman's view of this:

Q: How do people choose their church?
A: Usually, the woman follows her husband. Even if you don't want to go you still go because it's difficult to get husbands these days.

The churches, then, though controlled by men, are packed with women worshippers.

In many ways the churches have already supplanted the village and the extended family as the centres of social groupings. Sundays reveal small groups of families walking considerable distances in search of their chosen brand of liturgy or doctrine. It is the church leaders, for example, and not the village headmen who these days organise initiation ceremonies, whether of the orthodox Anglican, Catholic and Presbyterian varieties or of the neo-traditional forms practised by the Ethiopian churches. Marriages and funerals take place under Christian auspices. The priests or pastors receive 'tribute' in the form of a weekly offering and they are in charge of its redistribution. Most significant of all is the question of land. Like John Chilembwe, the churches give approval to inheritance through the male line. Reminded by me that this conflicts with Lomwe custom, spokesmen for the Anglican, Presbyterian and Ethiopian churches all agreed: 'That is finished!'

This has happened not as a result of missionary onslaught but as a response from within to changing conditions since the disappearance of *thangata*. At first, the money from cash-cropping and labour migration posed a challenge to custom as the men sought security for their investments. Meanwhile, population increase reduced most family holdings to between two and three acres, making older patterns of settlement seem less and less viable. It is the churches, in all their apparent disparity, which have agreed on the new custom to be followed, defining fresh divisions of responsibility within the household.

At the same time, the churches have supplied a doctrine which is the third ingredient in their unspoken agreement with each other. Villagers today are locked in a poverty from which there is little chance of escape through business, wage labour or education. During the years of *thangata* after the Chilembwe rising's failure, they found emotional and imaginative relief within their village systems, falling back on a cultural conservatism which helped to maintain their self-respect. Today's poverty is different. Land shortage means the villages can never be self-sufficient. Land shortage makes wage labour inevitable, forcing villagers to confront their poverty. The churches offer a different kind of self-respect, the vision of a society in which poverty is not a rebuke, in which the equality denied them by the Malawian system is reasserted within the Christian community.

At Mpotola, Florence Liponda sang me a funeral hymn, 'There will be no darkness when Jesus comes.' The final verse promised:

John Chilembwe will make everything shine
John Chilembwe will make everything shine
John Chilembwe will make everything shine
   To take his beloved
   To take his beloved
   To take his beloved
John Chilembwe will make everything shine
   To take his beloved

In this account, Chilembwe is no longer the radical opponent of economic and political injustice. He is waiting in heaven to receive sinners who have borne their sufferings without complaint.

It is easy to demonstrate the irony of this, much harder to suggest alternatives. One very recent initiative is the interest taken in the area by the American Christian charity World Vision International. This is a fundamentalist body which gives aid to village and slum communities in developing countries through their church leaders. World Vision's Namadzi Development Project began work in 1985. Eighty thousand dollars have been committed over five years, 'to enable the needy people of Namadzi to respond to the Gospel of Jesus Christ and reach their God-given potential through a holistic development project'. A concrete bridge is being built across the river at Mpawa, a homecraft centre constructed and 'vocational training' offered to 'school dropouts' in carpentry, tin-smithing, tailoring, poultry farming and bricklaying. The most lasting and useful benefit is likely to be the sinking of three boreholes.

This programme will strengthen the role of the churches, whose 'ministry will be enhanced' and increase the opportunities of the marginally richer farmers to expand their trade. It is difficult to see what more can be achieved, given the necessity to work within Malawi's policies on agriculture and education. The villagers are delighted to be noticed but with unintended humour the charity is already known as 'World Division'.

Simultaneously, the Diocese of Southern Malawi is building on the site once cleared for the purpose by Bishop Mackenzie a large brick church in simplified Gothic. The foundations, laid in concrete with provision for a bell tower, are a few yards from the present grass church. Morning service there on my last Sunday in Malawi was not an easy occasion for me. The hymns were long and unbearably sad and the mud floor hard to my knees. Thirty men and women crammed the hut with an overspill outside. The readings were from Deuteronomy 15 ('For the poor shall never cease out of the land') and 1 John 4 ('Herein is our love made perfect that we may have boldness in the day of judgement'). Edwin Gabriel preached without rhetoric on the theme of Dives and Lazarus.

Towards the end of the service I was formally welcomed. The congregation was told what they already knew, that I had been with them for several months collecting their history and that I was with them here today. Why was I here today? It was a moment before I realised this was not a rhetorical question and that I was expected to answer. Why was I present, continued Edwin Gabriel. Was it to share their worship? Or just to record music?

It was a fair question. The true answer was that I was looking for an ending for the book I was going to write about them. Yet only someone who shared their worship could have made such an ending work. I was moved to be where Chigunda and the missionaries had played out their tragedy, but I did not believe that the seeds sown by those events were today bearing fruit. This was not my view of history.

Was I an Anglican? 'No,' I said truthfully. Then, feeling the burden of expectancy, I added lamely, 'but worship is the same in all languages.' It was the first time in my months of questioning that anyone had asked me about myself. I could not share their belief. Yet, given the story I had been unravelling, the long inheritance of Christianity, Civilisation and Commerce, I could not avoid feeling rebuked by it. Searching for an answer that was accurate I continued, 'I am from York. Where Procter came from. Where the Archbishop came from who visited you here.' This was true. Archbishop Fisher had visited the mission site briefly in 1960 during Dr Banda's detention. It was also a good reply. Edwin Gabriel beamed with pleasure and scribbled swiftly in his notebook. The service ended with a blessing and with photographs. Photographs at Magomero could allay all doubts.

Afterwards, I climbed Nanyungwi hill and took more photographs. In many ways I now knew more about the villages than most people living there. In other ways, I knew nothing. Our contact had been as superficial as all such contacts since 1859. Jaisoni Siliya from Mpawa climbed up beside me and watched while I wrote in my notebook the description with which this book begins. He had accompanied me on most of my interviews, insisting always on carrying my tape-recorder. As I shut my notebook, he pointed out unerringly something I had missed. Down on the river bank was a tiny grass hut. It was an initiation hut and the two boys inside it were singing and beating sticks to warn off passers-by.

We sat on boulders in the cold, sharing my sandwiches. Suddenly, below us, a tiny whirlwind passed from right to left. It roared through the compounds, an angry spiral of dust and leaves crackling like a fire, and passed up the road towards Nasawa, turning its rage inwards though on each side the air and trees remained perfectly still and untroubled.

Sources

Parts of this story have been told before in two outstanding books. Owen Chadwick's *Mackenzie's Grave* (1959) is an entertaining, sensitive account of the events at Magomero and Chibisa's from 1861 to 1864. *Independent African: John Chilembwe and the Nyasaland Rising of 1915* by G. Shepperson and T. Price (1958) is a pioneering study of African nationalism. Both books have set me challenging standards, Chadwick for his appreciation of character and his humour and Shepperson and Price for their breadth of scholarship and mastery of detail.

My own account differs in three ways. First, I have linked together what were earlier told as two separate stories. Chadwick's book closes in 1864, the future a matter of metaphor, while Shepperson and Price resolutely play down connections between the activities at Magomero of the two Livingstones, David and 'Listonia', never once referring to Bishop Mackenzie. The second difference is of perspective. *Mackenzie's Grave* is essentially a story of European endeavour while in *Independent African* the Lomwe who fought for Chilembwe are relegated to the background as a 'violent vacillating lumpen-proletariat'. My own account tries to recreate the experience of the Africans living on the Namadzi river during these two episodes and up until the present day. The third difference is what has made the first two possible, namely, that I have been able to draw on archival and oral evidence not available to historians writing in the 1950s. Of these, the most important are files held in the Malawi National Archives and in the Public Record Office, London, and interviews conducted under the Zomba History Project organised by the History Department of the University of Malawi.

In the description of my sources which follows, archival and oral sources predominate and the list of published materials is not meant to be exhaustive. Readers who wish to follow up references may consult E. Brown and C. Fisher, *A Bibliography of Malawi* (1965) or R. B. Boeder, *Malawi* (World Bibliographical Series, 1980).

Part I

The earliest accounts of the UMCA mission were *The Occasional Paper of the Oxford, Cambridge, Dublin and Durham Mission to Central Africa* (1862), H. Goodwin's *Memoir of Bishop Mackenzie* (1864) and H. Rowley, *The Story of the Universities' Mission to Central Africa* (1867). Meanwhile, D. and C. Livingstone had published their *Narrative of an Expedition to the Zambezi and its Tributaries* (1865). Much fuller information, however, is available in journals and letters published from 1952 onwards, namely, J. P. R. Wallis (ed.), *The Zambezi Journals of James Stewart* (1952), and *The Zambezi Expedition of David Livingstone 1858–1863* (2 vols., 1956), E. C. Tabler (ed.), *Richard Thornton's Zambezi Papers 1858–1863* (2 vols., 1963), R. Foskett (ed.), *The Zambezi Journal and Letters to Dr John Kirk* (2 vols., 1965), and N. R. Bennet and M. Ylvisaker (eds.), *The Central African Journal of Lovell J. Procter 1860–1864* (1971).

The best biography of David Livingstone remains T. Jeal's *Livingstone* (1973). Other useful sources dealing with central Africa in the nineteenth century include E. D. Young, *The Search after Livingstone* (1868) and (with H. Waller), *Nyassa: a Journal of Adventures* (1877), D. MacDonald, *Africana: or the Heart of Heathen Africa* (2 vols., 1881), J. Buchanan, *The Shire Highlands: East Central Africa as Colony and Mission* (1885), and H. Drummond, *Tropical Africa* (1891).

Horace Waller's unpublished diaries, letters, notes and sketches are held at Rhodes House, Oxford (MSS Afr. s.16), and Bishop Mackenzie's journal at the USPG archive, London (Box A1 (I) A), together with additional journals, an album kept by Mrs Burrup (Box A1 (I) B), and letters from H. Rowley and H C. Scudamore (Box A1 (II) A).

The Zimbabwe National Archives hold an extensive collection of David Livingstone's correspondence (LI 1/1/1 and 2/1/1), Charles Livingstone's correspondence (LI 3/1/1) and correspondence of the UMCA (UN 2/1/1). A further selection of D. Livingstone's unpublished letters ([ed. I. Schapera) is held at the Southern African Archive of the University of York.

A consequence of the expulsion of the Mang'anja people from the Shire Highlands in 1863 is that it is not possible to collect oral testimony referring specifically to the mission at Magomero (though M. Schoffelleers has collected traditions from the Shire valley about their settlement at Chibisa's). I have drawn, however, on interviews conducted for the Zomba History Project of the University of Malawi by Megan Vaughan in 1978–79 and by Kings Phiri with C. Chidzero and G. Makuza in 1979.

The village of Mangasanja, now situated in Mozambique on the Ruo river, is given in the missionaries' accounts as Manasomba. The correct name occurs in a serial article on Mulanje district in the *British Central Africa Gazette* I, 5–7 (April–May, 1894).

Where not already indicated in the text the passages quoted in part I are from the following souces: pp. 8–9, Kirk, 239–40; p. 25, Procter, 99; p. 26, Waller Diary, 5 August 1861; p. 35, Rowley, 147; pp. 41–2, Procter, 120–1; p. 44, Goodwin, 254 with Procter, 133; p. 45, Procter, 141–2; p. 50, Malawi National Archives, *Zomba District book*, I, 25; p. 54, Goodwin, 388; p. 58, Rowley, 258–9; p. 66; Stewart 102–3; p. 70, Young, *Nyassa*, 184.

Part II

The principal sources for all three chapters of Part II are (a) a series of seventy interviews and recordings made in the relevant villages during July–September 1982 and September 1985, and (b) documents held at the Malawi National Archives in Zomba, Malawi.

The interviews include historical and biographical material supplemented by stories, proverbs and some 340 songs. They were recorded and translated with the assistance of Coretta M'meta, Doris Kadzamira and Irene Machowa, all then of the University of Malawi. Copies are deposited in the university library and in the Southern African Archive of the University of York. Original recordings are held by the author but are available on request. The interviews are listed by village and informant and with one exception (see below) all passages cited in Part II are identified in the text.

The value of material held at the Malawi National Archives is limited in three ways. A fire in 1919, together with a 40-year restriction on access means that with a few exceptions material is effectively available from 1919 to 1945. For those who, like myself, have been given special permission to consult documents for the period 1945–65, the lack of an adequate catalogue makes research a hit or miss affair. Thirdly, until the 1950s colonial officials were surprisingly incurious about what was happening on the private estates and had limited powers of intervention. No estate records are yet held at MNA and little of the data recorded for Crown (later Trust) Land areas is available. Events on the A. L. Bruce Estates Ltd, however, were impossible to ignore, especially in 1915, 1938–9 and 1945–53.

I have consulted *District Books* for Blantyre, Zomba and Mulanje districts 1907 –, for Chiradzulu sub-districts 1910–23, and for Chiradzulu district 1923 –, together with Annual and Monthly Reports for Blantyre district (NSB 7/1/6 and 7/3/1–4), Annual and Monthly Reports for Zomba district (NSZ 4/1/1–7, S1/21/19, S1/1128/19 and S1/521/20), and Annual and Quarterly Reports from Chiradzulu district (NSD 2/1/1–4 and 2/2/2): also Correspondence, Chiradzulu (NSB 2/2/1), Chiradzulu District Native Association (NS 1/3/5) and *Ulendo*, Zomba (NSZ 4/4/1–2).

Files on the Chilembwe rising include evidence presented to the Commission of Enquiry (COM 6/2/1–3), Judges and Magistrates records (COM 6/3/3/1 and 6/3/4/1), records of the PIM (COM 6/3/2/3), statements (S10/1/1–7), despatches (GOA 2/4/14–15) and Mrs Livingstone (S1/3008/23). Chilembwe's death, described here for the first time, is from J2/9/3. Some subsequent information about the PIM is available in NS 1/19/6 and NS 1/19/12.

W. J. Livingstone testified in Cause 2 of 1903/04 (J5/2/1) and Kincaid-Smith to the Tobacco Industry Commission of 1938 (COM 7/1/1/1 to 7/5/1/1). The Kincaid-Smith affair is covered in GOB/G 187 with a comic sequel in file 21130 3–14–10^F box 1719. The sale of the Magomero estate, including balance sheets and a review of recent company history, is covered in 11861 2–8–9^F box 1476, 11861^I 3–2–8^F box 1270, 11861^{II} 2–8–9^F box 1476, 11861^{III} 16–6–9^F box 4953, 18497 2–29–12^R box 2679, S1/2767 23 and 1A/1010. For the aftermath, including the Land Settlement Scheme and police reports, see 23675 4–6–4^R box 4674, 1–7–6^F box 10733, 1–7–7^R box 10735 and 7–6–8^E with additional information about land purchase in 11967 2–8–9^F box 1476, 3–2–8^F box 1271, 7–6–8^F box 13227, 16–6–9^F box 4954, 2–17–7^F box 878, and 17–7–3^R box 17549.

A large number of files deal with land and labour. Cox v. ALC is in L3/20/11 and Native Affairs v. B & EA Co. in J5/2/1. For tax, *thangata* and land, see also L3/12/2, L3/20/11, L3/25/1–3, L3/35/7, S1/2308/21, S1/131/23, S1/1339/25, S1/596/26, S1/519/29, S1/108/32, S1/411^{II}/33 and 11542 3–14–12 box 2325. Much information on coffee, cotton, tobacco and tea is available in A1/1/1–3, A1/3/1, A2/1/1, A3/3/143, A5/2/1, AB/2/263, 1A/207, 1A/139/9, 1A/801, 1B/85, 1C/65 and NSZ 1/1/2. The Tobacco Industry Commission of 1938 contains much historical and personal testimony (COM 7/1/1/1 to 7/5/1/1). There are devastatingly critical histories of the Blantyre and East African Company and the British Central Africa Company in 12405 19–3–7^F box 1568 and 12258 19–3–6^R box 1567.

Megan Vaughan generously put at my disposal notes on the 1922 and 1949 famines derived from S1/244/22, S1/296/22, S1/377/22, S1/1852/22 and AFC 3/2/1. Key newspapers are the *British Central Africa Gazette* (1894–) and the *Central African Planter* (later *Central African Times*, later *Nyasaland Times*, 1895–).

In Malawi, I also consulted Annual Reports filed by the Blantyre and East African Company and the British Central Africa Company at the Registrar General's office in Blantyre, and on A. L. Bruce Estates Ltd held at solicitors Wilson & Morgan, Blantyre. The archive of the B & EA Co. held at Lauderdale Estate, Mulanje district, was also consulted but none of the very diverse material it contains has proved relevant for this book.

In Zimbabwe, much early correspondence on British Central Africa/Nyasaland is held at the National Archives. I have consulted Harry Johnston's correspondence (JO 1/1/1), In Letters, Nyasaland (CT 1/11/3/19–20 and CT 1/16/2–6), Out Letters, Nyasaland (CT 2/8/1) and In Letters African Lakes Company (CT 1/11/5/1).

In Britain, there is little official documentation bearing directly on twentieth-century village history, but I have consulted with profit files in the FO 84/1634–2141 series (1883–91) and CO 525/41–137 series (1912–30), held at the Public Record Office, London, file 8650, A. L. Bruce Estates Ltd held at the Scottish Record Office, Edinburgh, and register of Deeds OD/V 2555/2–32 (Alexander Low Bruce, 17 January 1894) at General Register House, Edinburgh.

Material on Mozambique is drawn from Leroy Vail and Landeg White, *Capitalism and Colonialism in Mozambique: a Study of Quelimane District* (Heinemann Educational Books, 1980). I am deeply indebted to books, theses, dissertations and articles on Malawi by C. A. Baker, D. G. Bettison, M. Chanock, J. E. R. Emtage, J. Hodgson, J. A. K. Kandawire, Z. D. Kadzamira, J. Kydd, I and J. Linden, E. Mandala, J. MacCracken, H. Macmillan, C. J. Mitchell, L. Msukwa, M. Page, B. Pachai, D. D. Phiri, K. Phiri. A. Ross, M. Schoffeleers, R. Tangri, H. L. Vail, M. Vaughan and D. Williams.

Where not already indicated in the text the passages quoted in Part II are from the following sources: p. 78, Nunan judgement MNA J5/2/1; p. 82, *(C)entral (A)frican (P)lanter* 15 October 1896; p. 82, General Register House, Edinburgh, Register of Deeds OD/V 2555/2–32; p. 83, *CAP* 3 November 1895; p. 85–6, *(B)ritish (C)entral (A)frica (G)azette* 1 June 1895; p. 89, MNA COM 6/2/1/3 testimony of Bismarck; p. 109, PRO 525/65 K. Livingstone to Bonar Law 9 July 1915; p. 123, *Central African Times* 8 December 19128 p. 128, MNA S1/3008/23; pp. 133–4, MNA COM 6/2/1/1 testimony of Wallace-Ross; p. 138, MNA S1/10/3 cases 240 and 241; p. 140–1, quoted in Shepperson and Price, 246; p. 141, MNA COM 3/3/3/1 case 29; p. 145, MNA J2/9/3 Enquiry into the death of John Chilembwe; p. 149, MNA NSB 7/3/3 March 1916; p. 155, Zomba History Project, Chikowi Historical Texts no. 9; pp. 171, MNA COM 7/2/1/1 memorandum by Kincaid-Smith (n.d.); p. 192, MNA S1/411^{II}/33 Tennett to DC Cholo 4 November 1935; p. 203, MNA 1A/1019 'Extracts from Col. Bruce's letters' (n.d.)

Index

Printed in the United States
66242LVS00004B/106-153